William Haslam

From Death into Life

Twenty Years of my Ministry

William Haslam

From Death into Life
Twenty Years of my Ministry

ISBN/EAN: 9783337389246

Printed in Europe, USA, Canada, Australia, Japan

Cover: Foto ©Lupo / pixelio.de

More available books at **www.hansebooks.com**

BALDHU CHURCH AND ITS SURROUNDINGS.

FROM

DEATH INTO LIFE:

OR,

Twenty Years of my Ministry.

BY

REV. W. HASLAM

(*Late Incumbent of Curzon Chapel, Mayfair*),

AUTHOR OF "BUILDING FROM THE TOP—TWENTY-FOUR TRUE TALES OF CONVERSION," "THE THREEFOLD GIFT OF GOD," ETC.

TO THE

RIGHT HONORABLE

FRANCIS ALEXANDER,

THE EARL OF KINTORE,

MY STEADY AND UNCHANGING FRIEND,

THIS VOLUME

𝔍𝔰 𝔞𝔣𝔣𝔢𝔠𝔱𝔦𝔬𝔫𝔞𝔱𝔢𝔩𝔶 𝔦𝔫𝔰𝔠𝔯𝔦𝔟𝔢𝔡

AS A

TOKEN OF REGARD.

INTRODUCTION.

THIS volume is not so much a history of my own life, as of the Lord's dealings with me; setting forth how He wrought in and by me during the space of twenty years. It will be observed that this is not, as biographies generally are, an account of life on to death; but rather the other way—a narrative of transition from death into life, and that in more senses than one.

I had been given over by three physicians to die, but it pleased the Lord, in answer to prayer, to raise me up again. My restored health and strength I thankfully devoted to a religious and earnest life. In the height and seeming prosperity of this, the Lord awakened me to see that I was dead in trespasses and sins; still far from Him; resting on my own works; and going about to establish my own righteousness, instead of submitting to the righteousness of God. Then He quickened me by the Holy Ghost, and raised me up into a new and spiritual life.

In this volume the reader will meet with the respective results of (what I have called) the Religious, as distinguished from the Spiritual, life. The former produced only outward and ecclesiastical effects, while the latter brought forth fruit in the salvation of souls, to the praise and glory of God.

One object in writing this book is to warn and instruct earnest-minded souls, who are, as I was once, strangers to the experience of salvation, seeking rest where I am sure they can never find it, and labouring to do good to others when they have not yet received that good themselves. They are vainly "building from the top;" trying to live before they are born; to become holy before they have been justified; and to lead others to conversion before they have been converted themselves.

A second object is—to draw the attention of every earnest, seeking, or anxious soul, to consider the Lord's marvellous goodness in first bearing with me in my religious wanderings, and then using me for His glory in the salvation of hundreds.

Another desire I have is—to cheer the hearts of believers who are working for God, by relating to them what He has done through me, and can do again, by the simple preaching of the Gospel. Here the reader will meet with narratives of the Lord's work in individual cases, in congregations, and in parishes—wonderful things which are worthy of record.

I have not shunned to tell of the mistakes I fell into after my conversion, hoping that others may take heed and profit by them; and then I shall not have written in vain.

CONTENTS.

CHAPTER I.
The Broken Nest—Illness—Recovery—Devotion . . . PAGE 1

CHAPTER II.
Religious Life—"Tracts for the Times"—Outward Profession . 8

CHAPTER III.
Ordination—First Parish—Country Choir—Church Restoration . 16

CHAPTER IV.
Perranzabuloe—The Lost Church Found—Cornish Crosses—Ministry Rejected 24

CHAPTER V.
New Parish—Temporary Church—Rev. R. S. Hawker—Baldhu Church Built 34

CHAPTER VI.
Building from the Top—A Picture—Extempore Preaching—Rev. J. Berridge's Experience—Awakening—The Happy Gardener 42

CHAPTER VII.
Visit to Rev. R. Aitken at Pendeen—"Are You Satisfied?"—"The Parson's Converted!"—"God stop the Man that's Wrong!" 53

CONTENTS.

CHAPTER VIII.
The Revival—Wonderful Scenes—Noisy Demonstrations . . 65

CHAPTER IX.
A Cornish Funeral—The Necessity of Conversion—A Visitor—Solemn Conversation 72

CHAPTER X.
The First Christmas—Schoolmaster's Conversion—The Clerk—The Ringer 80

CHAPTER XI.
Remarkable Dreams and Visions—Their Fulfilment . . 87

CHAPTER XII.
Billy Bray—His Visit to the Parsonage—His Story—Unusual Demonstration of Joy 99

CHAPTER XIII.
Frank—His Wonderful Conversion—Cottage Meetings—The "Wise Woman"—Her Warnings 110

CHAPTER XIV.
Open Air Services—Preaching on Perran Beach—Letting Down the Net—Fish Caught—The Young Lady—The Pet Kid—Rose-in-Vale—Preaching in the Garden—The Coastguardsmen—Mount Hawke—Preaching on a Common—Remarkable Manifestation of the Spirit's Work—A Continuous Meeting for Eight Days. 118

CHAPTER XV.
Two Professors of Religion—Their Conversion—Drawing-room Meeting—The Mayor Saved—Meeting in Town Hall—The Vicar's Disapproval 128

CHAPTER XVI.
Offence of the Cross—Opposition—Clerical Meetings—Sermons—Newspapers—Pamphlets—"Little Doggie Barking at an Elephant" 134

CONTENTS.

CHAPTER XVII.

Midnight Conversion—Popular Preacher—Not a Common Sinner—The Broken Leg—Sins Forgiven—The Uncommon Sinner—Revival 145

CHAPTER XVIII.

The Mill Pond and the Sea—Visit to Veryan—A Memorable Sunday—Service in a Fish Cellar—The Devil's Baits and Hooks 152

CHAPTER XIX.

Mission in the "Shires"—Devonshire—Dorsetshire—A Jesuit—Preaching in a Minster—"Bring him Back!"—"Very Remarkable!" 161

CHAPTER XX.

A Lady from London to see a Revival—Reformation not Conversion—The Child of God—A Relative—An Invitation . 173

CHAPTER XXI.

Golant Mission—The Lord's Preparation—Water Party—Burning an Effigy—Lecture on Pilgrim's Progress—Visit to a Neighbour 182

CHAPTER XXII.

The High Church Rector and his Curate—Dr. Pusey's Sermon—Sam's Testimony—Dangerous Drive—Great Joy . . 193

CHAPTER XXIII.

Rev. R. Aitken in Staffordshire—Bishop of Lichfield—Invitation—Preaching—Its Results 201

CHAPTER XXIV.

Dissatisfaction with the Work—New Discoveries in the Bible—Sanctification—The Dream 208

CHAPTER XXV.

Believers' Hope opened to View—Popish Legend—Three Judgments—The Tripod 218

CHAPTER XXVI.

Invited to Plymouth—Three Mountains Removed—Resignation of Baldhu—The Bishop's Refusal to Institute—Disappointment . 225

CHAPTER XXVII.

High-Church Services—The "Monk that Paints Apostles"—The Dream of Fire—Christ, not the Crucifix . . . 234

CHAPTER XXVIII.

Devonport—Conversion of Two Clergymen—Rejection by their Father Confessor—The Dying Lady—Removal to the Country 243

CHAPTER XXIX.

A Mission to the North of England—The Miner in Church—Edward's Grave—Visit to C.—The Churchwarden—"Paul Pry"—"Now or Never!"—The Conversion of Mr. F. . 250

CHAPTER XXX.

Tregoney—Opposition—The Mud Patch—The Revival—The Vicar and the M.P.—The Testimonial 264

CHAPTER XXXI.

Secessions to Rome—Their Mistake—False Interpretations of Scripture—Instituted to a Living—Unsettled . . . 271

CHAPTER XXXII.

Removal to Hayle—Infidels—Determined to Preach Christ Crucified—Success of the Work—Remarkable Dream—All Night Services 278

CHAPTER XXXIII.

The Church—Dissolving Views—Bible Classes—Grave Clothes . 290

CHAPTER XXXIV.

The Bethel Flag—Infidels' Club Broken Up—Raking the Cinders—Conversion of an Infidel 299

CHAPTER XXXV.

Rev. R. Aitken's Visit to Hayle—Its Great Result—Dismissal—The Last Christmas—The Farewell . . . 310

FROM DEATH INTO LIFE.

CHAPTER I.

The Broken Nest.

1841.

AT the time in which this history begins, I had, in the providence of God, a very happy nest; and as far as temporal prospects were concerned, I was provided for to my liking, and, though not rich, was content. I had taken my degree; was about to be ordained; and, what is more, was engaged to be married: in order, as I thought, to settle down as an efficient country parson.

With this bright future before me, I went on very happily; when, one evening, after a hard and tiring day, just as I was sitting down to rest, a letter was put into my hand which had been following me for several days. "Most urgent" was written on the outside. It told me of the alarming illness of the lady to whom I was engaged, and went on to say that if I wished to see her alive I must set off with all haste. It took me a very short time to pack my bag and get my travelling coats and rugs together, so that I was all ready to start by the night mail. At eight o'clock punctually I left London for the journey of two hundred and eighty miles. All that night I sat outside the coach; all the next day; and part of the following night. I shall never forget the misery of mind and body that I experienced, for I was tired before starting; and the fatigue of sitting up all night, together with the intense cold of the small hours of the morning, were almost beyond endurance. With the morning, however, came a warm and bright sunshine, which in some degree helped to cheer me; but my bodily suffering was so great that I could never have held up, had it not been for the mental eagerness with which I longed to get forward. It was quite consonant with my feelings when the horses were put into full gallop, especially when they were tearing down one hill to get an impetus to mount another.

At length, the long, long journey was over; and about thirty hours after starting, I found myself staggering along to the well-known house. As I approached, the door was softly opened by a relative who for several days had been anxiously watching my arrival. She at once conducted me upstairs, to what I expected was a sick chamber, when, to my horror, the first thing I saw was the lid of a coffin standing up against the wall, and in the middle of the room was the coffin, with candles burning on either side.

I nearly fell to the ground with this tremendous shock and surprise. There was the dear face, but it seemed absorbed in itself, and to have lost all regard for me. It no longer turned to welcome me, nor was the hand stretched out, as heretofore, to meet mine. All was still; there was no smile—no voice—no welcome—nothing but the silence of death to greet me.

The sight of that coffin, with its quiet inmate, did not awaken sorrow so much as surprise; and with that, something like anger and rebellion. I was weak and exhausted in body, but strong in wilful insubordination. Murmuring and complaining, I spoke unadvisedly with my lips.

A gentle voice upbraided me, adding, that I had far better kneel down in submission to God, and say, "Thy will be done!" This, however, was not so easy, for the demon of rebellion had seized me, and kept me for three hours in a tempest of anger, filling my mind with hard thoughts against God. I walked about the room in the most perturbed state of mind, so much so, that I grieved my friends, who came repeatedly to ask me to kneel down and say, "Thy will be done!" "Kneel down—just kneel down!" At length I did so, and while some one was praying, my tears began to flow, and I said the words, "Thy will be done!" Immediately the spell was broken, and I was enabled to say from my heart, again and again, "Thy will be done!" After this, I was conscious of a marvellous change in my mind; rebellion was gone, and resignation had come in its place. More than that, the dear face in the coffin seemed to lie smiling in peace, so calm and so lovely, that I felt I would not recall the spirit that was fled, even if it had been possible. There was wrought in me something more than submission, even a lifting-up of my will to the will of God; and withal, such a love towards Him that I wondered at myself. God had been, as it were, a stranger to me before. Now I felt as though I knew and loved Him, and could kiss His hand, though my tears flowed freely.

The funeral took place the same morning: it was a time of great emotion; sorrow and joy met, and flowed together. I thought of the dear one I had lost, but yet more of the God of love I had found; and to remember that she was with Him was an additional comfort to me. The funeral service was soothing and elevating beyond expression; and yet, when it was all over, such a sense of desolation came upon me, that I felt utterly forlorn and truly sad.

My nest was now completely stirred up; but instead of bemoaning its broken state, I could see the eagle fluttering over her young ones (Deut. xxxii. 11). I was conscious that God was looking on, and that He had not forsaken me in this great wreck.

The strain and excitement I had undergone naturally brought on an illness. I was seized with inflammation of the lungs, and was dangerously ill. From this, and other complications which supervened, the doctor pronounced that I could not recover, and bade me prepare for eternity.

Judges and doctors, when they pass sentence of death, seem to regard religion as a necessary preparation for it. Too common, also, is this idea, even among those who do not belong to these respected professions. My own opinion was much the same at that time.

Having received this solemn warning, I took down the Prayer-book, and religiously read over the office for the Visitation of the Sick. I became so interested in this exercise, that I determined to read it three times a day. The prayer for a sick child especially commended itself to my mind, so that, by changing a few words, I made it applicable to my own case, and used it not only three, but even seven, times a day. In substance, it petitioned that I might be taken to heaven if I died; or that, if it should please God to restore my health, He would let me live to His glory. I did not at that time expect my days would be prolonged, nor had I any wish to live, for the world was now perfectly blank and desolate to me. I felt as if I could never be happy again; to be with God would be far better!

I little dreamed that if I had died in that unpardoned

and Christless state, I should have been lost for ever; for I was profoundly ignorant of the necessity of change of heart—perfectly unconscious that I must be born again of the Spirit. This vital truth had never come to my mind; I felt a love for God, and in my ignorance I wished to die.

One morning the thought came to me, as I was sitting all alone by the fire, "What have I been praying for?—that the Lord would take me to heaven if I died; or, if I lived, that He would let me live to His glory?" Why, this is heaven both ways!—heaven in heaven, or heaven on earth—whichever way it pleases God to answer my prayer. Somehow I felt certain that He would answer it. I was exceedingly happy, and could not help thanking Him. From that day I began to feel better, and became impressed with the idea that I was to live, and not die. The doctor smiled at me when I told him so, for he did not believe it. He, and two other physicians, had told me that my lungs were diseased; indeed, six months afterwards, all three sounded me, and declared that one lung was inoperative, and the other much affected.

Yet, notwithstanding the doctor's discouraging announcement—for he told me, also, that " it was one of the fatal signs of consumption for the patient to feel or think he was getting better "—I had a certain conviction that I was to recover. As soon as the medical man had gone, I put on my coat and hat, and went out for a walk. I trembled much from weakness, and found it necessary to move very slowly and stop often; but under the shelter of a wall, courting the warmth of the bright shining sun, I managed to make my way to the churchyard.

While I was sitting there alone, the great bell struck out unexpectedly, and caused me to shake all over; for I was in a very weak condition. It was the sexton tolling to announce the departure of the soul of some villager from the world. Having done this, he came out with his boards and tools to dig the grave. He did not observe me sitting by; so he at once commenced, and went on diligently with his work. The ground had so often been broken before, that it did not take him long to accomplish his task: he gradually got deeper and deeper into the ground, till he disappeared altogether from my sight. I crept to the edge of the narrow pit in which he was, and looking into it, I could not help thinking of those words of Kirke White—

> "Cold grave, methinks, 'twere sweet to rest
> Within thy calm and hallowed breast!"

I had no fear of death, but rather felt that I should welcome it even more than restoration to health.

I have even now a most vivid remembrance of this, and place it on record to show how delusive are our feelings: because I did not feel any danger, I took it for granted that there really was none. That day, however, was an eventful one in my life; for, in the gladness of my heart, I gave *myself* to God, to live for Him. I had given my *will* before, and now I gave my life, and was happy in the deed. I did not know at that time that faith does not consist in believing that I have given myself, even if I meant it ever so sincerely; but in believing that God has taken or accepted me.

At the outset, I began with the former—a merely human faith—and its result was consequently imperfect. I was spiritually dead, and did not know it. Alas! what multitudes there are who are utterly unconscious of the fact of this spiritual death, though there are few things more plainly declared and revealed in the Word of God.

The full meaning of the word DEATH is too often misunderstood and overlooked. There are three kinds referred to in the Word of God—spiritual, natural, and everlasting. The first is a separation of the soul from God; the second, that of the body from the soul; and the last, that of the unbelieving man, body and soul, from God for ever.

It will be seen that there is one characteristic which is common to all three kinds—that is, *separation;* and that there is no idea of finality—death is not the end. When the Lord God created man, we suppose that He made him not merely in the form of a body, but a man with body and soul complete; and afterwards that He breathed into this *living man* the Spirit, and he became a *living soul*. As such, he communed with the eternal God, who is a Spirit. In this spiritual state he could walk and converse with God in the garden of Eden. When, however, he disobeyed the command which had been given to him, he incurred the tremendous penalty. The Lord God had said, "In the day that thou eatest of the tree of the knowledge of good and evil, thou shalt surely die." He did eat and he died there and then; that is, he forfeited that spirit which had quickened his soul, and thus became a dead soul; though, as we know, he remained a living man for nine hundred years before his body returned to its dust.

By his one act of disobedience, Adam opened in an instant (as an earthquake opens a deep chasm) the great gulf, the impassable gulf of separation which is fixed between us and God. By nature, as the children of Adam, we are all on the side which is away from God; and we are become subject also to the sentence pronounced against the life of the body. We know and understand that we are mortal, and that it is appointed unto men once to die; but we do not seem to be aware of the more important fact of the death of our souls. Satan, who said to our first parents, "Ye shall not surely die," employs himself now in deceiving men by saying, "Ye are not dead;" and multitudes believe him, and take it for granted that it is actually true. Thus they go on unconcerned about this awful and stupendous reality.

CHAPTER II.

Religious Life.

ITH returning health and strength, I did not think of going back into the world, but rather gave myself more fully to the purpose for which I supposed that my life had been restored. I felt a thankfulness and joy in my recovery, which confirmed me more and more in my determination to live to the glory of God.

When I was able to return to the South, I did so by easy stages till I got back to the neighbourhood of London; and there it was ordered that I should be shut up for the remainder of the winter.

During this season of retirement, I spent my time most happily in reading and prayer, and found great delight in this occupation. I was able to say, with the Psalmist, " I love the Lord, because He has heard my voice and my supplication;" and, like him, I could say, " I will call upon Him as long as I live ; I will walk before Him in the land of the living ; and I will take the cup of salvation and call upon the name of the Lord." That is, in secret or private life ; in social intercourse with my fellow-men ; and in the worship of the sanctuary, I will seek the glory of God.

I used to have much pleasure every day in asking God to give me a deeper sense of His love, that I might unfeignedly thank Him, and show forth His praise with my life as well as my lips.

All this, be it observed, was because God had saved not my soul, but my life; for as yet I had not, like the Psalmist, felt any trouble about my soul. I knew nothing of what he describes as the "sorrows of death and the pains of hell." I had not been awakened by the Spirit to know the danger and sorrow of being separated from God (which is spiritual death). I was perfectly unconscious that between God and myself there was the "impassable gulf" I have already referred to, and consequently I had not experienced such overwhelming anxiety as made the Psalmist cry out, "O Lord, I beseech Thee, deliver my soul." I knew nothing of the necessity of passing from death to life, and therefore I could not say, "The Lord has delivered my soul from death, mine eyes from tears, and my feet from falling."

The only thing I knew was that God was good to me, and therefore I loved Him, and was thankful, not for the sake of getting His favour, but because I thought I had it. I turned over a new leaf, and therewith covered up the blotted page of my past life. On this new path I endeavoured to walk as earnestly in a religious way, as I had before lived in a worldly one.

This mistake into which I fell was natural enough, and common as it is natural; but for all this it was very serious, and might have been fatal to me, as it has proved to multitudes. I did not see then, as I have since, that turning over a new leaf to cover the past, is not by any means the same thing as turning back the old leaves, and getting them washed in the blood of the Lamb.

I have said before that I did not know any better; nor was I likely to see matters in a clearer light from the line of study in which I was chiefly occupied. I was absorbed for the time, not so much in the Bible as in the "Tracts for the Times"—a publication which was engaging much attention. These Oxford tracts suited me exactly, and fitted my tone of mind to a nicety. Their object was the restoration of the Church of England from a cold, formal condition, into something like reality—from a secular to a religious state; this also was my own present object for myself. I read these writings with avidity, and formed from them certain ecclesiastical proclivities which carried me on with renewed zeal.

I suppose I learned from the perusal of them to interpret the Bible by the Prayer-book, and to regard the former as a book which no one could understand without the interpretation of the Fathers. Certain it is, that I did not look to the Bible, but to the Church, for teaching, for I was led to consider that private judgment on the subject of Scripture statements was very presumptuous. I got, moreover, into a legal state, and thought my acceptance with God depended upon my works, and that His future favour would result upon my faithfulness and attention to works of righteousness which I was doing. This made me very diligent in prayer, fasting, and almsdeeds; and I often sat and dreamed about the works of mercy and devotion which I would do when I was permitted to go out again.

Like persons in this state of mind, I also relied on ordinances, and was subject to them. I took it for granted that I was a child of God, because I had been baptized and brought into the Church; and having been confirmed and admitted to the Lord's Table, I concluded that I was safely on the way to Heaven. I see now the error of this very earnest devotion, and that I was going about to establish my own righteousness instead of submitting to the righteousness of God. I like to remember these days and tell of them, not because I am proud of them—far otherwise; but because they show the kind forbearance and patience of God towards me, and, besides this, they give me a clearer idea of the state of very many earnest people I meet with, who enter upon a religious path in much the same way.

Such persons make the two mistakes already referred to They start with believing in their surrender of themselves, instead of God's acceptance of it; and secondly, they make their continuance therein depend upon their repeated acts of devotion. They live and walk by their own works, not by faith in the finished work of Christ. What shall I say to these things? Shall I denounce them as delusions or superstitious legality? No. I would far rather that people should be even thus religious than be without religious observances—far rather that they should be subject to the Prayer-book teaching than be the sport of their own vain imaginings. If men have not given their hearts to God and received forgiveness of sins, it is better that they should give themselves to a Church than yield themselves to the world and its vanities.

If I had to go over the ground again under the same circumstances, I do not think I could take a better path. Church teaching by itself, with all its legalities, is superior to a man's own inventions; and the form of godliness required by it, even without spiritual power, is better than no form or profession of religion.

To say the least, Church teaching, when it is correctly followed, instructs the conscience, restrains and guides the will, and imparts a practical morality which we do not find in any other system. I have more hope of people who rest in some distinctive and positive dogmas than of those who merely deal with negations. The former may be reached by spiritual teaching; the latter are but shadowy adversaries with whom it is impossible to engage.

Therefore, when I see a man, for conscience towards God, giving up the world, and taking up with reverential worship, with even superstitious veneration for ecclesiastical things, because they are so—when I see a man, who was careless before, become conscientious and true in all his outward dealings, very particular in his observance of private and public prayer, exercising self-denial, living for others rather than himself, bearing and forbearing in all quietness and meekness—I cannot do otherwise than admire him. This, surely, is far more lovely and admirable than the opposite of these things.

Instead of joining in the outcry against such persons, I feel rather in sympathy, and have a desire in my heart to win them to still better things, and to show them "the way of God more perfectly." I feel that they are stirred as I was, and are struggling in self-righteousness, not because they wilfully prefer it to God's righteousness, but because they are yearning for true and spiritual reality. They are in a transition state, and the more restless they are, the more assured I am that they will never attain real rest and satisfaction to their souls till they have found God, and are found of Him in Christ Jesus.

But the question may be asked, "Is it possible for unsaved people (spiritually dead) to be so good and religious? Is not such a state an indication of spiritual vitality?" I answer, without hesitation, that it is possible. Religion by itself, irrespective of the subject-matter of a creed, may have a quieting and controlling effect upon the soul. The Hindoo, the Moslem, the Jew, the Romanist, as well as the Protestant, may each and all be wonderfully self-possessed, zealous, devout, or teachable, or even all these together, and yet remain dead souls.

As a boy in India, I remember being greatly struck with the calmness of the Hindoos, as contrasted with the impatience and angry spirit of the English. On one occasion I observed one of the former at his devotions. He, with others, had been carrying me about in a palankeen all day in the hot sun. In the evening, he most reverently took from his girdle a piece of mud of the sacred river Ganges, or Gunga, as they call it, and dissolving this in water, he washed a piece of ground, then, having washed his feet and hands, he stepped on this sacred spot, and began to cook his food. While it was preparing, he was bowed to the ground, with his face between his knees, worshipping towards the setting sun. A boy who was standing by me said, "If you touch that man he will not eat his dinner." In a thoughtless moment I did so with my hand, and immediately he rose from his devotions; but instead of threatening and swearing at me, as some might have done who belong to another religion, he only looked reproachfully, and said, "Ah, Master William!" and then emptying out the rice which was on the fire, he began his ceremony all over again. It was quite dark before he had finished his "poojah," or worship, and his meal. This man's religious self-possession made a greater impression on me than if he had abused or even struck me, for hindering his dinner. I thought to myself, "I will be a Hindoo when I grow up!" And truly I kept my word, though not in the same form; for what else was I in my earnest, religious days!

This is an important question to settle, and, therefore, I will give three examples from Scripture.

No one can doubt the zeal of Saul of Tarsus. His was no easy-going, charitable creed, which supposes all good men are right. He was sure that if he was right, as a natural consequence Stephen was wrong, even blasphemous, and as such worthy of death. Therefore, he had no scruples about instigating the death of such an one. Notwithstanding all this uncompromising and straightforward religiousness, he needed to be brought from death to life.

Again: look at Cornelius, who was "a devout man that feared God with all his house, which gave much alms to the people, and prayed to God alway" (Acts x. 2). There can be no mistake about this man with such a testimony; and yet he also needed to hear words whereby he and all his house should be saved (Acts xi. 14).

Next: Nicodemus, I suppose it will be admitted, was an earnest and religious man. Evidently, he was one of those who "believed in the name of Jesus, because he saw the miracles which He did" (John ii. 23). This man, humble and teachable as he was, came to Jesus, and said, "Rabbi, we know that Thou art a teacher come from God, for no man can do these miracles that Thou doest, except God be with him." Yet he was told, "Except a man be born again, he cannot see the kingdom of God." "Marvel not that I said unto thee, Ye must be born again" (John iii.). As surely as all mankind are dead in Adam, so surely every man needs spiritual life. In this respect it was no new thing which the Lord Jesus propounded to Nicodemus. The spiritual change of heart He referred to has always been the one condition of intercourse with God. All God's saints, even in the Old Testament times, had experienced this. Hence the Lord's exclamation, "Art thou a master of Israel, and knowest not these things?"

It may be urged that these three men were not in the Christian dispensation. Let this be granted; but the point at hand is that they needed spiritual life, though they were such good religious men. It will not be very hard to prove that even baptized men in the Christian dispensation need to be raised from death unto life just as much as any other children of Adam. It is clear, both from Scripture and experience, that baptism, whatever else it imparts, does not give spiritual vitality.

St. Peter's testimony is this, "Of a truth I perceive that God is no respecter of persons; but in every nation he that feareth Him and worketh righteousness is accepted with Him" (Acts x. 34, 35). Accepted to be saved, not because there is any merit in his works, but because God sees that there is real sincerity in his living up to the light he has. The heathen who know there is a God, and do not worship Him as God, are given over to idolatry (Rom. i.); but, on the other hand, those who do worship Him, and give Him thanks, are taken in hand to be guided into life and truth. Therefore are we justified in hoping that earnest and religious men, though they be dead, if their religion is really towards God, will be brought to spiritual life.

It was a happy winter to me, however, notwithstanding my spiritual deficiencies; and the recollection of it still abides in my memory. I had now no desire for the world and its pleasures. My mind had quite gone from such empty amusements and frivolities; even the taste I used to have for these things was completely taken away.

I was happier now than ever I had been before, so that I am convinced from personal experience that even a religious life may be one of joy, though by no means so satisfying and abiding as a truly spiritual one. I was happy, as I have already said, and longed for the time when I could be ordained, and devote my energies to work for God in the ministry.

CHAPTER III.
Ordination and First Parish.
1842.

IN the returning spring, as I was feeling so much stronger, and altogether better, I thought I would go and see the physician who had sounded me some months before. He, after a careful examination, still adhered to his previous opinion, and gave very little hope of my recovery, but suggested that if I went to the north coast of Cornwall there might be a chance for me.

On my return home, I took up an "Ecclesiastical Gazette," though it was three months old, and looked over the advertisements. There I observed one which invited a curate for a church in that very neighbourhood. It was a sole charge; but, strange to say, a title for holy orders was offered also. In reply to this I wrote a letter, asking for particulars, in which I stated my Church views, and that I was ordered to that part of the country for the benefit of my health.

The Vicar, who resided in another parish, thirty miles off, was so eager to get help for this one, that he wrote back to say he had sent my letter to the Bishop, with one from himself, and that I should hear from his lordship in a few days.

I was surprised at this precipitation of affairs, and all the more so when I received a note from the Bishop of Exeter (Phillpotts), bidding me come to him immediately, that I might be in time for the Lent ordination.

Accordingly, I started westward, and having passed my examination, I was sent with letters dimissory to the Bishop of Salisbury (Denison), to whom I was also sent, a year afterwards, for priest's orders. I was very weak, and much exhausted with travelling, but still went on, though I know not how.

The long-desired day at length arrived, and I was duly ordained; but instead of being full of joy, I became much depressed in mind and body, and could not rouse myself from dwelling upon the Bishop's address, which was very solemn. He told us that we were going to take charge of the souls of our parishioners, and that God would require them at our hands; we must take heed how we tended the Lord's flock. Altogether, it was more than I had calculated upon; and feeling very ill that afternoon, I thought that I had undertaken a burden which would certainly be my ruin. "What could I do with souls?" My idea of ordination was to be a clergyman, read the prayers, preach sermons, and do all I could to bring people to church; but how could I answer for souls which had to live for ever? and what was I to do with them?

In the evening, I so far roused myself as to go amongst the other candidates, to sound them, and ascertain what were their feelings with regard to the Bishop's solemn address! They merely thought that it was very beautiful, and that he was a holy man; and then some of them proposed that we should all go in a riding party, to see Stonehenge, the next day. It was especially thought that a drive on the Wiltshire plains would do me a great deal of good, if I did not feel strong enough to ride on horseback. I agreed to this, and went with them to see this famous temple of Druidical worship ; and after that set off for Plymouth, on my way to the far west. But, alas ! the charm of ordination had fled, and I was more than half sorry that I had undertaken so much. It had been done so precipitately too, for even now it was only ten days since I had seen the physician.

After resting a day, I proceeded to Truro, and then took a post-chaise and drove out to my first parish, called Perranzabuloe, which was situated about eight miles from Truro, on the north coast of Cornwall. I alighted at an old manor house, where I was to have apartments with a farmer and his family. Being much fatigued, I soon retired to bed, anything but happy, or pleased with the bleak and rough-looking place to which I had come.

I slept well however, and the next morning felt considerably better, and was revived in spirits. After making many inquiries about things in general, I obtained the keys, and made my way to the parish church, which was about ten minutes' walk from the house. Here, again, I was greatly grieved and disappointed to see such a neglected churchyard and dilapidated church ; and when I went inside, my heart sank, for I had never seen a place of worship in such a miserable condition. Moreover, I was told that the parish was seven miles long, and that its large population of three thousand souls was scattered on all sides, excepting round the church.

I had left my friends a long way off, and was alone in a strange place, with an amount of work and responsibility for which I knew I was thoroughly unprepared and unfit. However, I sauntered back to my lodgings, and began to ruminate as to what was to be done.

I had now sole charge of this extensive parish, for the uties of which I was to receive the very moderate stipend of forty pounds a year; but of this I did not complain, for my board and lodging, with washing, and the keep of a horse included, was only twelve shillings a week, leaving me a margin of nearly ten pounds for my personal expenses. The questions that troubled me were—what was I to do with three thousand people? and how was I to reach them?

In due course Sunday morning arrived, and with the help of a neighbouring clergyman, who kindly came over, as he said, "to put me in the way," I got through the service (being the only one for the day at that time), having about a score of listless people, lounging in different parts of the church, for a congregation. This was my first Sunday in my first parish.

Just at this time a book was sent me by a kind friend, entitled "The Bishopric of Souls," which terrified me even more than the Bishop's charge had done; for I felt that, notwithstanding my ardent desire to serve and glorify God, I had not the remotest conception how to do it, as regards winning souls. The author of this book took it for granted that every one who had the office of a pastor, had also the spiritual qualification for it; but experience proves that this is by no means the case. My ordination gave me an ecclesiastical position in the parish; the law maintained me in it; and the people expected me to do the duties of it: but how to carry all this out, except in a dry and formal way, I did not know.

As time went on, my parochial duties increased. I had to baptize the children, marry the young, visit the sick, and bury the dead; but I could not help feeling how different was this in action, to what it was in theory. I had had a kind of dreamland parish in my head, with daily service, beautiful music, and an assembly of worshipping people; but instead of this, I found a small, unsympathizing congregation, who merely looked upon these sacred things as duties to be done, and upon me as the proper person to do them. When I went to visit the sick I had nothing to say to them; so I read a few Collects, and sometimes gave them a little temporal relief, for which they thanked me; but I came out dissatisfied with myself, and longed for something more, though I did not know what.

Notwithstanding all these trials and disappointments, my health was gradually improving. I found that the air of this place was like meat and drink, and gave me an appetite for something more substantial. I very often frequented the beach, with its beautiful cliffs, and was much exhilarated by the bracing sea air; indeed, I had, and still retain, quite a love for the place. As my strength and energy increased, I rode about the parish all day, making the acquaintance of the people, and inviting them to come to church.

During my visits, I found out that the churchwarden was a good musician, and that he knew others in the parish who were able to play on various instruments; so in order to improve the services, and make them more attractive, I urged him to invite these musical people to his house to practise; and in due course we had a clarionet, two fiddles, and his bass viol, with a few singers to form a choir. We tried over some metrical psalms (for there were no hymn-books in those days), and soon succeeded in learning them. This musical performance drew many people to church. The singers were undeniably the great attraction, and they knew it; consequently I was somewhat in their power, and had to submit to various anthems and pieces, such as "Vital Spark," "Angels Ever Bright and Fair," and others, not altogether to my taste, but which they evidently performed to their own praise and satisfaction.

Finding that the people were beginning to frequent the church, I thought it was time to consider what steps should be taken about its restoration, and made it the subject of conversation with the farmers. It awakened and alarmed many of them when I said that the church must be restored, and that we must have a church rate. The chief farmer shook his head, saying, "You cannot carry that;" but I replied, "According to law, you are bound to keep up the fabric, and it ought to be done. I will write to the Vicar at once about it." He was a non-resident pluralist.

The farmer smiled at that, and said, laughing, "I will pledge myself that we will do as much as he does." It so happened that the Vicar, equally incredulous about the farmers doing anything, promised that he would do one half, if they would do the other.

Having ascertained this to my satisfaction, I immediately sent for the mason of the village, who played the clarionet in the church, also his son, who was "one of the fiddles," and consulted with them as to how this matter was to be accomplished. They, being in want of work at the time, readily advised me in favour of restoration. The church-warden (the "bass viol") said "that he had no objection to this proceeding, but that he would not be responsible. In two months," he added, "would be the annual vestry meeting." "That will do," I said, interrupting him; and I made up my mind that I would at once restore the church, and let the parishioners come and see it at that time.

Having made all necessary preparations, we commenced one fine Monday morning with repairing the roof and walls; and while the men were employed outside, we took out the windows and opened all the doors, to let the wind blow through, that the interior of the building might be thoroughly dried. This done, we next coloured the walls, also the stone arches and pillars (they were far too much broken to display them); and having cleaned the seats and front of the gallery, we stained and varnished them, matted the floor, carpeted the sacrarium, and procured a new cloth for the Communion Table, and also for the pulpit and reading-desk.

All this being completed, I painted texts with my own hands on the walls, in old English characters. I had great joy in writing these, for I felt as if it was to the Lord Himself, and for His name, and finished with Nehemiah's prayer, " Remember me, O my God, concerning this ; and wipe not out my good deeds that I have done for the house of my God, and for the offices thereof" (Neh. xiii. 14).

Altogether, it was a pretty church now, and a pretty sum was to be paid for it. I told the vestry that I alone was responsible, but that the Vicar had promised to pay one half if the vestry would pay the other. It seemed to be such a joy to them to get anything out of him, that they made a rate at once ; and upon the Vicar's letter, raised the money and paid off the debt.

The people were much pleased with their church in its new aspect, and brought their friends and neighbours to see it. Besides this, I observed something which gratified me very much. It was that when they entered the church they did so with reverence, taking off their hats and walking softly, in place of stamping with their heels and coming in with their hats on, as they too often had previously done, without any respect or concern whatever. A neglected place of worship does not command reverence.

My church now began to be the talk of the neighbourhood. Numbers of people came to see it, and among them several clergymen, who asked me to come and restore their churches.

There were many places where the people could not afford to rebuild the structure. In such, I was invited to exercise my skill in repairing, as I had done with my own ; in others, I was asked to give designs for restoring portions of the edifice ; and in some, for rebuilding altogether.

In this district, schools were not built nor parsonage-houses enlarged without sending for me.

For several years I was looked upon as an authority in architectural matters. I rode about all over the county from north to west, restoring churches and designing schools, and was accounted the busiest man alive; and my horse, my dog, and myself, the "three leanest things in creation," we were to be seen flying along the roads, day and night, in one part or another.

The Bishop of Exeter, who at that time presided over Cornwall, appointed me to make new "Peel" districts.* I designed nineteen, and made all the maps myself, calling on the Vicars and Rectors for their approbation. I was at this time a very popular man, and it was said that "the Bishop's best living" would be given to me in due time.

---

* The "Peel" districts were the new ecclesiastical districts created under the Church Extension Act, introduced by Sir Robert Peel.

CHAPTER IV.

Antiquarian Researches and Ministry.

1843—6.

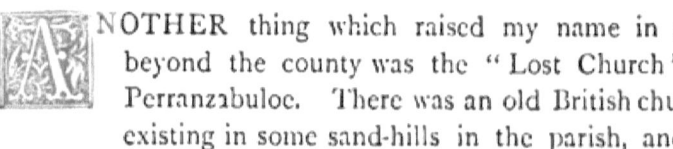 NOTHER thing which raised my name in and beyond the county was the "Lost Church" at Perranzabuloe. There was an old British church existing in some sand-hills in the parish, and it was said to be entire as far as the four walls. The hill under which it was buried was easily known by the bones and teeth which covered it. The legend said that the patron saint, St. Piran, was buried under the altar, and that close by the little church was a cell in which he lived and died. This was enough. I got men, and set to work to dig it up. After some days' labour we came to the floor, where we discovered the stone seats, and on the plaster on the wall the greasy marks of the heads and shoulders of persons who had sat there many centuries ago. We found the chancel step, and also the altar tomb (which was built east and west, not north and south). It was fallen, but enough remained to show the original shape and height of it.

I put a notice in the newspapers, inviting people to come and see the old church which had been buried for fifteen hundred years! In the presence of many visitors, clerical and lay, we removed the stones of the altar, and found the skeleton of St. Piran, which was identified in three ways. The legend said that he was a man seven feet high; the skeleton measured six feet from the shoulder-bones to the heel. Again, another legend said that his head was enshrined in a church forty miles away; the skeleton corresponded with this, for it was headless. Moreover, it was said that his mother and a friend were buried on either side of him; we also found skeletons of a male and female in these positions. Being satisfied on this point, we set the masons to work to rebuild the altar tomb in its original shape and size, using the same stones as far as they would go. We made up the deficiency with a heavy granite slab.

The "Lost Church," as it appeared in 1845.

On this I traced with my finger, in rude Roman letters, "Sanctus Piranus." The mason would not cut those crooked letters unless I consented for him to put his name in better ones in the corner. I could not agree to this, so his apprentice and I, between us, picked out the rude letters, which have since (I have heard) been copied for a veritable Roman inscription.

My name was now up as an antiquary, and I was asked to be the secretary (for the West of England) to the Archæological Society. I was supposed to be an old gentleman, and heard myself quoted as the "venerable and respected Haslam," whose word was considered enough to settle a knotty point beyond doubt. I was invited to give a lecture on the old Perran Church, at the Royal Institution, Truro, which I did; illustrating it with sketches of the building, and exhibiting some rude remains of carving, which are now preserved in the museum there.

The audience requested me (through their chairman) to print my lecture. This I undertook also; but being very young in literary enterprises, I added a great deal of other matter to the manuscript which I was preparing for the press. There was much in the book* about early Christianity and ecclesiastical antiquities. I imagined that this parish was, in British and Druidic times, a populous place, and somewhat important. There was a "Round," or amphitheatre, for public games, and four British castles; also a great many sepulchral mounds on the hills, the burial-place of chieftains. I supposed that St. Piran came here among these rude natives (perhaps painted savages) to preach the Gospel, and then built himself a cell † by the sea-shore, near a spring or well, where he baptized his converts. Close by, he built this little church, in which he worshipped God and prayed for the people.

The words of the poet Spenser do not inaptly describe this scene of other days:—

> "A little, lowly hermitage it was,
> Downe in a dale—
> Far from resort of people, that did pas

---

* "The Church of St. Piran." Published by Van Voorst.

† This little building still remains entire, under the sand. Some pieces of British pottery and limpet-shells were found outside the door.

> In traveill to and fro : a litle wyde
> There was a holy chappell edifyde,
> Wherein the hermite dewly wont to say
> His holy things each morn and eventyde ;
> Thereby a crystall streame did gently play,
> Which from a sacred fountaine wellèd forth away."

Here, then, more than fourteen centuries ago, people called upon God; and when their little sanctuary was overwhelmed with the sand, they removed to the other side of the river, and built themselves another church; but they still continued to bury their dead around and above the oratory and resting-place of St. Piran.

When my book was published, there ensued a hot controversy about the subject of it ; and some who came to see the " Lost Church " for themselves, declared that it was nothing more than "a modern cow-shed ;" others would not believe in the antiquity I claimed for it : one of these even ventured to assert his opinion in print, that " it was at least eight centuries later than the date I had fixed;" another asked, in a newspaper letter, " How is it, if this is a church, that there are no others of the same period on record ? "

This roused me to make further research; and I was soon rewarded by finding in the registry at Exeter a list of ninety-two churches existing in Cornwall alone in the time of Edward the Confessor, of which Lam-piran was one. With the help of another antiquary, I discovered nine in one week, in the west part of the county, with foundation walls and altar tombs, of which I published an account in the "Archæological Journal." This paper set other persons to work, who discovered similar remains in various parts of the country; and thus it was proved to demonstration that we had more ecclesiastical antiquities, and of earlier date, than we were aware of.

Next, my attention was directed to Cornish crosses ; about which I also sent a paper, with illustrations, as a good secretary and correspondent to the same Journal. My researches on this subject took me back to a very remote time. I found crosses among Roman remains, with inscriptions, something like those in the Catacombs near Rome—these were evidently Christian; but I found crosses also among Druidic antiquities. I could not help inquiring, "Where did the Druids get this sign?" From the Phœnicians. "Where did they get it?" From the Egyptians. "Where did they get it?" Then I discovered that the cross had come to Egypt with traditions about a garden, a woman, a child, and a serpent, and that the cross was always represented in the hand of the second person of their trinity of gods. This personage had a human mother, and slew the serpent which had persecuted her.*

Here was a wonderful discovery! The mythology of Egypt was based on original tradition, handed down from Antediluvian times! From further investigation, it was evident that the substance of Hindoo mythology came from the same source; as also that of the Greeks, Chinese, Mexicans, and Scandinavians. This is how the Druids got the cross also: it was in the hand of their demi-god Thor, the second person of their triad, who slew the great serpent with his famous hammer, which he bequeathed to his followers.

I was beside myself with excitement, and walked about the room in a most agitated state. I then made a table or harmony of these various mythologies, and when placed side by side, it was quite clear that they were just one and the same story, though dressed up in a variety of mythological forms, and that the story was none other than that of the Bible.

In my architectural journeys I used to entertain people

---

* These traditions came to the Egyptians from an ancestor who had come over the flood with seven others.

with these wondrous subjects; and one evening I had the honour of agitating even the Bishop of Exeter himself, who, in his enthusiasm, bade me write a book, and dedicate it to him. I did so. "The Cross and the Serpent" is the title of it, and it was duly inscribed to his lordship.

It excites me even now to think about it, though it is thirty-five years since I made these discoveries. The old librarian at Oxford declared that I was mad, and yet he could not keep away from the subject, and was never weary of hearing something more about it. This reverend Doctor said, "If you are right, then all the great antiquaries are wrong." I suggested that they had not had the advantage I possessed of placing their various theories side by side, or of making their observations from my point of view.

Notwithstanding all these external labours, which engrossed my earnest and deep attention, I did not neglect my parish. I felt, however, that my parishioners did not know anything about ecclesiastical antiquities or architectural science; and that they knew nothing, and cared less, about Church teaching. They did not believe, with me, that in order to be saved hereafter, they ought to be in the Church, and receive the Holy Communion—that there is no salvation out of the Church, and no Church without a Bishop. They were utterly careless about these things, and from the first had been an unsympathetic and unteachable people. I feel sure that had it not been for other interesting occupations which engaged my mind, I should have been altogether discouraged with them.

I tried to stir them up to a zeal worthy of their ancestors, who were such good and loyal Churchmen, that King Charles the First wrote them a letter of commendation, and commanded that it should be put up in all the churches. I had a copy of this letter well painted, framed, and placed in a conspicuous part of my church. Then I prepared an original sermon, which I preached, or rather read, to inaugurate the royal letter.

My text was taken from Heb. xii. 22 – 24, " Ye are come unto Mount Sion, and unto the city of the living God, the heavenly Jerusalem, and to an innumerable company of angels, to the general assembly and church of the first-born, which are written in heaven, and to God the Judge of all, and to the spirits of just men made perfect, and to Jesus the mediator of the new covenant, and to the blood of sprinkling, that speaketh better things than that of Abel." I applied these words to the Church of England, and rather reproached the Cornish people for not being more loyal and scriptural !

I think I was more roused by my sermon than any one else ; and no one asked me to print it, but I did for all that, with a copy of the king's letter. I am sorry to say that the public did not care sufficiently about it to buy copies enough even to pay for printing.

It fell very flat, but I attributed that to the degeneracy of the times, and of Cornish people in particular. The fact was, they understood that text far better than I did, and knew that " The Church of the first-born " was something more spiritual than I had any conception of.

From the commencement of my ministry I did not, as a general rule, preach my own sermons, but Newman's, which I abridged and simplified, for in that day I thought them most sound in doctrine, practical, and full of good common sense. Indeed, as far as Church teaching went, they were, to my mind, perfect. They stated doctrines and drew manifest conclusions ; but my people were not satisfied with them then ; and I can see now, thank God ! that, with all their excellences, they were utterly deficient in spiritual vitality.

The author was one whom I personally admired very

much, but by his own showing, in his "Apologia," he was a man who was searching not for God, but for a Church. At length, when he grasped the ideal of what a Church ought to be, he tried by the Oxford Tracts, especially No. XC., to raise the Church of England to his standard; and failing in that, he became dissatisfied, and went over to the Church of Rome.

Once, when I arrived at a friend's house in the Lake district, I was told that there was a most beautiful view of distant mountains to be seen from my window. In the morning I lifted the blind to look, but only saw an ordinary view of green fields, hedges, trees, and a lake. There was nothing else whatever to be seen. In the course of the day, a heavy mist which had been hanging over the lake was dispersed, and then I saw the beautiful mountains which before had been so completely veiled that it was difficult to believe in their existence.

So it was with me. I could see ecclesiastical things, but the more glorious view of spiritual realities beyond them, in all their full and vast expanse, was as yet hidden.

Whether my extracts from Newman's Sermons were more pointed, or whether I became more impatient with my congregation, I cannot tell, but it was very evident that my words were beginning to take effect at last; for as I went on preaching and protesting against the people and against schism, my "bass viol" called on me one day, and said, "If you go on preaching that doctrine, you will drive away the best part of your congregation." "Excuse me," I answered, "not the best part; you mean the *worst* part." "Well," he said, "you will see."

On the following Sunday, I gave out my text, and had scarcely read three pages of my manuscript when I heard a voice say, "Now we *will* go." With this, the "bass viol," the other fiddles, the clarionet, the ophicleide, and the choir, came stumping down the gallery stairs, and marched out. Some of the congregation followed their example, with the determination never to come back to the Church again. I waited till the noise was over, and then went on with my sermon meekly, and thought myself a martyr for Church principles.

I little thought that the people were being martyred; yet they were right, and enlightened in the truth, while I was altogether in the dark, and knew nothing about it. From this time there was a constant feud between the parishioners and myself. I *thought* that they were schismatics; and they *knew* that I was unconverted, and did not preach the Gospel.

One day, a Dissenter called to pay a burial fee for the funeral of his child, which he had purposely omitted paying at the proper time because he wished to tell me a piece of his mind. I was absent on the occasion on some architectural or archæological business, which was to me all important. "I know," he said, "why you went away and would not bury my child." "Do you?" I asked. "Yes; it was because I am a Dissenter." "Oh!" I said, "I would bury you all to-morrow if I could; for you are no good, and can do none either."

This went round the parish like wildfire, and did not advance my popularity, or do my cause any good.

Seriously at this time I thought that separation from the Church of England was a most deadly sin—it was schism. Idolatry and murder were sins against the Mosaic law; but this was a sin against the Church. I little dreamt then that many of the people with whom I thus contended, and whom I grieved so much, were real spiritual members of Christ, and had only ceased to be members of the Church of England because I did not preach the Gospel; that, in fact, I was the cause of their leaving the services; that I was the schismatic, for I was separated from Christ : they only, and that for a good reason, had separated from the communion of the Church of England, which I misrepresented.

The Church of England's teaching since the Reformation, like that of the primitive Church, is based not on baptism, but CONVERSION. Baptism was intended according to the Lord's commandment (Matt. xxviii. 19), for the purpose of making disciples*—that is, to graft members into the body of Christ's Church outwardly. Whatever special grace is given to infants and others at baptism, is given upon the condition of personal faith and repentance. Until a baptized person has been enabled by the Holy Ghost to repent and believe the Gospel, he is not really a new-born child of God, or raised from death unto life, though nominally, in the words of the Catechism, he has "been made a child of God."

Since the feuds and dissensions in my parish, the church was almost deserted, and left chiefly to myself, my clerk, and a few poor people, who, for the most part, were in ill favour in the chapels.

One day I was absorbed in writing, or rather re-writing, a text over the porch door of the church. It was, "This is none other but the house of God, and this is the gate of heaven." A man who was standing at the foot of the ladder said, "Heaven is a long way from that gate, I reckon." I pretended not to hear him, but his speech stuck to me. I knew only too well from this, and many other indications, that the people had no respect for the church under my ministrations.

---

* See *Greek*.

CHAPTER V.

The New Parish.

1846.

ABOUT this time the news reached us that the Vicar was dead; and thus ended my connection with Perranzabuloe. As the Dean and Chapter would not appoint me to succeed, I had no alternative but to make arrangements for my departure.

In one sense I was not sorry to go; but for various other reasons I much regretted having to leave a place where my health had been so wonderfully restored and sustained, and in which I had received so many tokens of God's favour. It is true that my labours were of an external character; but these I thought most important, and did them with all my might as unto the Lord. I took the work as from Him, and did it all to Him, and for Him, thanking Him for any token of success or commendation which I received.

I also regretted leaving the place before I had done any good to the people; for, with all my endeavours, I had not succeeded in persuading them to receive my idea of salvation by churchmanship.

However, the door was shut behind me; and this crisis happened at the exact time of another important event in my life. I was just engaged to be married, and therefore had an additional interest in looking for a sphere of labour which would suit me, and also the partner of my choice, who was in every respect likely to be an effectual helpmeet. This was soon found, and we agreed together to give ourselves to the Lord's work (as we thought) in it.

One of the "Peel" districts in the neighbourhood of Truro, which I had designed, called Baldhu, was on the Earl of Falmouth's estate: it came to his lordship's mind to take an interest in this desolate spot; so he bought the patronage from the commissioners, and then offered it to me, to be made into a new parish. This I accepted, with many thanks, and began immediately to dream out my plans for the future.

It was a time of great distress in that place amongst the tenants, on account of the failure of the potato crop; so his lordship employed some hundreds of the men in breaking up the barren croft for planting trees; there he gave me a good central site for a church.

Now I made up my mind to have everything perfect, and with my own rules and regulations, my surpliced choir, churchwardens, and frequent services, all after my own heart, it could scarcely fail to be otherwise. I thought that, having free scope, mine should be a model place. The district was in a barren part of a large parish: three thousand souls had been assigned to me; and I was to go and civilize them, build my church, school-house, and, indeed, establish everything that was necessary.

To begin with, I took a room which was used for a village school in the week, and for a service on Sunday. This succeeded so well, that in a few months I determined to enlarge the building in which we assembled, as speedily as possible. Having made all necessary plans, and procured stones, timber, and slate, we commenced operations at five o'clock one Monday morning, and by Saturday night had a chancel (which I thought most necessary) ready for Sunday use !

All the world came to see this sudden erection. This temporary church now held three hundred people; and with the addition of a new choir and hearty service, it was a great success, or, at least, so I imagined, for in those days I did not look for more.

I entered upon my work here with renewed energy and sanguine hope. I had, of course, gained more experience in the various duties of my ministry, and had, moreover, a clearer perception, as I thought, how sacramental teaching, under the authority of the Church, ought to work. I preached on holy living, not conversion, for as yet I knew nothing about the latter.

In 1847, I went on a visit to a very remarkable man, who had a great effect upon me in many ways. He was the Rev. Robert Hawker, of Morwenstow, in the extreme north of Cornwall.*

This friend was a poet, and a High Churchman, from whom I learned many practical lessons. He was a man who prayed, and expected an answer; he had a wonderful perception for realizing unseen things, and took Scripture literally, with startling effect. He certainly was most eccentric in many of his ways; but there was a reality and straightforwardness about him which charmed me very much; and I was the more drawn to him, from the interest he took in me and my work.

He knew many legends of holy men of old, and said that the patron saints of West Cornwall were in the calendar of the Eastern Church, and those in the north of Cornwall belonged to the Western. His own patron saint, Morwenna, was a Saxon, and his church a Saxon fane. He talked of

---

* See his " LIFE," by Rev. Baring Gould.

these saints as if he knew all about them, and wrote of them in a volume of poems thus:—

> "They had their lodges in the wilderness,
> And built them cells along the shadowy sea;
> And there they dwelt with angels like a dream,
> And filled the field of the evangelists
> With thoughts as sweet as flowers."

He used to give most thrilling and grand descriptions of the storms of the Atlantic, which broke upon the rocky coast with gigantic force, and tell thrilling stories of shipwrecks; how he saved the lives of some of the sailors, and how he recovered the bodies of others he could not save. Then, in the churchyard he would show you—there, a broken boat turned over the resting-place of some; here, two oars set up crosswise over several others; and in another part the figure-head of a ship, to mark the spot where the body of a captain was buried.

The Vicarage house was as original as himself. Over the door was inscribed—

> "A house, a glebe, a pound a day;
> A pleasant place to watch and pray.
> Be true to Church, be kind to poor,
> O minister, for evermore!"

The interior was furnished with old-fashioned heavy furniture, and the outside was conspicuous for its remarkable chimneys, which were finished off as models of the towers of churches where he had served. The kitchen chimney, which was oblong, perplexed him very much, till (as he said) "I bethought me of my mother's tomb; and there it is, in its exact shape and dimensions!"

He had daily service in his church, generally by himself, when he prayed for the people. "I did not want them there," he said. "God hears me; and they know when I am praying for them, for I ring the bell."

He had much influence in his parish, chiefly amongst the poor, and declared that his people did whatever he told them. They used to bring a bunch of flowers or evergreens every Sunday morning, and set them up in their pew ends, where a proper place was made to hold them. The whole church was seated with carved oak benches, which he had bought from time to time from other churches, when they were re-pewed with "deal boxes!"

On the Sunday, I was asked to help him in the service, and for this purpose was arrayed in an alb, plain, which was just like a cassock of white linen. As I walked about in this garb, I asked a friend, "How do you like it?" In an instant I was pounced upon, and grasped sternly on the arm by the Vicar. "'Like' has nothing to do with it; is it right?" He himself wore over his alb a chasuble, which was amber on one side and green on the other, and was turned to suit the Church seasons; also a pair of crimson-coloured gloves, which, he contended, were the proper sacrificial colour for a priest.

I had very little to do in the service but to witness his proceedings, which I observed with great attention, and even admiration. His preaching struck me very much; he used to select the subject of his sermon from the Gospel of the day all through the year. This happened to be "Good Samaritan Sunday," so we had a discourse upon the "certain man who went down from Jerusalem to Jericho" in which he told us that "the poor wounded man was Adam's race; the priest who went by was the Patriarchal dispensation; the Levite, the Mosaic; and the good Samaritan represented Christ; the inn was the Church; and the twopence, the Sacraments."

He held up his manuscript before his face, and read it out boldly, because he "hated," as he said, "those fellows who read their sermons, and all the time pretended to preach them;" and he especially abhorred those who secreted notes in their Bibles: "Either have a book, sir, or none!"

He had a great aversion to Low Church clergymen, and told me that his stag Robin, who ranged on the lawn, had the same; and that once he pinned one of them to the ground between his horns. The poor man cried out in great fear; so he told Robin to let him go, which he did, but stood and looked at the obnoxious individual as if he would like to have him down again and frighten him, though he would not hurt him—"Robin was kind-hearted."

"This Evangelical," he continued, "had a tail coat; he was dressed like an undertaker, sir. Once upon a time there was one like him travelling in Egypt, with a similar coat and a tall hat; and the Arabs pursued him, calling him the 'father of saucepans, with a slit tail.'" This part of his speech was evidently meant for me, for I wore a hat and coat of this description, finding it more convenient for the saddle, and for dining out when I alighted.

He persuaded me to wear a priestly garb like his, and gave me one of his old cassocks for a pattern; this I succeeded in getting made to my satisfaction, after considerable difficulty.

I came back to my work full of new thoughts and plans, determined to do what was "right;" and this in spite of all fears, whether my own, or those of others.

I now began to think more of the reality of prayer, and of the meaning of the services of the Church; I emphasized my words, and insisted upon proper teaching. I also paid more attention to my sermons, having hitherto disregarded them; for, as I said, "the Druids never preached; they only worshipped."

I held up my manuscript and read my sermon, like Mr. Hawker; and I wore a square cap and cassock, instead of the "saucepan" and the "tails." This costume I continued to wear for several years, though I was frequently laughed at, and often pursued by boys, which was not agreeable to flesh and blood; but it helped to separate me from the world, and to make me feel that I was set apart as a priest to offer sacrifice for the people.

In course of time I began to make preparations for my permanent church. I drew the designs for it, passed them, and obtained money enough to begin to build. There was a grand ceremony at the stone-laying, and a long procession. We had banners, chanting, and a number of surpliced clergy, besides a large congregation.

The Earl of Falmouth, who laid the stone, contributed a thousand pounds towards the edifice; his mother gave three hundred pounds for a peal of bells; and others of the gentry who were present contributed; so that upwards of eighteen hundred pounds was promised that day. Just twelve months after, July 20, 1848, the same company, with many others, and the Bishop of Exeter (Phillpotts) came to consecrate the "beautiful church."

In the meantime, between the stone-laying and the consecration, the Parsonage house had been built, and, more than that, it was even papered, furnished, and inhabited! Besides all this, there was a garden made, and a doorway, after an ecclesiastical mode, leading into the churchyard, with this inscription over it :—

> "Be true to Church,
> Be kind to poor,
> O minister, for evermore."

In this church there were super-altar, candles, triptych, and also a painted window; organ, choir, and six bells; so that for those days it was considered a very complete thing. "The priest of Baldhu," with his cassock and square cap, was quite a character in his small way. He preached in a surplice, of course, and propounded Church tactics, firmly contending for Church teaching. The Wesleyans and others had their distinctive tenets, the Church must have hers; they had their members enrolled, the Church must have hers; therefore he would have a "guild," with the view of keeping his people together. Outwardly there was an *esprit de corps*, and the parishioners came to church, and took an interest in the proceedings; but it was easy to see that their hearts were elsewhere. Still I went on, hoping against hope, "building from the top" without any foundation, teaching people to live before they were born!

CHAPTER VI.

The Awakening.

1848—51.

THE more earnestly I wrought among the people, and the better I knew them, the more I saw that the mere attachment to the Church, and punctual attendance at the services or frequency of Communion, was not sufficient. I wanted something deeper. I wanted to reach their hearts in order to do them good.

Whether this desire sprang up in the ordinary progress by which God was imperceptibly leading me, or from a story I heard at a clerical meeting, I know not—perhaps from both. My mind was evidently as ground prepared to receive the warning. The story was about a dream a clergyman had. He thought the judgment-day was come, and that there was, as it were, a great visitation—greater than the Bishop's. The clergy were mustering, and appeared in their gowns, but instead of being alone, they had part of their congregations with them. Some had a few followers, others had more, and some a great many; and all these received a gracious smile from the Judge when their names were called. The clergyman who dreamed was waiting, as he supposed, with a large number of people at his back.

When his turn came he went forward; but as he approached, he saw that the Judge's countenance was sad and dark. In a sudden impulse of suspicion he looked back; and lo! there was no one behind him. He stopped, not daring to go any further, and turning to look at the Judge, saw that His countenance was full of wrath. ·This dream had such an effect upon him that he began to attend to his parish and care for the souls of his people.

I also was beginning to see that I ought to care for the souls of my people—at least, as much as I did for the services of the Church. As a priest, I had the power (so I thought) to give them absolution: and yet none, alas! availed themselves of the opportunity. How could they have forgiveness if they did not come to me? This absolution I believed to be needful before coming to Holy Communion, and that it was, indeed, the true preparation for that sacred ordinance. I used to speak privately to the members of the Church Guild about this, and persuaded some of them to come to me for confession and absolution; but I was restless, and felt that I was doing good by stealth. Besides this, those whom I thus absolved were not satisfied, for they said they could not rejoice in the forgiveness of their sins as the Methodists did, or say that they were pardoned. In this respect I was working upon most tender ground, but I did not know what else to do.

I used to spend hours and hours in my church alone in meditation and prayer; and, while thinking, employed my hands in writing texts over the windows and on the walls, and in painting ornamental borders above the arches. I remember writing over the chancel arch, with much interest and exultation, "Now is come salvation, and strength, and the kingdom of our God, and the power of His Christ" (Rev. xii. 10).

I imagined, in my sanguine hope, that the kingdom of

Christ was come, and that the "accuser of the brethren" was cast down. I thought I saw, in the power of Christ given to His priests, such victory that nothing could stand against it. So much for dwelling on a theory, right or wrong, till it fills the mind. Yet I cannot say that all this was without prayer. I did wait upon God, and thought my answers were from Him; but I see now that I went to the Lord with an idol in my heart, and that He answered me according to it (Ezek. xiv. 3).

One day I saw a picture in a friend's house which attracted me during the time I was waiting for him. It was nothing artistic, nor was it over well drawn, but still it engaged my attention in a way for which I could not account. When my friend came down, we talked about other things; but even after I left the house this picture haunted me. At night I lay awake thinking about it—so much so, that I rose early the next morning, and went to a bookseller's shop, where I bought a large sheet of tracing-paper and pencil, and sent them out by the postman, with a note to my friend, begging him to give me a tracing of the picture in question.

I had to wait for more than a fortnight before it arrived, and then how great was my joy! I remember spreading a white cloth on my table, and opening out the tracing-paper upon it; and there was the veritable picture of the Good Shepherd! His countenance was loving and kind. With one hand He was pushing aside the branch of a tree, though a great thorn went right through it; and with the other He was extricating a sheep which was entangled in the thorns. The poor thing was looking up in helplessness, all spotted over with marks of its own blood, for it was wounded in struggling to escape. Another thing which struck me in this picture was that the tree was growing on the edge of a precipice, and had it not been for it (the tree), with all the cruel wounds it inflicted, the sheep would have gone over and perished.

After considering this picture for a long time, I painted it in a larger size on the wall of my church, just opposite the entrance door, so that every one who came in might see it. I cannot describe the interest with which I employed myself about this work; and when it was done, finding that it wanted a good bold foreground, I selected a short text— "He came to seek and to save that which was lost."

God was speaking to me all this time about the Good Shepherd who gave His life for me; but I did not hear Him, or suspect that I was lost, or caught in any thorns, or hanging over a precipice; therefore, I did not apply the subject to myself. Certainly, I remember that my thoughts dwelt very much on forgiveness and salvation, but I preached that these were to be had in and by the church, which was as the Ark in which Noah was saved. Baptism was the door of this Ark, and Holy Communion the token of abiding in it; and all who were not inside were lost. What would become of those outside the Church was a matter which greatly perplexed me. I could not dare to say that they would be lost for ever; but where could they be now? and what would become of them hereafter? I longed to save John Bunyan; but he was such a determined schismatic that it was impossible to make out a hope for him! Sometimes I was cheered by the thought that he had been duly baptized in infancy, and that his after-life was one of ignorance; but this opened the door too wide, and made my theory of salvation by the Church a very vague and uncertain thing. So deeply was the thought engrained in my mind that one day I baptized myself conditionally in the Church, for fear that I had not been properly baptized in infancy, and consequently should be lost hereafter. I had no idea that I was lost now; far from that, I thought I was as safe as the Church herself, and that the gates of hell could not prevail against me.

I had many conversations with the earnest people in my parish, but they were evidently resting, not where I was, but on something I did not know. One very happy woman told me, "Ah! you went to college to larn the *Latin;* but though I don't know a letter in the Book, yet I can read my title clear to mansions in the skies." Another woman, whenever I went to see her, made me read the story of her conversion, which was written out in a copybook. Several others, men and women, talked to me continually about their "conversion. I often wondered what that was; but, as I did not see much self-denial among these converted ones, and observed that they did not attend God's House nor ever come to the Lord's table, I thought conversion could not be of much consequence, or anything to be desired.

I little knew that I was the cause of their remaining away from church, and from the Lord's table. One thoughtful man told me, "Cornish people are too enlightened to go to church! A man must give up religion to go there; only unconverted people and backsliders go to such a place!" Yet this was a prayerful man. What did he mean? At various clerical meetings I used to repeat these things, but still obtained no information or satisfaction.

I made it a rule to visit every house in my parish once a week, taking from twelve to twenty each day, when I sought to enlighten the people by leaving Church tracts, and even wrote some myself; but they would not do. I found that the Religious Tract Society's publications were more acceptable. To my great disappointment, I discovered, too, that Evangelical sermons drew the people, while sacramental topics did not interest them. So, in my ardent desire to reach and do them good, I procured several volumes of Evangelical sermons, and copied them, putting in sometimes a negative to their statements, to make them, as I thought, right.

Now I began to see and feel that there was some good in preaching, and used the pulpit intentionally, in order to communicate with my people, carefully writing or compiling my sermons. But I must confess that I was very nervous in my delivery, and frequently lost my place—sometimes even myself; and this to the great confusion of the congregation.

I will tell how it pleased the Lord to deliver me from this bondage of nervousness, and enable me to open my lips so as to plainly speak out my meaning.

One day, a friend with whom I was staying was very late in coming down to breakfast; so, while I was waiting, I employed myself in reading the "Life of Bishop Shirley," of Sodor and Man. My eyes happened to fall on a passage, describing a difficulty into which he fell by losing his sermon on his way to a country church. When the prayers were over, and the psalm was nearly sung, he put his hand into his pocket for his manuscript, and, to his dismay, it was gone. There was no time to continue his search; so he gave out a text, and preached, as he said, in dependence upon God, and never wrote a sermon afterwards.

When my friend came to breakfast, he asked me what I had been doing all the morning. I told him. "Ah!" he said, quietly, "why do you not preach in dependence upon God, and go without a book like that good man?" "I preach like that!" I said, in amazement, terrified at the very thought. "Yes," he answered, mischievously, "you. Who needs to depend upon God for this more than you do?" Seeing that I was perturbed at his suggestion, he went on teasing me all breakfast time, and at last said "Well, what is your decision? Do you mean to preach in future in dependence upon God?" I said, "Yes; I have made up my mind to begin next Sunday." Now it was his turn to be terrified, and he did all he could to dissuade me, saying, "You will make a fool of yourself!" "No fear of that," I replied; "I do it already; I cannot be worse. No; I will begin next Sunday!"

I came back with the determination to keep my promise, but must confess that I grew more and more uneasy as the time approached. However, on Sunday, I went up into the pulpit, and spoke as well as I could, without any notes, and found it far easier than I had feared. In the evening it was still easier; and so I continued, week by week, gaining more confidence, and have never written a sermon since that day—that is, to preach it. Once I was tempted to take a book up into the pulpit, feeling I had nothing to say, when something said to me, "Is that the way you depend upon God?" Immediately I put the volume on the floor, and standing on it, gave out my text, and preached without hesitation. This going forward in dependence upon God has been a deliverance to me from many a difficulty besides this one, and that through many years.

One day I went, in my cassock and cap, to the shop of a man whom I regarded as a dreadful schismatic. He sold the publications of the Religious Tract Society. On entering, he appeared greatly pleased to see me, and took unusual interest and pains in selecting tracts, giving me a double portion for my money. His kindness was very embarrassing; and when, on leaving, he followed me to the door, and said "God bless you!" it gave me a great turn. A schismatic blessing a priest! This, indeed, was an anomaly. I was ashamed to be seen coming out of the shop, and the more so, because I had this large Evangelical parcel in my hand, I felt as though everybody was looking at me. However, the tracts were very acceptable at home, and in the parish. I even began to think there was something good in them. So I sent for more.

Three men, one after another, told me that they had been converted through reading them. One of these said that "the tract I had given him ought to be written in letters of gold;" and a few months after, this same man died most happily, rejoicing in the Lord, and leaving a bright testimony behind. I mentioned the conversion of these three men to many of my friends, and asked them for some explanation, but got none. Still, the thought continually haunted me—"What can this conversion be?"

I had made it a custom to pray about what I had to do, and anything I could not understand; therefore I prayed about this. Just then (I believe, in answer to prayer) a friend offered to lend me Southey's "Life of Wesley," and said, "You will find it all about conversion;" and a few days after came a tract, "John Berridge's Great Error Detected." This tract was carefully marked with pencil, and had several questions written in the margin. I found out that it came from a person to whom I had given it, and who was anxious to know its meaning.

I read it with much interest, for I saw that the first portion of the history of Berridge corresponded with mine; but as I went on reading, I wondered what he could mean by "Justification." What was that wonderful thing which God did for him and for the souls of his people? What could he mean by having his eyes opened to see himself a wretched, lost man? What was "seeing the way of salvation"? He said that he had preached for six years, and never brought a single soul to Christ; and for two years more in another place, and had no success; but now, when he preached Christ instead of the Church, people came from all parts, far and near, to hear the sound of the glorious Gospel; and believers were added to the Church continually. I grappled with this subject; but I could not, by searching, find out anything, for I was in the dark, and knew not as yet that I was blind, and needed the power of the Holy Spirit to awaken and bring me to see myself a lost sinner. My soul was now all astir on this subject; but, as far as I can remember, I wanted the information—not for myself; but because I thought I should then get hold of the secret by which the Wesleyans and others caught and kept their people, or rather my people.

Soon after, my gardener, *a good Churchman*, and duly despised by his neighbours for attaching himself to me and my teaching, fell seriously ill. I sent him at once to the doctor, who pronounced him to be in a miner's consumption, and gave no hope of his recovery. No sooner did he realize his position, and see eternity before him, than all the Church teaching I had given him failed to console or satisfy, and his heart sank within him at the near prospect of death. In his distress of mind, he did not send for me to come and pray with him, but actually sent for a converted man, who lived in the next row of cottages. This man, instead of building him up as I had done, went to work in the opposite direction—to break him down; that was, to show my servant that he was a lost sinner, and needed to come to Jesus just as he was, for pardon and salvation. He was brought under deep conviction of sin, and eventually found peace through the precious blood of Jesus.

Immediately it spread all over the parish that "the parson's servant was converted." The news soon reached me, but, instead of giving joy, brought the most bitter disappointment and sorrow to my heart. Such was the profound ignorance I was in!

The poor man sent for me several times, but I could not make up my mind to go near him. I felt far too much hurt to think that after all I had taught him against schism, he should fall into so great an error. However, he sent again and again, till at last his entreaties prevailed, and I went. Instead of lying on his bed, a dying man, as I expected to find him, he was walking about the room in a most joyful and ecstatic state. "Oh, dear master!" he exclaimed, "I am glad you are come! I am so happy! My soul is saved, glory be to God!" "Come, John," I said, "sit down and be quiet, and I will have a talk with you, and tell you what I think." But John knew my thoughts quite well enough, so he burst out, "Oh, master! I am sure you do not know about this, or you *would* have told me. I am quite sure you love me, and I love you—*that I do!* but, dear master, you do not know this—I am praying for the Lord to show it to you. I mean to pray till I die, and after that if I can, till you are converted." He looked at me so lovingly, and seemed so truly happy, that it was more than I could stand. Almost involuntarily, I made for the door, and escaped before he could stop me.

I went home greatly disturbed in my mind—altogether disappointed and disgusted with my work among these Cornish people. "It is no use; they will never be Churchmen!" I was as hopeless and miserable as I could be. I felt that my superior teaching and practice had failed, and that the inferior and, as I believed, unscriptural dogmas had prevailed. My favourite and most promising Churchman had fallen, and was happy in his fall; more than that, he was actually praying that I might fall too!

I was very jealous for *the Church*, and therefore felt deeply the conversion of my gardener. Like the elder brother of the Prodigal Son, I was grieved, and even angry, because he was restored to favour and joy. The remonstrance of the father prevailed nothing to mollify his feelings; in like manner, nothing seemed to give me any rest in this crisis of my parochial work. I thought I would give up my parish and church, and go and work in some more congenial soil; or else that I would preach a set of sermons on the subject of schism, for perhaps I had not sufficiently taught my people the danger of this great sin!

Every parishioner I passed seemed to look at me as if he said, "So much for *your* teaching! You will never convince us!"

CHAPTER VII.

Conversion,

1851.

THIS was a time of great disappointment and discouragement. Everything had turned out so different to the expectation I had formed and cherished on first coming to this place. I was then full of hope, and intended to carry all before me with great success, and I thought I did; but, alas! there was a mistake somewhere, something was wrong.

In those days, when I was building my new church, and talking about the tower and spire we were going to erect, an elderly Christian lady who was sitting in her wheel-chair, calmly listening to our conversation, said, "Will you begin to build your spire from the top?"* It was a strange question, but she evidently meant something, and looked for an answer. I gave it, saying, "No, madam, not from the top, but from the foundation." She replied, "That is right—that is right," and went on with her knitting.

This question was not asked in jest or in ignorance; it was like a riddle. What did she mean? In a few years this lady passed away, but her enigmatic words remained.

---

* See Tract, "Building from the Top," by Rev. W. Haslam.

No doubt she thought to herself that I was beginning at the wrong end, while I went on talking of the choir, organ, happy worship, and all the things we were going to attempt in the new church; that I was aiming at sanctification, without justification; intending to teach people to be holy before they were saved and pardoned. This is exactly what I was doing. I had planted the boards of my tabernacle of worship, not in silver sockets (the silver of which had been paid for redemption), but in the sand of the wilderness. In other words, I was teaching people to worship God, who is a Spirit, not for love of Him who gave His Son to die for them, but in the fervour and enthusiasm of human nature. My superstructure was built on sand; and hence the continual disappointment, and that last discouraging overthrow. No wonder that my life was a failure, and my labours ineffectual, inasmuch as my efforts were not put forth in faith. My work was not done as a thank-offering, but rather as a meritorious effort to obtain favour from God.

Repentance towards God, however earnest and sincere, without faith towards our Lord Jesus Christ, is not complete or satisfying. There may be a change of mind and will, producing a change of actions, which are done in order to pacify conscience, and to obtain God's favour in return; but this is not enough. It is like preparing the ground without sowing seed, and then being disappointed that there is no harvest. A garden is not complete or successful unless the ground has been properly prepared, nor unless flourishing plants are growing in it.

REPENTANCE with FAITH, the two together, constitute the fulness of God's religion. We have to believe, not in the fact that we have given ourselves—we know this in our own consciousness—but in the fact that God, who is more willing to take than we to give, has accepted us. We rejoice and work, not as persons who have surrendered ourselves to God, but out of loving gratitude, as those who have been changed by Him to this end.

I will go on now to tell how I was brought at this critical period of my life to *real* faith towards our Lord Jesus Christ. This was done in a way I knew not, and moreover, in a way I little expected. I had promised a visit to Mr. Aitken, of Pendeen, to advise him about his church, which was then building; and now, in order to divert my thoughts, I made up my mind to go to him at once. Soon after my arrival, as we were seated comfortably by the fire, he asked me (as he very commonly did) how the parish prospered. He said, "I often take shame to myself when I think of all your work. But, my brother, are you satisfied?"

I said, "No, I am not satisfied." *

"Why not?"

"Because I am making a rope of sand, which looks very well till I pull, and then, when I expect it to hold, it gives way."

"What do you mean?"

"Why," I replied, "these Cornish people are ingrained schismatics."

I then told him of my gardener's conversion, and my great disappointment.

"Well," he said, "if I were taken ill, I certainly would not send for you. I am sure you could not do me any good, for you are not converted yourself."

"Not converted!" I exclaimed. "How can you tell?"

He said, quietly, "I am sure of it, or you would not have come here to complain of your gardener. If you had been converted, you would have remained at home to rejoice with him. It is very clear you are not converted!"

---

* See Tract, "Are you Satisfied?" by Rev. W. Haslam.

I was vexed with him for saying that, and attempted to dispute the point; but he was calm and confident; while I, on the other hand, was uneasy, and trying to justify myself.

In the course of our conversation, he said, "You do not seem to know the difference between the natural conscience and the work of the Spirit." Here he had me, for I only knew of one thing, and he referred to two. However, we battled on till nearly two o'clock in the morning, and then he showed me to my bed-room. Pointing to the bed, he said (in a voice full of meaning), "Ah! a very holy man of God died there a short time since." This did not add to my comfort or induce sleep, for I was already much disturbed by the conversation we had had, and did not enjoy the idea of going to bed and sleeping where one had so lately died—even though he was a holy man. Resolving to sit up, I looked round the room, and seeing some books on the table, took up one, which happened to be Hare's "Mission of the Comforter." Almost the first page I glanced at told of the difference between the natural conscience and the work of the Spirit. This I read and re-read till I understood its meaning.

The next morning, as soon as breakfast was finished, I resumed the conversation of the previous night with the additional light I had gained on the subject. We had not talked long before Mr. Aitken said, "Ah, my brother, you have changed your ground since last night!"

I at once confessed that I had been reading Hare's book, which he did not know was in my room, nor even in the house. He was curious to see it.

He then challenged me on another point, and said, "Have you peace with God?" I answered, without hesitation, "Yes,"—for, for eight years or more I had regarded God as my Friend. Mr. A. went on to ask me, "How did you get peace?" "Oh," I said, "I have it continually. I get it at the Daily Service, I get it through prayer and reading, and especially at the Holy Communion. I have made it a rule to carry my sins there every Sunday, and have often come away from that holy sacrament feeling as happy and free as a bird." My friend looked surprised, but did not dispute this part of my experience. He contented himself by asking me quietly, "And how long does your peace last?" This question made me think. I said, "I suppose, not a week, for I have to do the same thing every Sunday." He replied, "*I thought so.*"

Opening the Bible, he found the fourth chapter of St. John, and read, "Whosoever drinketh of this water shall thirst again." "The woman of Samaria drew water for herself at Jacob's well, and quenched her thirst; but she had to come again and again to the same well. She had no idea of getting water, except by drawing, any more than you have of getting peace excepting through the means you use. The Lord said to her, 'If thou knewest the gift of God, and who it is that saith to thee, Give me to drink; thou wouldest have asked of Him, and He would have given thee living water,' which should be 'a well of water springing up into everlasting life'" (John iv. 10—14). My friend pointed out the difference between getting water by drawing from a well, and having a living well within you springing up.

I said, "I never heard of such a thing."

"I suppose not," he answered.

"Have you this living water?" I continued.

"Yes, thank God, I have had it for the last thirty years."

"How did you get it?"

"Look here," he said, pointing to the tenth verse: "Thou wouldest have asked of Him, and He would have given thee living water."

"Shall we ask Him?" I said.

He answered, "With all my heart;" and immediately pushing back his chair, knelt down at his round table, and I knelt on the opposite side. What he prayed for I do not know. I was completely overcome, and melted to tears. I sat down on the ground, sobbing, while he shouted aloud, praising God.

As soon as I could get up, I made for the door, and taking my hat, coat, and umbrella, said that "I was really afraid to stay any longer." With this I took my departure, leaving my carpet-bag behind. It was seven miles to Penzance, but in my excitement I walked and ran all the way, and arrived there before the coach, which was to have called for me, but brought my carpet-bag instead. In the meantime, while I was waiting for it, I saw a pamphlet, by Mr. Aitken, in a shop window, which I bought, and got into the train to return to Baldhu. My mind was in such a distracted state, that I sought relief in reading. I had not long been doing so, when I came to a paragraph in italics: "*Then shall He say unto them, Depart from Me; I never knew you.*" The question arrested me, What if He says that to you?

Ah, that is not likely.

But, what if He does?

It cannot be. I have given up the world; I love God; I visit the sick; I have daily service and weekly communion.

But, what if He does?—what if He does?

I could not bear the thought; it seemed to overwhelm me.

As I read the pamphlet, I saw that the words were spoken to persons who were taken by surprise. So should I be. They were able to say, "We have eaten and drunk in Thy presence, and Thou hast taught in our streets: in Thy name we have cast out devils, and done many wonderful works." Yet, with all this, He replied, "Depart from Me, I never knew you." I did not see how I could escape, if such men as these were to be rejected.

Conviction was laying hold upon me, and the circle was becoming narrower. The thought pressed heavily upon me, "What a dreadful thing, if I am wrong!" Added to this, I trembled to think of those I had misled. "Can it be true? Is it so?" I remembered some I had watched over most zealously, lest the Dissenters should come and pray with them. I had sent them out of the world resting upon a false hope, administering the sacrament to them for want of knowing any other way of bringing them into God's favour. I used to grieve over any parishioner who died without the last sacrament, and often wondered how it would fare with Dissenters!

My mind was in a revolution. I do not remember how I got home. I felt as if I were out on the dark, boundless ocean, without light or oar or rudder. I endured the greatest agony of mind for the souls I had misled, though I had done it ignorantly. "They are gone, and lost for ever!" I justly deserved to go also. My distress seemed greater than I could bear. A tremendous storm of wind, rain and thunder, which was raging at the time, was quite in sympathy with my feelings. I could not rest. Looking at the graves of some of my faithful Churchmen, I wondered, "Is it really true that they are now cursing me for having misled them?"

Thursday, Friday, and Saturday passed by, each day and night more dark and despairing than the preceding one. On the Sunday, I was so ill that I was quite unfit to take the service. Mr. Aitken had said to me, "If I were you, I would shut the church, and say to the congregation, 'I will not preach again till I am converted. Pray for me!'" Shall I do this?

The sun was shining brightly, and before I could make up my mind to put off the service, the bells struck out a merry peal, and sent their summons far away over the hills. Now the thought came to me that I would go to church and read the morning prayers, and after that dismiss the people. There was no preparation for the Holy Communion that day, and I had deputed the clerk to select the hymns, for I was far too ill to attend to anything myself. The psalms and hymns were especially applicable to my case, and seemed to help me, so that I thought I would go on and read the ante-communion service, and then dismiss the people. And while I was reading the Gospel, I thought, well, I will just say a few words in explanation of this, and then I will dismiss them. So I went up into the pulpit and gave out my text. I took it from the Gospel of the day—"What think ye of Christ?" (Matt. xxii. 42).

As I went on to explain the passage, I saw that the Pharisees and scribes did not know that Christ was the Son of God, or that He was come to save them. They were looking for a king, the son of David, to reign over them as they were. Something was telling me, all the time, "You are no better than the Pharisees yourself—you do not believe that He is the Son of God, and that He is come to save you, any more than they did." I do not remember all I said, but I felt a wonderful light and joy coming into my soul, and I was beginning to see what the Pharisees did not. Whether it was something in my words, or my manner, or my look, I know not; but all of a sudden a local preacher, who happened to be in the congregation, stood up, and putting up his arms, shouted out in Cornish manner, "The parson is converted! the parson is converted! Hallelujah!"* and in another moment his voice was lost

---

* This scene is well depicted in the accompanying Illustration.

"The Parson is Converted!"

See page 60.

in the shouts and praises of three or four hundred of the congregation. Instead of rebuking this extraordinary "brawling," as I should have done in a former time, I joined in the outburst of praise; and to make it more orderly, I gave out the Doxology—" Praise God, from whom all blessings flow "—and the people sang it with heart and voice, over and over again. My Churchmen were dismayed, and many of them fled precipitately from the place. Still the voice of praise went on, and was swelled by numbers of passers-by, who came into the church, greatly surprised to hear and see what was going on.

When this subsided, I found at least twenty people crying for mercy, whose voices had not been heard in the excitement and noise of thanksgiving. They all professed to find peace and joy in believing. Amongst this number there were three from my own house; and we returned home praising God.

The news spread in all directions that "the parson was converted," and that by his own sermon, in his own pulpit! The church would not hold the crowds who came in the evening. I cannot exactly remember what I preached about on that occasion; but one thing I said was, "that if I had died last week I should have been lost for ever." I felt it was true. So clear and vivid was the conviction through which I had passed, and so distinct was the light into which the Lord had brought me, that I knew and was sure that He had "brought me up out of an horrible pit, out of the miry clay, and set my feet upon a Rock, and put a new song into my mouth" (Ps. xl.). He had "quickened" me, who was before "dead in trespasses and sins" (Eph. ii. 1).

I felt sure, as I said, that if I had died last week I should have been lost for ever. This was a startling and an alarming word to many of my earnest people, who said,

"What then will become of us?" I replied, "You will be lost for a certainty if you do not give your hearts to God."

At the end of this great and eventful day of my life—my spiritual birthday, on which I passed from death to life by being "born from above"—I could scarcely sleep for joy. I awoke early the next morning, with the impression on my mind that I must get up and go to a village a mile off, to tell James B—— of my conversion. He was a good and holy man, who had often spoken to me about my soul; and had been praying for three years or more on my behalf.

I had scarcely gone half-way before I met him coming towards me: he seemed as much surprised to see me as I was to meet him. He looked at me in a strange way, and then, leaning his back against a stone fence, he said, "Are you converted?"

"Why do you ask me?" I replied. "I am just on my way to your house, to tell you the good news—that I have found peace. My soul is saved."

The dear man said, "Thank God!" and it came from the very depths of his heart. Shedding tears of joy, he went on to say, "This night I woke up thinking of you; you were so strongly in my mind, that I got up and began to pray for you; but I could not '*get hold:*' I wrestled and cried aloud, but it was all of no avail; I begged the Lord not to give you up; but it seemed I could not pray. After trying for more than two hours, it came to my mind that perhaps *you were converted.* This thought made me so happy, that I began to praise the Lord; and then I had liberty, and shouted so loud that it roused up the whole house, and they came rushing into my room to know whatever was the matter with me. 'I am praising God,' I said; 'praising God—the parson is converted!—I feel sure he is. Glory be to God! Glory be to God!' They said, 'You must be dreaming; you had better lie down again, and be quiet.' But it was of no use, I could not sleep; and so soon as the light began to break, I dressed myself, and have come out to see whether it is true."

"Yes," I said, "*it is true;* the Lord has saved my soul; I am happy!" I thanked him then and there for all the help he had been, and for the patience he had so long exercised towards me. We spent a happy time together, thanking and praising God, and then he returned home to tell his friends and neighbours the news.

After breakfast a visitor arrived, who was on an errand of quite another kind. The report had by this time spread far and wide, that I was converted in my own pulpit, and by means of my own sermon; also, that I had said, "If I had died last week, I should have been lost for ever!" My friend having heard this, immediately mounted his horse and rode over to see me about it. He at once put the question, "Did you say, last night, in your pulpit, that you were saved; and that if you had died last week you would have been lost for ever?"

I answered, "Yes, indeed, I did; and I meant it."

He looked quite bewildered, and stood for a long time arguing with me; then taking a chair he sat down, and began to sympathize and pity me, saying how grieved he was, for he could see madness in my eyes. He tried to divert my thoughts, and begged that I would go out for a ride with him. Seeing that he made no impression by his various arguments, and that he could not prevail upon me to recall my words, he ordered his horse; but before mounting, he said, "I cannot agree with you, and will oppose you as hard as I can."

"Very well," I replied; "but let us shake hands over it: there is no need that we should be angry with one another."

Then mounting, he started off, and had not gone more than a few yards, when, suddenly pulling up, he turned, and placing his hand on the back of his horse, called out, "Haslam, God stop the man who is wrong!"

I answered, "Amen," and off he trotted.

On the Friday following he broke a blood-vessel in his throat or chest, and has never preached since. His life was in danger for several weeks, though in course of time he recovered, but I have heard that he has never been able to speak above a whisper. God has most undoubtedly stopped him; while He has permitted me to preach for the last nine-and-twenty years, on the average more than six hundred times a year.

From that time I began to preach the Gospel, and was not ashamed to declare everywhere what the Lord had done for my soul. Thus from personal experience I have been enabled to proclaim the Word, both as a "witness" and a "minister."

I, who before that time used to be so weak, that I could not preach for more than fifteen or twenty minutes for three consecutive Sundays without breaking down, was now able to do so each day, often more than once, and three times every Sunday.

CHAPTER VIII.

The Revival.

1851—4.

IN the providence of God, my conversion was the beginning of a great revival work in my parish, which continued without much interruption for nearly three years. At some periods during that time there was a greater power of the divine presence, and consequently more manifest results, than at others; but all along there were conversions of sinners or restoration of backsliders every week—indeed, almost every day.

I was carried along with the torrent of the work, far over and beyond several barriers of prejudice which had been in my mind. For instance, I made a resolution that if I ever had a work of God in my parish, it should be according to rule, and that people should not be excited into making a noise, as if God were deaf or afar off; also, that I would prevent their throwing themselves into extraordinary states of mind and body, as though it were necessary that they should do so in order to obtain a blessing. I intended to have everything in most beautiful and exemplary order, and that all should be done as quietly and with as much precision as the working of a machine. No shouting of praises, no loud praying, no hearty responding; and, above all, no extravagant crying for mercy, such as I had witnessed in Mr. Aitken's parish.

But notwithstanding my prudence and judicious resolutions, "the wind blew as it listed; we heard the sound thereof, but could not tell whence it came, or whither it went" (John iii. 8). In spite of all my prejudices, souls were quickened and born of the Spirit. I was filled with rejoicing, and my heart overflowed with joy to see something doing for the Lord.

Anything is better than the stillness of death, however æsthetic and beautiful, however reverential and devout a mere outward ceremonial may appear. Imposing pageants and religious displays may excite enthusiastic religiosity or devotionism; but they do not, and never can, promote spiritual vitality. Far from this, they draw the heart and mind into a channel of human religion, where it can sometimes overflow to its own satisfaction; but they never bring a sinner to see himself lost, or unworthy by nature to be a worshipper, and consequently, as such, utterly unfit to take any part in religious ceremonies.

On the Monday after my conversion we had our first week-day revival service in the church, which was filled to excess. In the sermon, I told them once more that God had "brought me up out of an horrible pit, out of the miry clay, and set my feet upon the Rock, and . . . put a new song in my mouth" (Ps. xl. 2—3). I had not spoken long, when some one in the congregation gave a shriek, and then began to cry aloud for mercy. This was quickly followed by cries from another and another, until preaching was altogether hopeless. We then commenced praying for those who were in distress, and some experienced men who were present dealt with the anxious.

I cannot tell how many people cried for mercy, or how

many found peace that night; but there was great rejoicing. I, who was still in my grave-clothes, though out of the grave, was sorely offended at people praying and praising God so heartily and so loudly *in the church*. I thought that if this was to become a regular thing, it would be akin to "brawling," and quite out of order. Practising singing and rehearsing anthems in the church, I did not think much about; but somehow, for people to cry out in distress of soul, and to praise God out of the abundance of their hearts, was too much for me. I was sadly perplexed!

At the close of the service, I told the people I would have a short one again the next evening, in the church, and that after that we would go into the schoolroom for the prayer meeting. Thus ended the second day of my spiritual life.

On Tuesday evening we assembled in the church, and then went to the schoolroom for the after-meeting. There the people had full liberty to sing, praise, and shout too, if they desired, to their hearts' content, and truly many availed themselves of the opportunity. In Cornwall, at the time I speak of (now twenty-nine years ago), Cornish folk did not think much of a meeting unless it was an exciting and noisy one.

In this schoolroom, evening by evening, the Lord wrought a great work, and showed forth His power in saving many souls. I have seldom read of any remarkable manifestations in revivals the counterpart of which I did not witness in that room; and I saw some things there which I have never heard of as taking place anywhere else. I was by this time not afraid of a little, or even much noise, so long as the power of the Lord's presence was evident. The shouts of the people did not hinder me, nor did their loud praying, nor their hearty responses.

There were some subjects on which it was impossible

to venture without eliciting vehement demonstrations. A friend of mine, who had come from some distance on a visit, went with me on one occasion to an afternoon Bible-class. I asked him to address the people, and in a quiet way he proceeded to talk of heaven. As he described the city of gold, with its pearly gates, its walls of jasper, its foundations of sapphire and precious stones, and to tell them that " the city had no need of the sun, neither of the moon, to shine in it; for the glory of God did lighten it, and the Lamb is the light thereof" (Rev. xxi. 2—3), I began to feel somewhat uneasy, and feared that he was venturing on tender ground, when all at once there was heard a shriek of joy, and in a moment almost the whole class was in an ecstasy of praise. My friend was greatly dismayed, and also frightened at the noise, and seizing his hat, he made hastily for the door. "Stop! stop!" I said; "you must stand fire better than that." I quietly gave out a hymn, and asked some of them to help me sing, and then we knelt down to pray. I prayed in a low voice, and soon all was still again, excepting the responsive "Amens," and the gaspings of those who had been thus excited.

It may be asked, why did I permit such things? I lived amongst a people who were accustomed to outward demonstrations; and by descending to them in their ways I was enabled to lead many of them to higher things, and to teach them to rest not so much on their feelings, as on the facts and truth revealed in the Word of God. But theorize as we would, it was just a question, in many cases, of no work, or of decided manifestation. We could not help people being stricken down, neither could they help it themselves; often the most unlikely persons were overcome and became excited, and persons naturally quiet and retiring proved the most noisy and demonstrative. However, it was our joy to see permanent results afterwards, which more than reconciled us to any amount of inconvenience we had felt at the time.

When the power of God is manifestly present, the persons who hear the noise, as well as those who make it, are both under the same influence, and are in sympathy with one another. An outsider, who does not understand it, and is not in sympathy, might complain, and be greatly scandalized. For my own part, I was intensely happy in those meetings, and had become so accustomed to the loud "Amens," that I found it very dull to preach when there was no response. Prayer-meetings which were carried on in a quiet and formal manner seemed to me cold and heartless. "They that go down to the sea in ships, that do business in great waters; these see the works of the Lord, and His wonders in the deep" (Ps. cvii. 23, 24). Some spiritual mariners never venture out of a calm millpond, and rejoice in very quiet proceedings; they do *not look* like rejoicing at all. They resemble the people who are going through a formal duty, and, "like a painted ship upon a painted ocean," they are never tossed. Most undeniable it is that many trying things happen in the excitement of a storm.

I was hardened against criticism, and only wished that my criticizing friends could show me a more effectual way of working, and a way in which God's glory might be advanced, without giving offence.

The very remembrance of these times warms my heart as I write; and though I do not know whether I am still young enough to enter into such things in the same way, yet I am sure that the manifest presence of the Lord, under any circumstances, would still stir and rejoice my spirit. My friend Mr. Aitken used to rise above it all most majestically, and shout as loud as the loudest. It was grand to see his great soul at full liberty rejoicing in the Lord. He was quite at home in the noisiest and stormiest meetings, and no doubt he thought me a promising disciple, and a very happy one, too.

Oh, what tremendous scenes we witnessed whenever Mr. Aitken came to preach at Baldhu! The church, which was built to seat six hundred, used to have as many as fifteen hundred packed into it. Not only were the wide passages crowded, and the chancel filled, even up to the communion table, but there were two rows of occupants in every pew. The great man was king over their souls, for at times he seemed as if he was endued with power whereby he could make them shout for joy, or howl for misery, or cry aloud for mercy. He was by far the most effective preacher I ever heard, or ever expect to hear. Souls were awakened by scores whenever he preached, and sometimes the meetings continued far into the night, and occasionally even to the daylight of the next morning.

To the cool, dispassionate outside observers and the newspaper reporters, all this vehement stir was very extravagant and incomprehensible, and no doubt they thought that it was done for excitement; certainly they gave us credit for that, and a great deal more. They did not esteem us better than themselves, and consequently we had the full benefit of their sarcasm and invective.

Cornish revivals were things by themselves. I have read of such stirring movements occurring occasionally in different places elsewhere, but in Cornwall they were frequent. Every year, in one part or another, a revival would spring up, during which believers were refreshed and sinners awakened. It is sometimes suggested that there is a great deal of the flesh in these things—more of this than of the Spirit. I am sure this is a mistake, for I am quite satisfied that neither Cornish nor any other people could produce revivals without the power of the Spirit, for they would never be without them if they could raise them at pleasure. But, as a fact, it is well known that revivals begin and continue for a time, and that they cease as mysteriously as they began.

Sometimes I have known the children of the school commence crying for no ostensible reason; when a few words about the love of God in giving His Son, or the love of Christ in laying down His life, would prove enough to kindle a flame, and they would begin to cry aloud for mercy forthwith. I have seen a whole school of more than a hundred children like this at the same time. An awakening of such a character was generally a token of the beginning of a work of God, which would last in power for four or five weeks, if not more; then the quiet, ordinary work would go on as before. Sometimes, for no accountable reason, we saw the church thronged with a multitude of people from various parts, having no connection with one another, all equally surprised to see each other; and the regular congregation more surprised still to see the unexpected rush of strangers. After a time or two we began to know the cause, and understood that the coming together of the people was by the Spirit of the Lord, and so we prepared accordingly, expecting a revival to follow.

On these occasions it was very easy to preach, or pray, or sing; we had only to say, "Stay here, or go to the schoolroom;" "Stand and sing;" or, "Kneel and pray;" and it was done at once: such was the power of the Spirit in melting the hearts of the people into entire submission for the time.

CHAPTER IX.

The Visitor.

1851.

IN the midst of these things, we had a scene quite characteristic of Cornwall, which was the funeral of my late gardener and friend, John Gill. This man's conversion, it will be remembered, was the event by which it pleased God to bring my religious state to a crisis. After my sudden exit from John's cottage, which I have already described, he continued to pray for me, as he said he would, until the following Sunday, when he heard of my conversion. Then he praised God, and that with amazing power of mind and body for a dying man. Day by day, as his life was prolonged, he was eager to hear of the progress of the work.

At last the day of his departure arrived, and he was quite content and happy to go. A large concourse of people assembled at the funeral, dressed in their Sunday best. They gathered by hundreds in front of John's cottage, several hours before the time fixed for the service. During this interval they sang hymns, which were given out two lines at a time. Then they set out for the church, singing as they went along.

In the West it is not the custom to carry the coffin on the shoulders, but by hand, which office is performed by friends, who continually relieve one another, that all may take part in this last mark of respect to the deceased. At length, they arrived at the "lych" gate, and setting the coffin upon the lych stone (a heavy slab of granite, put there for the purpose), they sang their final hymn. At the conclusion of this, I came out with my clerk to receive the funeral party and to conduct them into the church. After the service I was about to give an address, when I was told that there were more people outside than within the church. In order, therefore, not to disappoint them, we came to the grave-side in the churchyard, and from thence I addressed a great concourse of people.

I told them of dear John's conversion, and of my disappointment and distress on account of it; then of my own conversion, and John's unbounded joy; taking the opportunity to enforce the absolute necessity of this spiritual change, and the certain damnation of those who die without it.

This funeral caused a solemn feeling, and as the people lingered about, we re-entered the church, and further improved the occasion. Then we went to the schoolroom for a prayer-meeting, and many souls were added to the number of the saved.

Among the strangers present was a gentleman who had come all the way from Plymouth, in order to witness for himself the wonderful work, of which he had read an account in the newspaper. After attending several of our services, he came up to speak to me, and said that he had seen an account of "the fall of a High Churchman into Dissent," which was regarded as a very extraordinary thing, for at that time some Dissenters were becoming High Churchmen, or what used to be called then "Puseyites." Having seen me, and heard for himself of my conversion, and my adherence to the Church, he was satisfied, and asked me to spare time for a little conversation with him.

He came to my house the next morning, and commenced by asking, "Do you really think you would have been lost for ever, if you had died before you were converted?" This he said looking me full in the face, as if to see whether I flinched from my position.

I answered, "Most certainly; without a doubt."

"Remember," he said, calmly, "you have been baptized and confirmed; you are a communicant, and have been ordained; and do you really think that all this goes for nothing?"

"Most assuredly, all these things are good in their place, and fully avail for their respective purposes, but they have nothing whatever to do with a sinner's salvation."

"Do you mean to say," he continued, "that *the Church* is not the very ark of salvation?"

"I used to think so," I replied, "and to say that 'there was no Church without a Bishop, and no salvation out of the Church;' but now I am sure that I was mistaken. The outward Church is a fold for protecting the sheep, but the Church is not the Shepherd who seeks and finds the lost sheep."

"Well," he said, "but think of all the *good men* you condemn if you take that position so absolutely."

Seeing that I hesitated, he went on to say that he "knew many very good men, in and out of the Church of England, who did not think much of conversion, or believe in the necessity of it."

"I am very sorry for them," I replied; "but I cannot go back from the position into which, I thank God, He has brought me. It is burned into me that, except a man is converted, he will and must be lost for ever."

"Come, come, my young friend," he said, shifting his chair, and then sitting down to another onslaught, "do you mean to say that a man will go to hell if he is not *converted*, as you call it?"

"Yes, I do; and I am quite sure that if I had died in an unconverted state I should have gone there; and this compels me to believe, also, that what the Scripture says about it is true for every one."

"But what does the Scripture say?" he interposed.

"It says that 'he that believeth not is condemned already, because he hath not believed' (John iii. 18); and in another place, 'He that believeth not shall be damned' (Mark xvi. 16). As surely as the believer is saved and goes to heaven, as surely the unbeliever is lost and must go to hell."

"Do you mean Gehenna, the place of torment?"

"Yes, I do."

"This is very dreadful!"

"More dreadful still," I said, "must be the solemn reality; and therefore, instead of shrinking from the thought, and putting it off, I rather let it stir and rouse me to warn unbelievers, so that I may, by any means, stop them on their dangerous path. I think this is the only true and faithful way of showing kindness; and that, on the other hand, it is the most selfish, heartless, and cruel unkindness to let sinners, whether they are religious, moral, reformed, or otherwise, go on in an unconverted state, and perish."

"Do you believe, then," said my visitor, "in the fire of hell? Do you think it is a material fire?"

"I do not know; I do not wish to know anything about it. I suppose material fire, like every other material thing, is but a shadow of something real. Is it not a fire which shall burn the soul—a fire that never will be quenched—where the worm will never die?"

"Do you really believe all this?"

"Yes," I said, "and I have reason to do so." I remembered the anguish of soul I passed through when I was under conviction, and the terrible distress I felt for others whom I had misled.

"When our blessed Lord was speaking to the Jews, and warning them against their unbelief and its fearful consequences, He did not allow any '*charitable hopes*' to hinder Him from speaking the whole truth. He told them of Lazarus, who died, and went to Paradise, or Abraham's bosom; and of Dives, who died, and went to hell, the place of torment" (Luke xvi.)

"But," he said, interrupting me, "that is only a parable, or figure of speech."

"Figure of speech!" I repeated. "Is it a figure of speech that the rich man fared sumptuously, that he died, that he was buried? Is not that literal? Why, then, is it a figure of speech that he lifted up his eyes in torment, and said, 'I am tormented in this flame'? (Luke xvi. 24). My dear friend, be sure that there is an awful reality in that story—a most solemn reality in the fact of the *impassable gulf*. If here we do not believe in this gulf, we shall have to know of it hereafter. I never saw and felt," I continued, "as I do now, that every man is lost, even while on earth, until he is saved, and that if he dies in that unsaved state he will be lost for ever."

My unknown visitor remained silent for a little time, and I could see that he was in tears. At last he burst out and said, "I am sure you are right. I came to try you upon the three great 'R's'—'Ruin,' 'Redemption,' and 'Regeneration,' and to see if you really meant what you preached. Now I feel more confirmed in the truth and reality of the Scriptures."

I thought I had been contending with an unbeliever all

along, but instead of this I found that he was a man who scarcely ventured to think out what he believed to its ultimate result—he believed God's Word, but, like too many, alas! held it loosely.

This gentleman had experienced the truth of the three "R's"—that is to say, he had been awakened to know himself to be lost and *ruined* by the fall, *redeemed* by the blood of Christ, and *regenerated* by the Holy Ghost. In other words, he had been converted, and he knew it.

I found out that at the time of his conversion he was a beneficed clergyman, and that, as such, not being responsible to any rector or vicar, he began to preach boldly the things he had seen. His changed preaching produced a manifest result, and the people were awakened, even startled, and it would appear he was startled too. Instead of thanking God and taking courage, he became alarmed at the disturbance amongst his congregation, and finding that his preaching made him very unpopular, he was weak enough to change his tone, and speak smooth things. Thus he made peace with his congregation, and gained their treacherous good-will; but as a living soul he could not be satisfied with this state of things. He knew that he was not faithful to God or to his people; so being a man of competent means, he resigned his living, and retired into private life—"beloved and respected," as they said, for being a good and peaceable man!

At this distance of time I continue to thank God for his visit to me; it helped to fix the truth more firmly in my own soul, and to confirm me in the course in which I was working, and even contending, in the face of much opposition. I must say that I have had no reason to waver in my conviction, and still feel that I would not, for ten times that man's wealth, and twenty times the amount of good-will which he enjoyed (if he did enjoy it), stand in his place.

After long observation, I perceive that it is not the sword of the Word which offends congregations, for preachers are commended and promoted for declaring the whole truth, so long as it is *judiciously* put, and with "much discretion," so as not to wound the prejudices of the people. The majority of congregations rather like to see the sword drawn out to its full length and flashed with dexterity, and they do not always object to being hit with it, and even hit hard, so long as it is done with the flat of the sword; but they very quickly resent a touch with its edge, and more a thrust with its point. They admire sheet lightning, which is beautiful, as it is harmless; but forked lightning is something to be dreaded and avoided. For instance, a man may preach most eloquently and acceptably on the three "R's," if he does not apply the subject too pointedly, by telling the people, both in the pulpit and out of it, that they are now ruined and lost; and that, having been redeemed, they are responsible before God; and that, if they will not be regenerated by the Spirit, they will be damned. They do not object to your saying, "You hath He quickened," but to turn these same words into a personal question is too often considered impertinent; though, indeed, it is the sincerest kindness and truest Christian love.

"This is a faithful saying, and worthy of all acceptation, that Christ Jesus came into the world to save sinners" (1 Tim. i. 15). He came, and is spiritually present now, everywhere, for this purpose. His real presence with power is particularly promised to the preacher of the Gospel (Matt. xxviii. 20). The Lord Jesus is ever present to take especial interest in the result of preaching. How disappointing then must it be to Him, to find His servants so often spending their time and energies upon other objects, however great or good they may be! When they do preach the Gospel, it must grieve Him to see that their object is too often not the same as His; and when He does apply the Word by the power of the Spirit, it must also grieve Him to see that they are afraid of the result.

Gospel preaching should not be to entertain people, nor even to instruct them; but first to awaken them to see their danger, and to bring them from death into life, which is manifestly the Lord's chief desire.

This was the definite object of my work; I preached for and aimed at it; and nothing short of this could or would satisfy my longings. In the church, in the schoolroom, or in the cottages, we prayed that the Holy Spirit would bring conviction upon sinners, and then we sought to lead them to conversion with the clear ringing testimony, "You must be born again, or die to all eternity."

CHAPTER X.

The First Christmas.

1851—2.

THE first Christmas-day, during the revival, was a wonderful time. The people had never realized before what this festival was, beyond regarding it as a season for domestic rejoicing. It surprised many to see that their past Christmases were a true representation of their past lives—that they had cheered and tried to make themselves happy without Christ, leaving Him out of their consideration in His own world, as they had on His own birthday. What a Christless and hopeless life it had been! What a Christless religion! Now we praised the Lord together for His marvellous goodness to us, and desired that we might henceforth live unto Him, singing in heart and life, "Glory to God in the highest, and on earth peace, good-will towards men."

When New Year's eve arrived we had a midnight gathering, and dedicated ourselves afresh to God's service. It was a blessed season, and several hundreds were there, who, together with myself, were the fruits of the revival during the previous two months.

The new year opened upon us with fresh manifestation

of divine power and larger blessings. I endeavoured to show the people that the Lord was called Jesus, not that He might save us from hell or death, but from our sins; and this while we lived on earth—that our heart and all our members being mortified from all carnal lusts, we might live to His glory; that Christ's religion was not intended for a death-bed, but for a happy and effectual Christian life—a life showing forth the power of His grace.

After the Christmas holidays, our schoolmaster and his wife returned. They came back full of disdain and prejudice against the work, and even put themselves out of the way to go from house to house, in order to set the people against me and my preaching. They said that they could bring a hundred clergymen to prove that I was wrong; but their efforts had just the contrary effect to what they expected. It stirred the people to come more frequently to hear, and contend more zealously for what they knew to be right. The master was particularly set against "excitement" and noise. He said, "It was so very much more reverent to be still in prayer, and orderly in praise; it was not necessary to make such an unseemly uproar!" I had, however, discovered, long before this time, that the people who most objected to noise had nothing yet to make a noise about; and that when they had, they generally made as much or more noise than others.

If a house is seen to be on fire, people cannot help making an outcry; which they do not, when they only read about it. Witnessing a danger stirs the heart; and when people's eyes are open to see souls in eternal danger, they cannot help being stirred up, and crying out. I am sometimes asked, "Is there not such a thing as a feeling which is too deep for expression?" It may be that at times people are so surprised and astonished at some sudden announcement of good or bad news, that they are stunned, and for a time unable to give vent to their joy or grief; but soon there is a reaction, and then expression is given. Generally speaking, these so-called "deep feelings" are only deep in the way of being low down in the vessel—that is to say, very shallow, and by no means sufficient to overflow.

We read, that "the whole multitude of the disciples began to rejoice, and praise God with a loud voice, for all the mighty works that they had seen" (Luke xix. 37). And we are told, over and over again, in the Psalms, to "praise God with a loud voice," and to "shout." When we lift up our voice, the Lord can stir our hearts; and surely the things of the Lord have more right, and ought to have more power, to stir and arouse the soul of man, than a boat-race, or a horse-race, or a fictitious scene on the stage. I think people would be all the better for letting out their hearts in praise to God. It may be it is trying and exciting to some, but perhaps they are the very ones who need such a stimulus, and this may be the best way of bringing it out.

Notwithstanding the schoolmaster's opposition, he still came to church, and was very attentive to the sermons, taking copious notes. One Sunday, when I had been preaching on the text, "Cut it down; why cumbereth it the ground?" he was heard to say, "Thank God, I am not cut down yet;" and then he proceeded for the first time to the after-meeting in the school-room.

When I entered I saw him low down on his knees, and said how happy I was to see him there. "Oh," he cried, "I fear there is no mercy—the sentence is surely gone forth against me, 'Cut him down! cut him down!'" And then the poor man howled aloud in his distress. The people prayed for him with shouts of thanksgiving, while he threw himself about in agony of mind, and made a great noise, which only drew still louder acclamations from the people. In the midst of this tremendous din he found peace, and rejoiced with the others in unmistakable accents, and as loud as the loudest. Evidently he was not ashamed or afraid of excitement and noise now.

While he was thus engaged I went round to his house to see his wife, and tell her the news. I found her sitting on the stairs in profound dismay, as if some dreadful calamity had happened. She was literally dumb with fear and astonishment. When she could speak, she said, "What will happen to him now? Will he die? What will become of us?" When I assured her that her husband was only just beginning to live, she said, "Must we be Dissenters now? Oh, what will become of us?" Her sister, who was staying with her, became very angry at hearing of the master's conversion. Finding that I could not do much with these two, I left them, and returned to the schoolroom, where the people were even more uproarious and happy than before; several others having also found pardon and peace.

The Sunday after, the master was seen moving out of church as quickly as he could; and when he reached the churchyard he was observed to run, and then leap over a wall, and next over a hedge into a field. They could not hear him, but he was shouting all the time as well as running. He afterwards said that the Prayer-book was full of meaning; it was like a new book to him; and that if he had stayed in church, he should have disturbed the whole congregation. He became a very earnest Christian, and took much pains and interest in the religious instruction of the children. There were several revivals in the school while he was there, and many of the children were converted. It was not long before he was able to rejoice over the conversion of his wife, and her sister also.

I had been anxious about my clerk for some time; he was a good man in his way, and most attentive to his work in and out of church; he was also a regular communicant, and exemplary in his life; but, with all this, he was unconverted. I often warned him of his danger; and one day it came to my mind to tell him of the man who went in to the marriage supper without the wedding garment. I said, no doubt he thought himself as good as others, but when the King came in to see the guests, he was speechless; and because he was so, and had not on the wedding garment, the King commanded that he should be bound hand and foot, and put into outer darkness. Now, I continued, the King has often come in to see us, and we have rejoiced before Him; but you have never spoken to Him, or asked for mercy. It is a very hardening thing to hear so much as you do, and remain unsaved; and a very deadening thing to come to the Lord's table as you do, going through the form without any real meaning. You receive the bread and wine in remembrance that Christ died for you, and yet you do not believe enough to thank Him. I was led to say, "I must forbid your coming to the Lord's table till you have given your heart to God. You know it is right to do it, and that you ought to be converted. I will not have you come here again till you are."

The man looked at me as if to see whether I meant it, and then appeared so sorrowful that I nearly relented. All through the service he was low and dejected, and went away at the time of the administration of the ordinance, and sat at the other end of the church. My heart ached for him, for I had never seen him so touched about anything. Afterwards, when he came into the vestry, I could see that he had been crying. "Ah, friend," I said, "it is bad to be left out from the Lord's table here; what will it be to be left out of heaven?"

In the evening he was more miserable than ever, and at the close of the service came into the schoolroom, where he broke down, and asked the people to pray for him, for he was a hard-hearted, miserable sinner. "Pray the Lord to melt my heart." We did so: and soon the poor broken-hearted man sobbed and cried aloud for mercy; and it was not long before, to our great joy, he found peace. He afterwards told us that he had been getting hardened by forms ever since he had been clerk, reading solemn words without any meaning, which at first he trembled at doing. He was right; it is good to hear the Gospel, good to attend the means of grace, good to assemble in the company of God's people; but to rest in the habit of doing these good things, without conversion, is most dangerous, and calculated to deaden the heart. He said that he felt it very much when 'master' was converted (meaning myself), and was also dreadfully condemned; for he had believed in the *necessity of conversion* all his life; and though he knew that I was unconverted, yet he never told me, but rather encouraged me to go on as I was. He said that he had had many sleepless nights about it; "but now, thank God," he added, "it is all right; my feet are on the Rock, my soul is saved. I can praise the Lord in the congregation."

The clerk's conversion did not stop with himself, for it was a call to some of the ringers; they were still outside and unsaved, though they knew as well as he did, that they ought to be otherwise. One of these men began to attend the meetings regularly, but we could not get him to pray, or speak a word. I said to him one evening, "You will never have a sound from the bell till you move it or its tongue; in like manner, you must move your tongue, for you will have nothing until you speak, nor get an answer until you pray." Still he remained silent, and shut up to himself; till one night, as we were putting out the lights at ten o'clock, the meeting being over, I said to him as he stood by, "James, I wonder when you will ever give your heart to God?" He looked at me and said, "Now." "That is right," I replied; "thank God! let it be so. I at once stopped the extinguishing of the lights, and invited him to pray with me, but he took no heed. It was evident he had deliberately made up his mind what he would do, for he took off his coat, undid his neck-tie, turned back his shirt-sleeves, and then, setting a form about nine or ten feet long, square with the room, he knelt down and began to say, "Lord, have mercy upon me!" "Lord, have mercy upon me!" This he repeated with every returning breath, faster and louder as he went on, till at last he worked himself up to a condition of frenzy. He went on without cessation for two hours, and then stopped in an exhausted state, gasping for breath. I pointed him to the cross, and told him of God's mercy in giving His Son to die for sinners; but he was quite absent, and did not appear to hear me, or take the least notice. After a little rest, he commenced again praying as before, and got into terrible distress. What with his noise, and the energy he put forth, it was frightful to see the struggle. He cried and beat the form till I thought his arms would be black and blue; then he took up the form and beat the floor with it, till I expected every moment it would come to pieces. The noise he made brought some of the neighbours out of their beds in a fright, to see what was the matter.

At two o'clock in the morning, four hours after he began, he laid himself across the form, and begged with tears that the Lord would not cast him off. I told him that the Lord was actually waiting for him. At last he found peace, or felt something, and, springing up, he began to shout and praise God; and we all joined with him. When this was done, he put on his coat and neck-tie, and saying "Good night," went home. From this time he became a changed man, and an earnest and steadfast believer.

CHAPTER XI.

Dreams and Visions.

1851—4.

DURING the revival, the outpouring of the Spirit of God was very manifest and unmistakable, and was seen in various ways. It was not, of course, by power or might of men, but by divine influence, that souls were awakened to see themselves in their true condition. The candle of the Lord was lighted, and there was a searching of and for immortal souls, as typified by our blessed Lord in the parable of the lost piece of silver.

We read that the woman with her lighted candle discovered her treasure; so the Divine Spirit, by awakening and searching hearts, found souls, though they had been buried under sins, worldliness, and neglect, and that for many years. It was astonishing to hear persons who had been dull and silent before, break out into full and free expression of spiritual truth; and their liberty and power in prayer were not less remarkable. It was truly an opening of eyes to see, and ears to hear, and hearts to understand— a raising of the dead to spiritual life and animation. It was as wonderful as the speaking of tongues on the day of Pentecost, with this difference—that those people spoke what they knew, in tongues they had not known; and these, in their own speech, declared things which they had never seen or known before.

We had another distinctive sign of Pentecost, which was, that while believers rejoiced with overflowing joy, and sinners were pricked to the heart, and cried out, "What must I do to be saved?" there were those who mocked, saying, "These men are mad, or drunk." But, as St. Peter testified long ago, these men, women, and children were not drunk, but under the influence and power of the Holy Ghost.

We had yet another sign. The prophet Joel predicted, "It shall come to pass that I will pour out my Spirit upon all flesh; and your sons and your daughters shall prophesy, your old men shall dream dreams, your young men shall see visions; and also upon the servants and upon the handmaids in those days will I pour out my Spirit" (Joel ii. 28, 29). And I think my narrative would be very incomplete, and I should be holding back the truth, if I did not tell of some of the dreams and visions which continually happened at this time amongst us.

Every week, almost every day, we heard of some remarkable dream or striking vision. Such things may be called "superstitious" by incredulous people, but I merely state what actually took place without attempting to explain or account for it. My own feeling is, that I would rather be among the superstitious than the incredulous; for I think that the former lose nothing by believing, and the latter gain nothing by their unbelief.

Among the people who are alive to spiritual realities these remarkable tokens are not suspected or doubted. To believe nothing but what you can understand or account for, is to believe nothing at all. Cornish people at that time—and they may still be the same—lived in a spiritual atmosphere, at least in their own county; so much so, that I have often heard them complain, when they returned from the "shires," of the dryness and deadness they felt there. I can certainly set my seal to this testimony, and declare that those of us who had visions in Cornwall have not had them in the same way out of that district.

I will give a few specimens, but only one of a kind, for it would fill a volume if I told all; the reader can judge if there was meaning or import in some of them or not.

At one time, when there was a depression or check in the congregation, and preaching was hard, praying formal, and singing flat, I invited the people to join with me in prayer, that the Lord would show us what was the hindrance in the way of the work. They prayed with one accord, and without consulting one another, almost in the same words, whether in the school-room or in the cottages; the substance of their petition was, that we might know and put away the obstacle to spiritual blessing, whatever that obstacle might be.

One night I dreamt that I was in the church, feeling very desolate and forsaken; there were very few people there, but soon my eyes lighted on an ugly-looking stranger, who tried to evade me. He was a very disagreeable, sullen-looking man. When I spoke to him he gnashed his teeth, and, as I approached, he drew out a knife and held it out before me. I pursued him notwithstanding, when he backed towards the door and went out. I followed him through the churchyard till he was outside the lych-gate. As soon as he was gone, I saw a troop of happy people, all dressed in white, come in at the same gate, leaping and running like so many joyful children, and swinging their arms for gladness: they went into the church and began to sing. The dream was as vivid to me as a daylight scene.

I went out the next evening, intending to tell it at the school-room meeting; but before I began to do so, I observed that the people sang more freely than usual, and I also noticed that two men who prayed omitted to offer the usual request for hindrances to be removed. When I told my dream, a man arose and said, "I know all about that; there has been one among us who we thought was a good man, but instead of this we have discovered that he was most immoral and deceitful, doing a deal of mischief, secretly undermining the faith of some, and misleading others; he has been detected, and is gone." Sure enough our old happy freedom returned, and there was liberty in preaching, praying, and singing, and souls were saved.

Another time, when I was getting a little impatient with the people, I took a leaf out of my Scripture-reader's book, and preached a furious sermon about "damnation," representing God as pursuing the sinner to cut him down, if he did not repent there and then. I thought I had done it well, and went home rather satisfied with myself, supposing that I now knew how to make the congregation feel. The next morning, a woman called to me as I was passing her cottage, and said, "Master, what d'yer think? I dreamt last night that the devil was a-preaching in your pulpit, and that you were delighted at it!" A sudden fear fell upon me—so much so, that I returned to the church, and shutting the door, begged God's forgiveness: and thanking Him for this warning, asked that I might remember it, and never transgress again.

As my Scripture-reader continued to denounce wrath and vengeance, instead of preaching the Gospel, I parted with him.

Next, let me tell of a vision which refers to others. My sister came to me one morning, and said, "William, I had a vision last night of a young man in a tall hat with a green-

and-red carpet-bag in his hand. I saw him so plainly, that I should know him again anywhere. He was walking up the road when you met him, shook hands, and returned with him to the house. Then you and F—— brought him in at the glass door. On the hall table there stood a basket containing four beautiful and fragrant fruits. You took up the basket and offered it to the visitor, who, putting his hand upon one, said, 'Oh, thank you!' then touching the three others in order, said, 'That is for mother, and that for sister, and that for——.' I could not hear who. You may smile," she continued, "but I heard that, and saw it all as plainly as I see you now."

I was accustomed to hear such things, and consequently thought no more about it, but went on to speak of other subjects. In the course of the afternoon, as I was going out, I met a relative coming along the road, and took him back with me to the house; there my wife came out to him, and we led him in through the glass door. When he had sat some time, and had had some luncheon, my wife said, "I wonder whether this is the young man we heard about this morning?" "What young man?" asked our visitor, hastily; "what young man do you mean?" "I should not wonder if it is," I replied; "we will see presently." He seemed very suspicious, having heard before he came that some mysterious change had taken place in us, and so looked again and again to see if he could detect anything different.

"Come and see my sister," I said; to which he assented, and we went across to her house. As soon as we entered her room, she said, "How do you do? I saw you last night." "What do you mean?" he replied, withdrawing his hand. "Why, I was on board the steamer last night. "That may be," she said, "but you are the gentleman I saw. Have you not a green-and-red carpet-bag?

and did not William meet you on the road?" Poor young man! he looked dreadfully perplexed. "Never mind her," I said; "sit down and tell us about your journey."

After we had talked of this and other subjects, we returned home. I then told him that we were converted, and asked if he had given his heart to God. He said he had. Not being satisfied, I put the question in another form, and yet remained unsatisfied with his answer. "Do you doubt me?" he asked: "I will prove it to you." He then went up to his room for a little while, and returned with a paper in his hand, in which was a dedication of himself to God, duly signed and sealed. I had never seen an instrument of this kind before, and asked if he really believed in it?

"Yes, certainly," he replied; "and I mean it too."

"But," I said, "do you not see that faith does not consist in believing what you write, but in what God has written? The Word says that God is more willing to take than you are to give: you believe you have given; but do you believe that God has taken? He is far more ready to take your heart than you to give it; as surely as you have given, so surely He has taken. Cannot you see that?"

He replied, "I knew that there was something wrong about this, but I did not know what. Thank you! thank you!" Then thoughtfully folding up the paper, he went out of the room.

The bell was rung for dinner, but he did not appear; and then for tea, but he declined taking any. After we had gone to church, he found his way down and followed us there; and when the service was over, he returned again to his room. I was detained at the schoolroom that night, and until two o'clock in the morning, praying and talking with anxious souls, and returned home very tired. Going up to bed, I saw a light shining under my visitor's door, and hesitating there a few moments, I heard him pleading earnestly for mercy. I had a great mind to knock, but was afraid of disturbing him; so I prayed for him, and went to bed.

In the morning he came down smiling. "Thank God," he said, "it is all right now; I am saved." In his hand he held three letters—one to his mother, one to his sister, and the other to a cousin, in which he invited them earnestly to come to Jesus. Within the week all four were in our house, praising God for salvation.

As the vision indicated, we had nothing to do but hold the basket to him. He accepted it, and the fruit for himself and his relatives.

Amongst other people and characters I met with at this time was a good, respectable man, who had a remarkable dream. He came to me one day, after I had been speaking about Jacob's ladder, and said that my sermon had reminded him of his dream. I begged him to sit down and tell it to me. He said, "I dreamt that I and nineteen other young men were living in a beautiful house and place, where we had everything provided for us, and were free to enjoy ourselves as much as we pleased. We all understood that the premises belonged to Satan, and that we were his guests. As such, we were permitted to take our pleasure upon two conditions—one was, that we were not to pray; and the other, that we were not to go away. We smiled at this, and said it was not likely we should do the former, for we were not of the praying kind; and less likely that we should do the latter, for why should we be such fools as to forego or give up our enjoyments?"

I thought to myself, What a wonderful dream that is; and how true to reality! What numbers of young men there are, and young women too, besides many older people, who hold their worldly happiness on this tenure, and of course from the same master.

Well, to continue the story of the dream, he said, "In the course of time we all became heartily tired of the place and its pleasures, and longed to get away, but we could not. One of us made an attempt to do so, but he was captured and brought back, and made more of a slave than ever. At last, I and a few others agreed to pray at a stated time in different places, in the hope that if one was caught, yet the rest might escape. Upon a set day and time we began praying, each in his appointed place. I had fixed upon a dark corner in a large deserted room, where we had stowed away bales and bales of goods we did not care to open. Climbing over the top of these stores, I landed on the other side, and went to the spot I had chosen. I had not prayed long before I heard master coming, cracking his whip, and saying, 'I'll teach you to pray.' This made me tremble exceedingly, and pray all the harder; but hearing that he was very near and coming after me, I opened my eyes, and to my surprise there was a beautiful silver ladder before me. As quick as thought, I sprang with hands and feet upon it, and began to climb for dear life. 'Ha!' said master, 'I'll teach you to climb.' Then I felt the ladder shaking under me, and knew that he was coming up. I expected every moment to be seized and dragged back, so I climbed all the faster, and looked up to see how much farther I had to go. Oh, it was such a long way, and there was only a very small hole to get to at last. My heart began to fail me, so that I almost let go my hold, till I felt the master's sulphurous breath on the back of my neck, which made me rush forward more vehemently. At last I reached the top, and thrust my arm through the hole, then my head, and then my other arm; thus I got through altogether, leaving my old enemy blaspheming and cursing

A PREJUDICED GUEST.

down below. It was a most beautiful place that I was now in, and angels were flying about, just as the birds do in this world. I saw the Lord Himself, and fell down before Him to give Him thanks. As I remained a long time prostrate, He said to me, 'What is thy petition?' I answered, 'Lord, grant that that hole may be made larger, for I have nineteen friends down there in the power of the cruel master.' The Lord smiled, and said, 'That hole is quite large enough.' So I awoke."

Where there is a will, there is always a way of some kind; and if worldlings are really tired of Satan's service, they can easily call upon God to deliver them, and He will most surely do so when He sees they are in earnest. This dream had the effect of spiritually awakening the man who had it, and of bringing him to the foot of the cross for mercy and salvation.

I noticed that in dreams and visions in Cornwall the Lord Jesus very often appears, and the devil also; these are real persons to the Cornish mind, and their power is respectively acknowledged.

During the summer, a young gentleman, whom we invited to our house in the hope of reaching his soul, came to stay with us; and this in spite of his avowed prejudice against us and our proceedings. I took this as a token of encouragement, for I was sure that the devil would have hindered his coming, unless the young man had been constrained by a higher power. He spent his time in riding about or smoking, and made great fun of our meetings and services, though I observed that he was very attentive to hear the sermon whenever he did come.

One week-day evening, while we were sitting in the drawing-room, and little expecting it, he burst into tears, and cried out, "I don't know what to do; I shall be lost for ever!" We immediately sprang up to his help, always delighted at such opportunities of working for the Lord. We knelt down to pray, and as we continued to do so, he fell into great distress, and even agony of soul; he literally writhed as if in excessive pain, too great for utterance, and looked as if he was fainting with the struggle. We called all the servants into the room to help in prayer, and while I was praying by the side of my young friend, and pointing him to Christ, one of the servants rose up and walked straight across the room, and, with a firm hand pushing me aside, said, "The Lord is here Himself." I rose instantly and moved out of the way, while she stood with her hands together, adoring.

She afterwards told us that she saw the Lord stoop down to the low chair where my young friend was kneeling, and putting His hand on his head, He said something, and then stood up. Immediately upon this she saw the verandah crowded with ugly-looking devils, all with their eyes fixed on the young man as he knelt. The Lord then waved His hand, and the ugly company vanished. At that instant the young man lifted up his head, and turning towards the side on which she had discerned the Lord as standing, said, "Lord, I thank Thee," and then fainted away.

When the vision was over, the servant came, with tears in her eyes, to ask pardon for so rudely pushing me aside, but said that while the Lord was there she could not help herself: "Oh, He is so beautiful, so grand!" The young man was soon restored to animation, and began to speak in a voice and tone very different to his former utterance. He was altogether a remarkable instance of a change of heart and life.

One more case I will relate, with its solemn end, and then proceed with my narrative.

A careless, worldly man in my parish dreamt one night that he was in the market hall of a certain town. He was surprised to see, in a wall, a doorway, which he had never noticed before—so much so, that he went forward to examine it, and found that it really was a door, and that it opened to his touch. He went inside, and there he saw an impressive and strange scene. There were a number of men and women walking about, who appeared to be very woeful, and in great agony of pain. They were too distressed to speak, but he recognized most of them as persons who had been dead some time. They looked mournfully at him, as if sorry that he had come there, but did not speak. He was much alarmed, and made his way back to the door to escape, but was stopped by a stern, sullen-looking porter, who said, in a sepulchral voice, "You cannot pass." He said, "I came in this way, and I want to go out." "You cannot," said the solemn voice. "Look, the door only opens one way; you may come in by it, but you cannot go out." It was so, and his heart sank within him as he looked at that mysterious portal. At last the porter relented, and as a special favour let him go forth for eight days. He was so glad at his release that he awoke.

When he told me the dream I warned him, and begged him to give his heart to God. "You may die," I said, "before the eighth day." He laughed at the idea, and said he was "not going to be frightened by a dream." "When I am converted," he continued, "I hope I shall be able to say that I was drawn by love, and not driven by fear." "But what," I said, "if you have been neglecting and slighting God's love for a long time, and He is now moving you with fear to return to Him?" Nothing would do; he turned a deaf ear to every entreaty. When the eighth day arrived, being market day, he went to the hall as usual, and looked at the wall of which he had dreamed with particular interest, but seeing no door there, he exclaimed, "It's all right; now I will go and have a good dinner over it, with a bottle of wine!"

Whether he stopped at one bottle or not, I cannot tell; but late on Saturday night, as he was going home, he was thrown from his horse and killed. That was at the end of the eighth day.

Whether these dreams and visions were the cause or effect of the people's sensitive state, I do not know; but certainly they were very impressible, and even the cold and hardened amongst them were ready to hear about the mysteries of the unseen world. I attributed this to the spiritual atmosphere in which they were then living.

CHAPTER XII.

Billy Bray.

1852.

AFTER the events narrated in Chapter X., and when all the people who dwelt on the hill on which the church was built were converted, there came upon the scene a very remarkable person, who had evidently been kept back for a purpose. This was none other than the veritable and well-known "BILLY BRAY."*
One morning, while we were sitting at breakfast, I heard some one walking about in the hall with a heavy step, saying, "Praise the Lord! praise the Lord!" On opening the door, I beheld a happy-looking little man, in a black Quaker-cut coat, which it was very evident had not been made for him, but for some much larger body. "Well, my friend," I said, "who are you?"

"I am Billy Bray," he replied, looking steadily at me with his twinkling eyes; "and be you the passon?"

"Yes, I am."

"'Thank the Lord! Converted, are ye?"

"Yes, thank God."

---

* See "The King's Son; or, Life of Billy Bray," by F. W. Bourne.

"And the missus inside" (pointing to the dining room), "be she converted?"

"Yes, she is."

"Thank the dear Lord," he said, moving forward.

I made way for him, and he came stepping into the room; then making a profound bow to the said "missus," he asked, "Be there any maidens (servants)?"

"Yes, there are three in the kitchen."

"Be they converted too?"

I was able to answer in the affirmative; and as I pointed towards the kitchen door when I mentioned it, he made off in that direction, and soon we heard them all shouting and praising God together. When we went in, there was Billy Bray, very joyful, singing,

"Canaan is a happy place;
I am bound for the land of Canaan."

We then returned to the dining-room with our strange guest, when he suddenly caught me up in his arms and carried me round the room. I was so taken by surprise, that it was as much as I could do to keep myself in an upright position, till he had accomplished the circuit. Then he set me in my chair, and rolling on the ground for joy, said that he "was as happy as he could live." When this performance was at an end, he rose up with a face that denoted the fact, for it was beaming all over. I invited him to take some breakfast with us, to which he assented with thanks. He chose bread and milk, for he said, "I am only a child."

I asked him to be seated, and gave him a chair; but he preferred walking about, and went on talking all the time. He told us that twenty years ago, as he was walking over this very hill on which my church and house were built (it was a barren old place then), the Lord said to him, "I will give thee all that dwell in this mountain." Immediately he fell down on his knees and thanked the Lord, and then ran to the nearest cottage. There he talked and prayed with the people, and was enabled to bring them to Christ; then he went to the next cottage, and got the same blessing; and then to a third, where he was equally successful. Then he told "Father" that there were only three "housen" in this mountain, and prayed that more might be built. That prayer remained with him, and he never ceased to make it for years. The neighbours, who heard his prayer from time to time, wondered why he should ask for "housen" to be built in such an "ungain" place.

At last, after sixteen years, he received a letter from his brother James, to say that they were hacking up the "croft" to plant trees, and that they were going to build a church on the hill. He was "fine and glad," and praised the Lord. Again he did so, when his brother wrote to say there was a vicarage to be built on the same hill, and a schoolroom also. He was almost beside himself with joy and thankfulness for all this.

In the year 1848, when the church was completed and opened, he came on a visit to Baldhu, and was greatly surprised to see what a change had taken place. There was a beautiful church, a parsonage, with a flourishing garden, and also a schoolroom, with a large plantation and fields round them. He was quite "'mazed," for he never thought that the old hill could be made so grand as that! However, when he went to the service in the church, his joy was over; he came out "checkfallen," and quite disappointed. He told "Father" that there was nothing but an "old Pusey" He had got there, and that he was no good. While he was praying that afternoon, "Father" gave him to understand that he had no business there yet, and that he had come too soon, and without permission. So he went back to his place at once, near Bodmin, and continued to pray for the hill.

After three years his brother James wrote again; and this time it was to tell him that the parson and all his family were converted, and that there was a great revival at the church. Now poor Billy was most eager to come and see this for himself, but he obtained no permission, though he asked and looked for it every day for more than three months.

At last, one wintry and frosty night in January, about half-past eleven o'clock, just as he was getting into bed, "Father" told him that he might go to Baldhu. He was so overjoyed, that he did not wait till the morning, but immediately "put up" his clothes again, "hitched in" the donkey, and set out in his slow-going little cart. He came along singing all the way, nearly thirty miles, and arrived early in the morning. Having put up his donkey in my stable, he came into the house, and presented himself, as I have already stated, in the hall, praising God.

We were a long time over breakfast that morning, for the happy man went on from one thing to another, "telling of the Lord," as he called it, assuring us again and again that he was "fine and glad, and very happy"—indeed, he looked so. He said there was one thing more he must tell us; it was this—that he had a "preaching-house" (what we should now call a mission-room), which he had built years ago. He had often prayed there for "this old mountain," and now he should dearly love to see me in the pulpit of that place, and said that he would let me have it for my work. He went on to say that he had built it by prayer and faith, as "Father" sent him help, and that he and another man had built it with their own hands. One day he was short of money to buy timber to finish the roof; his mate said it would take two pounds' worth; so he asked the Lord for this sum, and wondered why the money did not come, for he felt sure that he was to have it. A farmer happened to look in the next morning, and Billy thought he had come with the money, but he merely asked them what they were doing, and then took his departure, without giving them help. All that day they waited in expectation, and went home in the evening without having done any work. The next morning the same farmer appeared again, and said, "What do you want two pounds for?" "Oh," said Billy, "you are come, are you? We want that money for the roof yonder." The farmer then went on to say, "Two days ago it came to my mind to give two pounds for the preaching house, but as I was coming down the hill on yesterday morning, something said to me, 'If you give one pound it will be handsome;' then I thought I would give only half-a-sovereign; and then that I would give nothing. Why should I? But the Lord laid it on my mind again last night that I must give you two pounds. There it is!"

"Thank the Lord!" said Billy, and proceeded immediately to get the required timber. In answer to prayer he also obtained "reed" for thatching the roof, and by the same means timber for the forms and seats.

It was all done in a humble manner, so that he did not dream of buying any pulpit; but one day, as he was passing along the road, he saw that they were going to have a sale at the "count-house" of an old mine. He went in, and the first thing which met his eye was a strong oak cupboard, with a cornice round the top. It struck him that it would make a grand pulpit, if only it was strong enough: on examination, he found it all he could desire in this respect. He thought if he could take off the top and make a "plat'" to stand upon, it would do "first-rate." He told "Father" so, and wondered how he could get it. He asked a stranger who was there, walking about, what he thought that old cupboard would go for? "Oh, for about five or six shillings," was the reply. And while Billy was pondering how to "rise" six shillings, the same man came up and said, "What do you want that cupboard for, Billy?" He did not care to tell him, for he was thinking and praying about it. The man said, "There are six shillings for you; buy it, if you will." Billy took the money, thanking the Lord, and impatiently waited for the sale. No sooner was the cupboard put up, than he called out, "Here, maister, here's six shillin's for un," and he put the money down on the table. "Six shillings bid," said the auctioneer—"six shillings—thank you; seven shillings; any more for that good old cupboard? Seven shillings. Going—going—gone!" And it was knocked down to another man.

Poor Billy was much disappointed and perplexed at this, and could not understand it at all. He looked about for the man who had given him the six shillings, but in vain—he was not there. The auctioneer told him to take up his money out of the way. He complied, but did not know what to do with it. He went over a hedge into a field by himself, and told "Father" about it; but it was all clear—"Father" was not angry about anything. He remained there an hour, and then went homewards.

As he was going along, much troubled in his mind as to this experience (for he still felt so sure he was to have that cupboard for a pulpit), he came upon a cart standing outside a public-house, with the very cupboard upon it, and some men were measuring it with a foot rule. As he came up, he heard them say, "It is too large to go in at the door, or the window either." The publican who had bought it said, "I wish I had not bid for the old thing at all; it is too good to 'scat' up for firewood." At that instant it came to Billy's mind to say, "Here, I'll give you six shillings for un." "Very well," said the man, taking the money; "you can have him." Then Billy began to praise the Lord, and went on to say, "'Father' as good as told me that I was to have that cupboard, and He knew I could not carry him home on my back, so He has found a horse and cart for me. Bless the Lord!" Promising to bring it back very soon, he led the horse down the hill, and put the old cupboard into the preaching house. "There it is!" he exclaimed, "and a fine pulpit he does make, sure enough! Now," said Billy, "I want to see thee in it. When will you come?" I could not fix for that day, or the next, but made arrangements to conduct a series of services the next week, and promised to have them in that place.

Before he left us, he made a particular inquiry about the two other houses which had been built, who lived in them, and especially if all the "dwellers were converted." Then he declared his intention to go and see the parties, and rejoice with them, and testify how fully the Lord had accomplished the promise He gave him upon that very hill, twenty years before.

According to promise, I went to Billy Bray's preaching-house, or mission-hall. It was the first time that I had preached anywhere outside my church and schoolroom since my conversion. There it pleased the Lord to give me much help, and a great work followed, such as Billy had never seen in that place before. Several times we were detained there all night through, with penitents crying aloud for mercy, and believers rejoicing.

As a rule, the Cornish man would remain at a meeting for hours, and come again the next day, and the day after, if needful, till he *felt* that he could cry for mercy, and then he would begin and continue crying until he *felt* he could believe.

At the conclusion of these services we returned to the schoolroom, where our meetings were continued.

Our friend Billy remained with us at Baldhu, and was very useful. He spoke in the schoolroom with much acceptance and power in the simplicity of his faith, and souls were added to the Lord continually.

At this time he was very anxious for a cousin of his, a man somewhat older than himself, of the same name. This Billy was as famous for his drunkenness and dissolute habits, as the other Billy was for his faith and joy. The former used to go by the name of the "lost soul." The very children in the lanes called after him, "Ah, Billy, you are a lost soul," and laughed at him. I was then in the freshness and power of my first love, and could not help regarding this pitiable object, and considering his case; for I could not imagine why any man should remain unsaved and without Christ.

Accordingly, one wet morning, when I felt pretty sure that old Billy would not be out working in the field, I made my way down to his house. As I expected, he was at home in his chimney corner; so setting down my dripping umbrella, I told him how glad I was to find him there, for I wanted to have a talk with him.

"Ah, it's all very well for you gentlemen, who have none else to do but to go about and talk; but we poor men must work." So saying, he rose up from his "settle" and went to the door.

"But, Billy, it is raining quite hard; you cannot work in rain like that."

"Can't help it; we must do our work," and so he slammed the door after him and departed.

His wife made all kinds of apologies for him, because "he was a very singular kind of man; he did not mean bad—he was 'that curious,' that he said and did curious things, and that I must not mind him."

I confess I was much disappointed at his abrupt departure from the house, but I remained a little longer, till the worst of the storm was over.

After the lapse of nearly a quarter of an hour, Billy crept back to the door, and lifting the latch quietly, whispered to his wife, " Is the passon gone ? "

" No, Billy," I said, " here I am. Come in out of the wet. I am so glad you have come back ? "

" What d'yer want with me ? " he inquired.

" I want to talk to you about your soul. I have been thinking much about you lately, Billy. They call you a ' lost soul.' "

" What's that to you ? "

" Ah, a great deal," I said, " because I have a message for lost people. I am not a doctor for the body; my business is about the soul."

" I ain't so bad as all that yet," he replied.

" But you are bad enough, Billy—bad enough."

" Yes, indeed," interposed his wife.

" You hold yer tongue ; you're no better."

I beckoned to her to be still, and went on to say, " You are bad enough, Billy, for an old man. How old are you ? "

" Up seventy years."

" Seventy years ! " I repeated. " Well, now, that's a great age—that's the age of man. Threescore years and ten ! It is like giving you notice to give up the keys of the old tabernacle. I wonder why God spares your life ? I am afraid you have been a cumberer of the ground all this time, Billy. Do you know why the good Lord has spared you for so long ? "

" I can't tell," he said, getting more and more impatient.

" Well, do you know, I think I can tell you. He is such a loving and merciful God, *He wants to have mercy on you!*

you could not have greater proof of it, could you? You set a horribly bad example; you do nothing but drink, and smoke, and swear. You have asked God to damn your soul over and over again, and yet here you are still. Why is this?"

He did not answer, but seemed interested; so I went on to speak of the forbearance of God towards him. I said, "Billy, do you know that I think the Lord wants to have mercy on you? He wants to save you!" As he listened, I went on to tell him that God loved him, and gave His Son to die for him. Then I proceeded to speak of the wonderful patience and long-suffering of God—a kind of crown upon His love; and what a shame it was to sin against such love as this.

Poor Billy looked at me with tears in his eyes, and said, "You are a dear man!"

"Dear man!" I answered. "What, then, is God, if I am 'dear' only for telling you of His love? Ah, Billy, take and give your heart to God at once. He is waiting for you. It is a shame to refuse such a God."

I knelt down and began to pray for him. He soon fell on his knees too, and sobbed aloud; then he commenced to pray in his own way. He needed much teaching, so when he rose from his knees I said to him, "Now, Billy, I have been to see you; it is your turn to come and see me next. When will you come?"

"This afternoon," he said.

"Very good; come this afternoon." And he did. More than that, this poor "lost soul" found peace in my study, to his great joy; and he was not ashamed to acknowledge it openly, nor afraid to praise God for His great goodness.

The same evening he stood up in the schoolroom meeting, and told the people what the Lord had done for his soul. There was great excitement that night, and well there might be, for every one knew what a daring and wicked man he had been. One man said that "if a corpse had come out of the churchyard and spoken, he could not have been more frightened" (more surprised, he meant).

Old Billy's conversion gave a new and fresh impetus to the work, and many more souls were added to the Lord.

This dear man lived for three months after this, verifying the words I was led to say to him at the beginning of our intercourse—that the Lord was keeping him alive in order to have mercy upon him. At the end of this time, his daughter came to me one morning in great haste, and said, "Father is dying, and does so want to see you. Will you come?" I went immediately. On reaching his house and entering his bedroom, his wife said, "You are too late; he is dead!" Softly I moved forward to the bed, and looking on that face once more, I thought that I could still see signs of life. Pressing his cold hand, I spoke a few words about the loving-kindness of the Lord. He knew me, and a smile brightened his face at the precious name of Jesus. While we stood silently round his dying bed, he said (evidently in reference to what he had heard), "Not dead: just beginning to live." Thus, with a sweet, triumphant smile, he departed.

CHAPTER XIII.
Cottage Meetings.

1852.

OUR steps were now directed to another part of the parish, where we commenced a series of cottage meetings in alternation with services in the church. These meetings were inaugurated in a very remarkable manner, in the house of a man named "Frank," who was well-known as an exceedingly wicked and careless fellow. His wife was among the fruits of the revival, and prayed much for him; but the more she did so, the worse he became. I used to try and comfort her with the thought that if he did not give himself to God to be made better, it was well that he got worse, for it was a proof that her prayers were telling; total indifference would have been a far more discouraging sign.

This was poor comfort to her, however, for he came home night after night drunk; or if not so, swearing about the revival in the church, and her praying. He often declared that if he ever caught me in his house, he would "give me something for myself." He was at all times a very irascible man, and being troubled with a wooden leg, it made him worse. As he was unable to work in the mine, he was dependent for his support on the parish authorities, who employed him to break stones on the road.

Notwithstanding his bad temper and ill-feeling towards me, I always stopped at his heap of stones when passing, and talked to him either about the weather or some other trivial subject, being quite satisfied that he knew the plan of salvation, as I had spoken to him about his soul at the time of his wife's conversion.

One day, when coming along, I observed Frank before me in the road, busy, as usual, breaking stones, and began to think what I would speak to him about, having no particular news to communicate. While I was thus pondering, I came to his place, when, to my great astonishment, he was not there. I looked around on all sides, and called, "Frank—Frank!" but in vain—no one answered. There was no hedge or tree within sight for him to hide behind; where could he be? All at once, I remembered that there was a small gravel-pit about twenty-five or thirty yards from the spot, but scarcely thought it possible he could be there. I went towards it, however, still calling, "Frank—Frank!" and yet received no answer. On looking in, sure enough, there was my man, lying down in the pit, close up to the side, with his face to the ground. I said, "Frank, is that you? What are you doing there? Are you ill?"

"No," he replied, "I'm not. What d'yer want with me?"

"Nothing in particular," I said; "but, to tell the truth, I was so surprised at your disappearance, that I could not pass on without looking for you. I was so sure that I saw you in the distance, sitting in your place; and then, when I came up, you were not there. I wondered whether I had seen your ghost instead of you, and whether you were dead, or what. Are you hiding away from me?"

Rising up, he said, "I had a terrible dream last night,

which frightened me very much. A voice said, 'Go and see Mr. Haslam about your soul.' I said, 'I will, I will, the first thing in the morning.' When the morning came, I thought the evening would do; and when I saw you coming, it made me tremble so, that I got up and hid myself here."

I said, "Frank, it is no use for you to fight against God, or stand out against your wife's prayers. You had far better give in."

He then told me that his dream referred to something in his past life, and sitting down on the bank or side of the gravel-pit, he said, "When I was ill with my leg (which was taken off), the doctor told me that I should die. I then cried to the Lord to have mercy on me, and said that if He would raise me up, I would give my heart to Him. I began to recover from that day, and kept on intending and intending to give my heart to God; but I never did it. I got quite well in health, but ever since that time I have been getting worse and worse in mind. When my wife was converted, it seemed as if the devil took possession of me altogether, and the Lord warned me again last night."

"Come now," I said, "you had better kneel down here and give up." It was a lonely road on a bare common. "Kneel down," I repeated, "and let us pray." He did so, and after prayer he said, "By God's help, I will give up."

"No," I replied, "that will not do. Say, 'Lord, take my heart. *I do*'—not '*I will*'—'give up.'"

After a short pause, he solemnly said, "I do; Lord, take my heart!" and then began to cry.

I gave him the text, "God so loved the world, that He gave His only-begotten Son, that whosoever believeth in Him should not perish, but have everlasting life" (John iii. 16). "Think over that," I said, "and come to the schoolroom to-night." He did so, and was saved, to the great joy of his soul. After the meeting was over, he remained behind a long time, and gave vent to his feelings with tears, when he remembered the goodness of God to him.

"This wooden leg of mine," he said, "is a moniment of God's mercy!"

"How is that?" I inquired.

"Several years ago," he said, "I was playing cards for money in a public-house, and was cheating in order to win, when the man I was playing with said, 'You would not have won that money if you had not cheated.' I swore at him, and said, 'God strike my limbs if I did so!" I knew I had; and the man would not believe that I had not. So we parted.

"The next morning, I was working in the mine, close to a very large piece of rock, which had been loosened with the blasting, when it slipped from its place, and carried me along with it into the shaft. As the heavy end was uppermost, it turned with its own weight, and fell across the shaft, pinning me against the side. This rock was not less than two or three tons weight. Notwithstanding the fearful shock, I retained my senses; but one leg was smashed, and the other severely wounded. 'God struck my limbs!' I cried for help; and when the men who were attracted by my screams found me, they saw at once that it was impossible to extricate me without moving the rock. There I remained for more than two hours, till they had put a sling round my body. Having done that, they adjusted a strong chain to the rock, and lifted the end. As soon as they succeeded in raising it, down it went, carrying plats, ladders, and all before it, to the bottom of the shaft, which was many fathoms deep, whilst I was left hanging in the sling. They then drew me up, and took me to the hospital, where one leg was taken off and the other set; but I was very ill for a long time. Oh, just think, if that rock had not pinned my legs to the wall of the shaft, I should have been in hell now! The Lord saved my life then—and has saved my soul now!"

Dear Frank became a very zealous Christian, and for many years preached the Gospel with much power and acceptance. After his conversion, he came one morning to beg my pardon for having forbidden me his house, and to ask if I would come and hold a meeting there for his neighbours.

I did; and there was such a crowd inside, and also outside the house, and so much blessing, that I was not satisfied with one visit, but went again and again.

The place was most inconveniently full; they turned out the chairs and tables to make standing-room inside, and opened the windows and doors for the people to hear outside; and sometimes, before the address was over, men and women cried aloud for mercy. We could not kneel down to pray—praying, singing, and hearing was done standing, and that very close together. The house was so uncomfortably thronged, that a miller in the neighbourhood, who had a large room in the mill, begged me to come and preach there instead. I accepted his invitation, and we went; but, alas! there was no power there; it was hard to pray or preach; and the people were not even attentive. Thus it was clearly seen that it is not by might or by power of men, but by the Spirit of the Lord; and that if the Lord was not present to work, no work was done. We went back to Frank's cottage, and there again the manifest presence of God was discernible; and every time we did so souls were saved.

Next door to Frank lived a tall, gaunt, gipsy kind of woman, whom they called "the wise woman." She had a marvellous gift of healing, and other knowledge, which made people quite afraid of her. This woman took a great interest in me and my work, and often came to church, besides attending the meetings at Frank's house.

One day, during these services, she paid a visit to the Parsonage, and said, "My dear, have you a lemon in the house?"

I went to inquire, and found that we had not.

"Well, then," she said, "get one, and some honey and vinegar, and mix them all together. You will want it. Mind you do, now," she said, drawing herself up to her full height; "mind you do, you will want it!" Then she put the bowl of her pipe into the kitchen fire, and having ignited the tobacco, went away smoking.

The servants were much frightened by her manner and her warning, and begged of me to get the lemon, saying, "It was about you, master; it was about you that she came."

I did not know where to get a lemon within three miles; but it so happened that a man came to the door with a net full, for sale, that same afternoon. We bought two, just to pacify the servants, and let them make the mixture, thinking nothing more about it.

In the course of the afternoon a very heavy thunderstorm fell upon us, deluging the roads and lanes; and before it ceased I had to go to the meeting. I took the precaution to put on thick shoes, and then set off and walked through the rain. When I arrived at the cottage, I thought my feet felt wet; but they were not cold, so that I soon forgot all about them, and went on with the meeting, which lasted till ten o'clock; then I returned home. On taking off my shoes, I was surprised to see how wet and muddy my socks were. I had been standing with wet feet all the evening. To guard against any ill effects, I put my feet in hot water before going to bed. However, at three o'clock in the morning I awoke, nearly choked with a severe fit of bronchitis: the thick, hard phlegm in my throat almost suffocated me; I had to struggle for breath and life. After an hour or more of the most acute suffering, my dear wife remembered the lemon mixture, and called the servant to get up and bring it. It was just in time. I was black in the face with suffocation; but this compound relieved, and, in fact, restored me. I was greatly exhausted with the effort and struggle for life, and after two hours I fell asleep. I was able to rise in the morning, and breathe freely, though my chest was very sore.

After breakfast, the "wise woman" appeared, standing outside the window of the drawing-room, where I was lying on the sofa.

"Ah, my dear," she said, "you were nearly gone at three o'clock this morning. I had a hard wrestle for you, sure enough. If you had not had that lemon, you know, you would have been a dead man by this time!"

That mysterious creature, what with her healing art, together with the prayer of faith and the marvellous foresight she had, was quite a terror to the people. One day she came, and bade me go to a man who was very worldly and careless, and tell him that he would die before Sunday.

I said, "You go, if you have received the message."

She looked sternly at me, and said, "You go! that's the message—you go!"

I went. The man laughed at me, and said, "That old hag ought to be hanged." I urged him to give his heart to God, and prayed with him, but to no effect. He was thrown from his cart, and killed the following Saturday, coming home from market.

Her sayings and doings would fill a book; but who would believe the things?

She was not always a bird of evil omen, for sometimes

she brought me good news as well as bad. One day she said, "There is a clergyman coming to see you, who used to be a great friend of yours, but since your conversion he has been afraid of you. He is coming; you must allow him to preach; he will be converted before long!" Sure enough, my old friend, W. B——, came as she predicted. He preached, and in due time was converted, and his wife also; but his story shall come in its own place.

The work at Frank's cottage stopped as suddenly as it began. I cannot theorize about the subject; I merely state that so it was. It began, it continued, and continued only in that house, and then it stopped.

Another remarkable thing may here be observed—that on visiting the cottages within a limited distance round Frank's house, people were softened, and it was easy to persuade them to yield themselves to Christ. They appeared to be quite ripe and ready. Just beyond this limit the people were as hard and careless as ever. It seemed as if the power of God overshadowed only a certain spot, and that all within that were under Divine influence for the time, though all were not converted. They acknowledged, however, that they felt the Spirit's power striving with them, and they knew afterwards that it was withdrawn. "The wind bloweth where it listeth."

CHAPTER XIV.

Open-air Services.

1852.

1. PERRANZABULOE.

S the summer advanced, it was laid on my heart to go and preach in the parish of Perranzabuloe, where I had ministered in my unconverted days. The vicar, however, would not consent to my having the church; but he told me, in writing, that he could not prevent my preaching on the common or the beach. I thanked him for his suggestion as to the latter. As soon as I was able I made arrangements, and giving due notice, went down to the old familiar place; but this time on a new errand, and it was to me a fresh start in my work. I took my gown for this first open-air service; and on arriving, found many hundreds of people already assembled at the appointed place, on Perran beach.

After giving out a hymn, which was most heartily sung, I prayed, thanking God for the change He had wrought in my soul, and begging Him to show that He had forgiven the past, by bestowing a manifest blessing upon the present service. All this was loudly responded to, in Cornish fashion, with hearty "Amens," and various other ejaculations to which I was well accustomed. Then I read the beginning of the fifth chapter of St. Luke, taking for my text the words, "Launch out into the deep, and let down your nets for a draught."

Having reminded the people how hard I had worked amongst them for four years without seeing any conversions, I went on to show them, by way of parallel, that Simon Peter had toiled all night and taken nothing, but that when he went forth at the Lord's command, he enclosed a great multitude of fishes. "Here," I said, "is encouragement for us to expect a blessing now. Why did Simon Peter fail at first? and why did he subsequently succeed? Why did he fail?—1, Because he went out in the night. 2, At his own desire. 3, In the wisdom of men. Why did I fail?—1, Because I preached and laboured in the night of my unconverted state. 2, I laboured at the bidding of the Church. And, 3, According to the wisdom and tradition of the fathers. Why did Peter succeed?—Because, 1, He went out in the morning. 2, At the Lord's bidding. 3, With the Lord's presence.

"I am come (I was thankful to be able to say) in the bright sunshine of my first love. Jesus, the Saviour, is the 'Sun of *my* soul, *my* Saviour dear.'" The people cheered me so much with their responding, that I felt as happy as they. The opening heaven seemed to shine around us, indeed, "with beams of sacred bliss." They shouted again and again, "Glory to God! Glory to God! Hallelujah!" "I am come now," I continued, "to tell you, from my own personal experience, about salvation and the forgiveness of sins." "Yes, yes!" "Thank the Lord!" "Bless Him!"

"I am come, dear friends, at the Lord's bidding. I feel sure that He put it into my heart to do so. Oh, how much I longed to do you good when I was your minister; but I could not, for I knew nothing about the Way myself. Now, that I do, I am constrained to tell you. The love of God within, and the Word of God without, compel me.

"I feel I have the Lord's presence, for He not only promised it where two or three are gathered together in His name; but also to those who preach the Gospel, He said, 'Lo, I am with you alway!' His presence is power. It is His word I bring you, not mine; I merely deliver it. He is here. And be sure He loves you, and, what is more, takes a deeper interest in this preaching than we can. He died for you, and shed His blood for your forgiveness; how, then, can He do otherwise than take an interest in the delivery of His message, and, more, in the result which is to follow?

"When Simon Peter let down his net, he was astonished; mark, it was a *net* he let down into the deep, something which enclosed the fish, in order that he might bring them out of their native element, the water. So I preach the Gospel, not merely for the sake of preaching, but to bring you from the power of Satan, in which we all are by nature, to God, that you may receive the forgiveness of your sins.

"We read that he enclosed a great multitude of fishes: I have faith to believe that the Lord will bring many to Himself to night."

With shouting and praise the address was concluded, and prayer was offered. At the close, we found at least fifty people in that great throng on their knees, crying for mercy. It was a most triumphant and joyful time, and the people were loth to separate. We slept that night at Porth, as that part of the village is called.

The next morning two fishermen came to my lodging, bringing a large basket of fish as a present. Their hearts had been cheered the preceding night, and taking my word in a natural as well as a spiritual sense, they went out once again and let down their nets. They had gone out many nights before and taken nothing; but this time their venture was crowned with success, and they came back rejoicing in the Lord, who had shown them that temporal as well as spiritual blessings come from Him. The basket of fish they brought me was an acknowledgment of their heartfelt gratitude.

After breakfast, as we were walking on the sea-shore, under the majestic cliffs which have stood as a wall against the Atlantic waves for centuries, we heard our good-natured Newfoundland dog barking at something on the rocks; we looked up, and behold! there was an exquisitely graceful fawn-coloured kid, with a scarlet collar and bells, bounding about playfully on the narrow ledges of the rocks. It seemed to us to be leaping about on the face of the cliff, for we could not see the little ledges on which it picked its way. It was quite out of the dog's reach, and appeared to know it, judging from the coquettish and defiant manner in which it was jumping about, in high glee at its independence. While we were standing watching the pretty and graceful creature, a young lady came out from behind other rocks, and called to her pet, which arched its little neck, and looked at her, then at the dog, as if it would say, "How can I come down?" I walked towards her, and on speaking, found that she knew me, and that I had seen her when she was a child. After a little talk about the playful kid, I asked if she had been to the meeting; she said "she had, and she had not!" I waited silently for an explanation. Presently, she said that her mamma had forbidden her to go to "such wild meetings," but that her father had asked her to walk with him under a wall in the garden, where they could and did hear every word; and she added, "I think papa has found peace—he is so very happy!"

"And have not you also?" I asked.

"Ah," she replied, "I wish I could."

The more I talked with her, the more convinced I felt she was in earnest, but that something stood in the way. She said she did not know what it was—that she really wished for salvation, and was willing to give up everything. I said, "Do you think your mother would let you return with us on a short visit? We are just going back to Baldhu."

She said, "Mamma is not at home: she has gone away for three days; but I think papa would let me go. Shall I ask him?"

She did; and soon returned saying that she might do so if we could promise to bring her back in two days. This being settled, she hastened to get her things ready, and sent her maid to fetch home her pet kid, which she bade her take great care of during her absence: then we set off.

On arriving at our house she went straight to her bedroom, and there on her knees implored God's mercy, and remained pleading and praying for five hours, before she found peace. Then she came down among us, rejoicing in the Lord. That evening she spent at the meeting, and the next day in visiting among the cottages. On the third day, after a happy visit, we took her home to her father, rejoicing in the liberty of the children of God.

Her mother returned the day after, and when she was told of the change in her husband and her daughter Lucy, she became exceedingly angry, and wrote, not to thank, but to forbid us the house; also prohibiting further intercourse. At the same time, she declared her intention to get all that nonsense out of her daughter's head as soon as possible. She dragged this poor girl out to parties and amusements of every kind, against her will, which had the effect of making her dislike them the more, and caused her to cleave steadfastly to the Lord in prayer.

Six months later, she was taken ill, and after a few weeks' suffering she died, rejoicing that her sins were pardoned, and that she was going home. It was evident that God would not trust that mother with a daughter whose soul she was determined to injure. He took His child away to Himself.

2. Rose-in-Vale.

The open-air preaching at Perran led to many similar services there, and at other places. I will tell of two only, to prevent sameness, and for fear of tiring the reader.

The former of these, was at a place called Rose-in-vale, in the same parish, on the lawn of the chief parishioner. He was an uneducated man, who had risen from the rank of a common miner to that of a mine captain. Being very shrewd and clever, he had succeeded in accumulating a considerable sum of money; and though he and his wife had a very large house, they chiefly occupied two of the smallest rooms. "Them fine things up in the parlours," he said, he "made no 'count of;" indeed he was anything but comfortable or easy in his state apartments. Being the wealthy man of the parish, he sat on Sunday in the large square pew; but beyond giving personal attendance, and that very regularly, I do not know what other heed he gave, either to the service or the sermon.

During this summer he invited me to give "a preaching" in his garden. Accordingly, on a fixed day, I went, and *tried* to speak, but found it most difficult to do so. I know not why; but again and again I felt as though I had lost the thread of my discourse, and was rambling—that I was at a loss for words, and could not hold the attention of the people. Perplexed, and greatly discouraged, I was not sorry when the time came to conclude; therefore I did not invite the people to remain for an after-meeting for prayer. Several persons came up and asked me why I had dismissed the assembly. "Ah!" I replied, "because there is no power. I could not get on at all!" They were surprised, and said they thought that I had been helped more than usual, and were quite sure that the Lord was working among the people. However, the congregation had gone now, and could not be recalled. This only made me feel more distressed than before.

The feeling was very strong with which I had been so burdened while speaking; and, to add to my perplexity, I observed three coast-guard men, who had come some five or six miles, behaving badly, and laughing all the time (as I thought) at my discourse, to the great discomfiture of my preaching. Open-air addresses were not common in those days, and for a man to set up (as some said) and pretend to be a second Whitefield or Wesley, was bad enough, but to fail was most humiliating!

Three years after this, I was travelling outside a coach, when a rough sailor-looking man came climbing up to the top, although he was told that there was no room. "Never mind," he said; "I will sit on the boxes. I want to talk to this here gentleman." So saying, he perched himself on the luggage, and offered to shake hands with me.

"Do you know me?" I asked.

"Oh yes, bless you, of course I do! Don't you remember three coast-guard men at Captain O——'s garden?"

"Yes," I said, "indeed I do, and am not likely to forget them easily; they behaved so badly, and disturbed me so much."

"Well," he continued, "I'm one o' them. I don't know why we laughed and made fun, for we all on us felt your words deeply, and went home to pray; and a few days afterwards we were all three converted—that we were.

Praise the Lord! After that, we volunteered for the navy, to go to the Crimea war. I've been in some hot scenes, sure enough. One day we got a little too near the Russian battery, and they peppered us brave—no mistake, I assure you; they cut our masts and rigging to pieces, and ploughed up our deck with their shots. Men were being killed on every side of me. I thought, now I shall see the King in His glory. My soul was so happy, I expected every moment to be cut down and sent into His presence; but not a shot touched me! I had not even a scratch; and here I be, safe and sound, all through mercy!"

Thus, these three men, who made me at the time so unhappy, and disturbed me to such a degree, turned out well, after all.

Since then, on several occasions, I have felt as discouraged in preaching as I was that day; and though again and again I have said that I will not heed it, I have nevertheless found it difficult to be unmoved under this mysterious influence. I write this, for the comfort and consolation of others who are afflicted under similar circumstances, that they may not be cast down by their feelings.

3. Mount Hawke.

The next occasion was very different, and quite a contrast in its results. I was invited to a neighbouring parish, which formerly used to be united with Perran at the time when I had sole charge of it. Here, on the appointed Saturday afternoon, I found not fewer than three thousand people assembled on the common. They had erected a kind of platform, with a canvas awning, to shelter me from the wind, which always blows with more or less violence in Cornwall, even when it is not raining.

There I stood and beheld this concourse of people,

evidently full of large expectation. I gave out the hymn—

> " Oh for a thousand tongues, to sing
> My great Redeemer's praise ! "

This was heartily sung; and after prayer for a blessing, I announced my text, and spoke from the fact, that Christ Jesus came into the world to save sinners. Upon enforcing this as worthy of all acceptation, I pressed the thought, that the Lord Jesus came more than eighteen hundred years ago, and that He is present still, and able to work greater miracles than He wrought then ; for indeed He only began then to do and to teach what He is doing and teaching continuously now.

A mighty power of the Spirit of the Lord came on the people, and several hundreds fell upon their knees simultaneously, and many began to cry aloud for mercy. The strange part was, that the power of the Lord appeared to pass diagonally through the crowd, so that there was a lane of people on their knees six or eight feet deep, banked up on either side by others standing. It extended from the left-hand corner near me, to the right-hand corner in the distance.

It was quite impossible to go on preaching, so I gave out a hymn, and then went in among "the slain of the Lord." After about an hour, some one suggested that we should go to the school-room, as it was getting dark. The clergyman of the parish was on horseback in the lane close by, watching proceedings. I asked him if we could have the use of the school-room. "Oh yes," he said ; "yes, certainly—certainly—anything." He seemed very frightened. The men and women in distress of soul were led to the room, crying and praying as they went. When I reached the place, I found it impossible to get in, for it was already full, besides a throng standing at the door. I was taken to a window at last, and getting in through that, I stood on the schoolmaster's table, which was near.

Against the wall the men had, in miners' fashion, set up with clay some candles, which were beginning to bend over with the heat of the room. The place was densely packed, and the noise of the people praying for mercy was excessive. I could do no more than speak to those who were near me round the table. As they found peace one by one, and were able to praise God, we asked them to go out and let others come. In this way the meeting went on till ten o'clock, when I left; and it continued to go on all night and all the next day without cessation. It will scarcely be credited, but that same meeting was prolonged by successive persons without any intermission, day or night, till the evening of Sunday, the eighth day after it began. This kind of thing was not unusual in Cornwall, for we had the same in our school-room at Baldhu for three days and nights; but eight days is the longest period of which I have any personal knowledge.

I went again and again to see how they were going on; but the people were too absorbed to heed my presence; and those who were then seeking mercy were strangers to me, and had not been present at the service on the previous Saturday.

CHAPTER XV.

Drawing-room Meetings.

1852—3.

ROM that time I did not confine myself so much to my own church, but frequently went out to preach in other places, as opportunities occurred; and these were, for the most part, brought about by remarkable and unsought-for incidents.

One Sunday a lady and gentleman came to my church from one of the neighbouring towns; they were professors of religion, and members of some Dissenting body. My sermon that evening was upon wheat and chaff—the former was to be gathered into the garner, the latter burned with fire unquenchable. I said that we were all either one or the other—to be gathered or burned. They went away very angry, and complained one to another of my want of charity; they also remarked that I took good care to let the people know that I was not amongst the chaff which was to be burned. The arrows of the Lord had evidently found them, and had pierced the joints in their harness. They could not sleep all night for anger and distress. In the morning the gentleman rose early, and before breakfast had his horse out, and galloped over eight miles to see me.

He came with the intention of finding fault, but instead of this he burst into tears, and told me that he was the greatest of sinners.

He was in sore distress, which increased all the more as he gave vent to his feelings. I could not help rejoicing, and told him that God had wounded him, but that He only wounds to heal, and kills to make alive.

"Ah," he said, "that is the first thought of comfort I have had; it is like balm to my soul."

We knelt down and prayed; then I had the privilege of leading him to Christ, and we praised God together.

I gave him some breakfast, and after that rode back with him to see his wife, whom he had left in the morning in great trouble of mind. We found her up, and rejoicing. It was most touching to witness the mutual surprise and joy of these two loving ones, when they discovered that they were now united in the Lord.

She told us, that after her husband's departure she was in such terrible trouble that she got up to pray, and that while she was on her knees she saw a vision on the bedcover. Before her was printed, in large visible letters, "Thy sins be forgiven thee;" she could scarcely believe her eyes, but with her own finger she traced the letters, and was sure they were there. Taking them as a message from Christ, she rose and thanked Him, and now felt quite sure she was saved. I could not help telling her not to believe in her eyes or her visions, but in Jesus, and the fact that He had died for her. Having thanked God together, they next began to think of their servants; so we sent for them, and both master and mistress told them what the Lord had done for their souls; and while we were praying, they all three cried aloud for mercy, and found peace.

This was the commencement of a good work in that town by drawing-room meetings, and many were gathered to the Lord. Amongst the number was the mayor of the town, who in his turn wished to have a meeting at his house. As soon as I was able to fix the day, he invited his friends, but on finding that so many more desired to come than he could accommodate, he announced that the meeting would be held at the Town Hall. Great interest was excited, and it was soon evident that even this building would not be large enough, so it ended in the Temperance Hall being selected. The vicar hearing about it, wrote to protest, and asked me to call on him before I went to the place of meeting. He said it was bad enough for me to come to his parish to private houses, but to come to a public room, and that a large one, was quite out of the question.

I endeavoured to show him that the lecture or address I had come to give was not an official or ministerial act; but he would not see that. I also suggested that there was no law against it. He, begging my pardon, said "The 'Conventicle Act' had not been repealed yet, and that no one could lawfully hold a meeting of more than twenty persons."

"But surely," I replied, "that is virtually repealed by the 'Toleration Act.' A clergyman ought not to be in greater bondage in England than a layman, or more restricted. Anybody else can come and preach the Gospel in your parish, and you cannot hinder it. Do not hinder me. It will do you no harm."

He said, "I cannot conscientiously allow it. It is against the Canons."

"Which Canon is it against?" I asked.

He took down a book and showed it me; but casting my eyes on one before, and another which followed, I found that we neither of us observed the one or the other. Why, then, be so zealous about this? "Besides," I said, "you are not responsible; you have not asked me, nor have I asked your consent. Your conscience need not be troubled about the matter."

"But," he said, impatiently, "I am determined that you shall not preach in this parish. I will inform the Bishop."

I replied, that "the Bishop had not any jurisdiction in this case; there is no law on the subject. The Conventicle Act only refers to worship, not to service or preaching."

He said, that he "could see no difference whatever between worship and service."

"But," I said, "I am sure the Bishop knows, and will acknowledge, the great difference between these two."

Then, changing his tone, he said, "Now, come, there's a good fellow, don't preach at the Town Hall."

"My dear man," I answered, "I am not a 'good fellow' at all. I cannot give it up."

"Then," he said, "at least please to defer your address for a week, till we can get the Bishop's decision."

He asked so kindly and earnestly, and made such a point of it, that I consented to wait for the Bishop's answer, and defer the preaching for the week. He was very pleased, and said that I was indeed a 'good fellow;' but the praise I got from him barely satisfied my conscience, and I was ashamed to meet my friends. I had not gone far, before my courage failed; so, going back, I said that "I must withdraw my consent to defer the meeting. I will take the consequences and responsibilities, and go on."

"No, no," said the vicar, "I will arrange for the postponement of your meeting. Look here, I have written out a notice for the crier; he shall go round the town at once, and tell the people that the meeting is unavoidably deferred for a week."

I was very reluctantly persuaded to yield, and then went to my friend and told him what I had done. He was very much vexed with me, and said, "Then we must go at once and tell the mayor before he hears the crier." We did so, and found that this personage was disappointed too, and advised me to go away out of sight of the people. Accordingly, my friend and I went to a house which commanded a good view of the town and principal streets, from whence we could see the people assembling and dispersing. A large gang of them stood opposite my friend's house, and asked if I would not preach to them in the open air; and when they ascertained that the vicar had hindered the preaching, they were much exasperated.

In the evening I went back to my own parish, and had the usual service, which I found very refreshing after so much bickering about technicalities.

The Bishop's letter arrived in due time. In it his lordship said, that he "always had entertained a great esteem for me and my obedience to authority, and highly commended me for postponing or giving up my service at the above town." As he did not say a single word of prohibition, I immediately wrote to the mayor to expect me on the following Tuesday, "for the Bishop had not forbidden me," and I also wrote to the vicar to the same effect. Large bills, with large letters on them, announced that "the Rev. William Haslam *will positively preach* in the Temperance Hall at three o'clock on Tuesday next."

The churchwardens of the parish were requested to attend the meeting, and protest, on behalf of the vicar, and also to present the archdeacon's monition. They stood beside me all the time, and after the service was concluded they showed me the archidiaconal instrument, with a great seal appended to it. They said that they "dared not stop that preaching," and so they took their monition back.

This gave rise to a long correspondence in the newspapers, some taking part on my side, and some against me. Thus the question was ventilated, and finally concluded, by a letter from some one, who said, "The Bishop of Exeter is one of the greatest ecclesiastical lawyers we have, and if he cannot stop Mr. Haslam, the question is settled; for be sure his lordship has all the will to stop this preaching, and would do so if he had the power."

From that time I never hesitated to preach the Gospel in any parish or diocese where I was invited. So few of the clergy asked me, that I was obliged to go out in spite of them, or, at any rate, without asking their consent, and in consequence of this, I am afraid I became obnoxious to many of my clerical brethren. Since then things are much changed. The Earl of Shaftesbury has succeeded in getting an Act passed through both Houses of Parliament, to settle the question about such services. Now any clergyman may preach in Exeter Hall, or any other public non-ecclesiastical building, without consulting the vicar of the parish. Besides this, a general disposition has arisen amongst the clergy, from one end of the land to the other, to have "missions," so that there is no need to work independently of clergymen, but *with* them, and very cheering it is to be thus employed. It was not pleasant to witness the scowl and the frown, nor to get the cold shoulder. Thank God, times are changed now; but I must needs tell of some of the scenes I was in, and the opposition I had to encounter, during the years that are gone by.

CHAPTER XVI.

Opposition.

1853.

 HAVE been telling hitherto of blessing and prosperity in the Lord's work. Many more cases might have been mentioned, and many other things of not less moment and interest; but enough has been said, I hope, to show the character of the work, and give some idea of the amount of blessing which attended it.

But it must not be supposed that the offence of the cross had ceased, or that the enmity of the carnal mind was never stirred; indeed, I always doubt the reality of a work which moves on without opposition. On the day of Pentecost, when the Holy Ghost was first given, while believers were rejoicing, and sinners were pricked to the heart, and some mocked, there arose the opposition of others, who resisted the influence of the Spirit; and being "cut to the heart," they gnashed with their teeth, and went forward in furious contention against the Lord's work. So it was with us.

The opposition ran very high, but I do not think it was of malice or hatred, but rather "righteous indignation."

The instigators of it were serious and earnest persons, who verily thought they were doing right. They tried first to save me from what they considered was my infatuation; and failing that, did all they could to save others from my bad influence. "I bear them record, that they had a zeal for God, but not according to knowledge." It was just such a zeal as I had before I was converted; therefore my heart's desire was drawn out towards them, and I made continual efforts to win them.

One dear friend of old time said he felt "so hurt" because I was changed, and often wondered why "God did not strike me dead for all the harm I had done to the Church." Another said that he "should not be surprised if the very ground opened and swallowed me up for my fraternizing with schismatics. The sin of Korah, Dathan, and Abiram was nothing to mine." At the Clerical Meeting, which I attended notwithstanding all this stir against me, I was beset on every side with something more than loving reproaches; for evidently my old friends were very much grieved, and could not forgive me for what they considered the betrayal of Church principles.

A special meeting or synod of the clergy was convened by the Rural Dean, to take into consideration, among other things, my defection, and to decide what public notice should be taken on the subject of this great scandal. I also attended this meeting, and found my brethren in a very angry and excited state. One after another got up and made grievous charges against me, about the proceedings in my church and parish. The burden of their distress, however, seemed to be noise and excitement.

They said that "There was brawling in my church, and howling in my schoolroom, women fainting, and men shouting in a most fanatical manner. They had not witnessed these scenes themselves, but they were credibly informed of them. Moreover, they asserted, on good authority, that I preached a very different doctrine to that which was authorized by the Church. I had declared that there was no salvation by the Church and Sacraments, but by simple faith in Christ; that any man—it did not matter what his previous life had been—if he only came to my preaching, and did as I told him, would be saved." These, and many other such charges, were made and supported by shouts of "Hear! hear!" and cries of "Shame!" The Rural Dean said he was glad Mr. Haslam was present to answer for himself; he had observed that I had sat very quietly to hear others, and he now hoped that a patient hearing would be given to me.

I rose, and said I was very thankful to be there, and to have this opportunity of testifying before them all that the Lord had converted my soul!

There was a little interruption here, but after a time I was permitted to go on. I said that before I was converted, I was even more zealous than any of them against this change, and greatly prejudiced against it. I actually flogged a big boy in my school for going to a chapel and professing to be converted; this I did before all the children, and he promised that he would "never be converted any more." I could, therefore, well understand their present feelings, and said that I was not angry with them, but rather prayed that they might, in their turn, be enabled to see these things as I now saw them, and be saved as I was.

Upon this, there arose a great disturbance. The Rural Dean gave me credit for candour, and said he thought I meant well, but that I implied too much against my brethren; however, he had said before, and would repeat it, that I had listened quietly to what others had said, and that now I was entitled to a patient hearing a little longer.

But this could not be, for I was stopped at every fresh statement I made, and had so many questions put to me, that I begged for only one at a time. I was enabled to stand my ground calmly, and endeavoured to answer the charges in order as they were brought out. To all appearance, I had to stand quite alone in that tumultuous party. We had met at twelve o'clock, and after four hours were still in the heat of the conflict.

At last, to conclude this extraordinary meeting, one of the clergy rose and said that he felt it was his painful yet necessary duty to propose that "a vote of censure be passed on Mr. Haslam." It was not seconded, and so fell to the ground. Whereupon, another rose "to record a protest against revival meetings, as contrary to the usage of the Church." This also failed; and as no one else had anything to say, the conclave of divines broke up. What they would have said or done, if I had not attended to be torn in pieces by them, I know not; all I can say is, that they separated without eating me up. Some of them came to me afterwards, and seemed pleased that I had stood my ground so good-naturedly, and thought that I had had a great badgering.

The opposition did not stop there—sermons were preached in several of the neighbouring churches, and people earnestly warned against attending certain services, and told not to countenance them by their presence. The newspapers also took up the matter, and public report was not behind in its usual exaggeration.

I give here an extract from a Letter I thought it necessary to write at this time, on "RELIGIOUS EXCITEMENT":

"MY DEAR SIR,—I have been seriously considering, for some time, the necessity of making a public statement respecting the work of God in this place; with a view partly of drawing attention to an all-important, though very neglected subject; and partly with a view of giving some definite and authoritative form to the various and varied reports which are in circulation. It is vain to pretend to know nothing about them, and it is equally vain to suppose that reports about our proceedings are likely to lose less by repetition, than those on other subjects of less moment.

"I embrace, therefore, the opportunity which your Sermon on RELIGIOUS EXCITEMENT offers, to make a statement.

"I do remonstrate against your publishing to the world a sermon avowedly against 'proceedings connected with a neighbouring church;' and that instead of encouragement, counsel, and co-operation in what I know is the work of God, I receive this public rebuke. I make this remonstrance the more earnestly, because several of the opinions you have expressed, are not, as I believe, consistent with the teaching of our Church; and lastly, I venture to be the remonstrant, because I am the person, and mine the church, which are the objects of your animadversions.

"You hold deservedly a high position among us in respect of rank and esteem for your piety and learning; but at the hazard of incurring the imputation of arrogance, I cannot, I must not, and I will not be unfaithful to the light in which I walk, by the grace of God; and therefore I do simply and plainly protest, in the first place, against the supposition that *Excitement* is a *means* which I am using, or an *end* I have in view; secondly, against the supposition that conversion is a *gradual* work, which is to be worked out by Sacraments and Means of Grace; and thirdly, against a teaching which supposes and actually declares, that a person may believe, may be pardoned, may be cleansed from sin, *yet not know it.*

"In the sense in which you censure Religious Excitement, namely, as a means to 'force, as it were, the Spirit of the Lord,' and 'for the purpose of strongly working on the animal feelings, etc.,' it may be justly censurable. Those who make excitement the end and object of their endeavours in a religious movement, must soon find the emptiness of it; they throw dust into their own eyes, and will ever verify your words that 'excitement lifts up for a moment and then lets fall again,' and that 'like dram-drinking, it leaves those that indulge in it weaker than before.'

"Those who really are engaged in the work of God, and especially *conversion work*, must meet with 'excitement.' It is impossible for a sinner, under conviction of sin, to remain in a calm imperturbable state, or when the despairing sinner comes to a knowledge of that

Saviour who made Atonement for him, to help being excited with joy. Noble or peasant, gentle or uneducated, I am sure there will be *excitement*, and overflowing joy and gladness.

"A man who never felt himself a lost sinner, and never knew his need of the Saviour, may reason gravely of the impropriety of 'excitement,' and the man who has never experienced the liberty of deliverance from the 'horrible pit, and the mire and clay,' may seem to be wise on the subject of Christian joy; but he knows it not. The outburst of joy in the new-born child of God, is as undiscriminating as the joyous mirth of children. But it becomes more subdued as the child grows on to 'the conquering young man,' and more chastened still when the 'young man' attains to that state which St. John terms 'father.' This I have no doubt is the kind of Christian joy you expect to see, and without which you are not satisfied.* But, dear friend, remember the perfect Temple was not built in one, but three days.

"We are at foundation work; and you rebuke us for an unfinished temple! Your rebuke is not undeserved in one sense: we ought to have attained to great advancements, and to have begun long ago; but God has had patience with us. In this beginning there seems to be confusion to superficial observers, and there must be 'excitement;' but this, as I said, is not the end in view, or the means we use. It is not long since I could reason against 'excitement,' and thought as many do now, that in connection with religion it is irreverent, and unbecoming.

"Oh, what a snare is this unfeeling 'propriety!' It is really a dislike of being aroused from sleep; a fearful hugging of oneself into apathetic security, and lying down in the arms of the Wicked One for a fatal slumber. Oh that I could 'excite' such persons! that I could arouse them! that by any means I could awaken these souls from the sleep of death! I would glory in the censure and rejoice in the blame. Would that I could reach your heart and the hearts of many of my other brethren; that we might unite together and raise a louder call! There should be a more excited blast, as from a trumpet, to stir the masses of those who come duly and regularly 'to hear us every Sunday,' a

---

* "I write unto you, little children, because your sins are forgiven you for His name's sake. I write unto you, fathers, because ye have known Him that is from the beginning. I write unto you, young men, because ye have overcome the Wicked One."—1 JOHN ii. 12, 13.

louder, stronger, and more urgent and thrilling cry, Repent! Repent! We want more fearless plain speaking, more personal appeal. It is not refined to preach of the grave and death, judgment and hell,—it is 'ranting:' but nevertheless let us 'rant;' let us be faithful; let us tell the sinner that he must die; and that he will die in his sins and perish for ever, except he repent and be converted that his sins may be blotted out. Let us tell him that he '*is condemned already*, because he hath not believed in the Name of the only-begotten Son of God' (John iii. 18): that 'the wrath of God abideth on him' (verse 35). Instead of arguments against 'excitement,' let us have a united cry against sin and frivolity wherever it is. There is excitement against 'excitement' now; let there be excitement, if you will, against indifference, and neglect of religion."

Many of the proceedings in our parish were, I confess, more tumultuous than I could justify, more noisy and exciting than I thought needful; but I could not control the people. If they had been educated to ideas of propriety and self-control, the impulse of Divine power, which really then *filled them*, might have found expression in a more quiet and orderly manner. To hinder their rejoicings therefore, though they were considered so obnoxious, would have been to withstand the Spirit of God. As the people had not been taught better, I could not interfere with them; I would rather bear the obloquy of men.

For instance, one day, by way of change, I had a meeting for the Bible Society, and invited some of the clergy who sympathized with its object. They attended, and others came out of curiosity "to see these revival people." We had a large gathering, and everything began smoothly. My Scripture-reader, who was naturally a most excitable and noisy man, tried to do his best before the clergy; he spoke of the sweet words which they had heard from the reverend speakers; it was charming, he said, to hear of a good cause supported in such "mellifluous accents," and so forth. He got a little wild towards the end, but on the whole he was to be praised for his kind efforts to give a quiet tone to the meeting. By this time, our friend "Billy Bray" had appeared on the scene, and gave us chapter and verse from one end of the Bible to the other, on the subject of "dancing for joy." He propounded his theory, that if a man did not praise God, he would not rise in the resurrection; if he only praised God with his mouth, he would rise like those things carved on the tombstones, with swelling cheeks and wings; if he clapped his hands (suiting his actions to the words) he would have a pair of hands as well at the resurrection; and if he danced with his feet, he would rise complete. He hoped to rise like that, to sing, to clap his hands, dance, and jump too. The worst of jumping in this world, he said, was that he had to come down again, but in heaven he supposed the higher he danced and jumped, the higher he would be; walking in heaven, to his mind, was praising God, one foot said "Glory," and the other "Hallelujah."

Under "Billy's" original theories the people were warming up, and becoming a little responsive, and "Billy" himself was getting excited. In reference to some remarks which had been made by a previous speaker about Samson, he said that he felt as happy and strong as Samson; then suddenly he put his arms round me, as I was standing gesticulating and making signs to the people to be still, and taking me up as he had done once before, he carried me down the schoolroom, crying out, "Here go the postés! Glory! hallelujah!" It was useless to resist, for he held me with an iron grasp; so I remained still, hoping at every step that he would put me down. I suppose he imagined himself to be Samson carrying off the gates of Gaza. The people got what they called "happy," and shouted and praised God most vociferously. I gave out a hymn, but the joy of the Cornish people could not be restrained within the bounds of a tune, or form of words. Some of them became very excited and unmanageable ; only those who have witnessed such scenes can understand what I mean. The power of God was great, though the demonstrations were very human. My visitors trembled with fear, and made their escape as precipitately as they possibly could. To those who are not in the power of the Spirit such rejoicings are unintelligible ; lookers-on are stumbled or offended because they only see and feel the human manifestation, and not the Divine power ; they are like people who get all the smoke, and none of the warmth of the fire.

I made up my mind for the worst, for we had a reporter there, and some others who were only too ready to make the most of such a scene. Nevertheless I would rather have the same thing over and over again, than have the most stately and orderly ceremonials conjoined with spiritual death. These things, with all their proprieties, are very chilling to living souls, and all the more hurtful because dead souls are satisfied by them instead of being disturbed.

Dear Mr. Aitken was very angry with us, when he heard the things which were reported ; and, like a good spiritual father, he came over to teach us better. He preached one of his own strong sermons, on the difference between emotion and principle, and after beating us down very hard, his dear heart relented, and he tried to cheer and lift us up. This last is always an easy thing to do in Cornwall. The people soon responded to his efforts, and began to praise God ; and then he took fire, and praised too. Mutually exciting and being excited, his powerful voice could be heard above the din of hundreds of shouting voices. The dear man was happy in his soul, and so was I, and we did not care a halfpenny for the outside world, newspapers, or anything else.

We had obloquy with opposition ; and even to my personal friends I could not give satisfactory explanations of these things. One suggested that I should read a paper at the next Clerical Meeting, and give a statement in exposition of my views and practices. This I consented to do, and Mr. Aitken kindly helped me to write it. On the appointed day I undertook to read it, on condition that no one interrupted me till I had finished. It was a hard task for them to sit still, but they did manage to do so; and at the end, burst out upon me in a volley of censure and disapprobation. I was obliged to tell them that they were not converted, and therefore could not understand these things.

I wrote a pamphlet to show that the Church of England's teaching was based on CONVERSION, and not on baptism; and that the Reformation was to the Church of England what Conversion was to the individual reformers. Taking my own change as an illustration, I said, that I used to rest on Baptism and the Church, and that now I was standing on the Rock, Christ Jesus. Once I worked *for* life, and now I worked *from* life; that is, because I possessed it. I declared that this was the characteristic difference between the Church of England as it is, and as it was when connected with the Church of Rome. This pamphlet would not satisfy them. I then wrote and published a letter to the Archdeacon, in which, in my young zeal, I charged the clergy with being unconverted, and doing the devil's work in hindering the salvation of souls, and that they seemed to stand on their parish boundaries and say, "This is my parish, and you shall not come here to disturb the sleep of death which now reigns." This poured no oil upon the waters.

I then wrote another pamphlet upon which I spent much time, thought, and prayer. I took the manuscript and read it to Mr. Aitken. He walked up and down in his large room, while I was reading, and ejaculated, as only he could, "Bless God! Glory be to God!" When I finished, I said, "Shall I print it?"

He said, "It is worth printing, but it will do no good. It is like a little doggie barking at a dead elephant. We shall never convert the Church as a body: we must try and get at individuals. I am quite convinced we shall not succeed unless we work in this way."

CHAPTER XVII.

Individual Cases.

1853.

AN Archbishop of Canterbury, in old times, contrasted public preaching with personal dealing in this way: When we preach, it is like dashing water from a bucket upon so many vessels which are arranged before us—some drops fall into one, and some into another, while others remain empty; but when we speak to individuals, it is like pouring water into the neck of a vessel.

I gave up writing and printing pamphlets, and went on as quietly as I could with my own work, looking out for individual cases as they presented themselves in the providence of God. In this way, without fomenting controversy or keeping up public excitement, I was able more effectually to impart my meaning, than by printed statements, which I found were misunderstood or distorted; and what is more, I was able to apply the truth with an individual " Have you?" It would take more space than I can afford to tell of the souls which were gained in this way. I will give here only a few instances, which are interesting, and which will sustain the thread of my narrative.

The first was in the case of one who began an argument on Baptismal Grace. I asked him what it was. "I know what converting or saving grace is; but what is this?" He did not say more, than that in Baptism he was made a member of Christ, a child of God, and an inheritor of the kingdom of heaven.

"But," I asked, "suppose you have not repented and believed, what then?" Receiving no answer, I continued, "Then, nothing; but the responsibility and the name."

A few days afterwards he came to me, saying that I had made him quite miserable, and asked me whether I meant to deny the necessity of baptism. I said, "Certainly not, but the condition of faith and repentance must be fulfilled. Whatever Baptismal Regeneration may be, Spiritual Regeneration is the work of the Spirit in those who believe in Christ Jesus." After a long talk and prayer, he appeared to understand that a conscious change should be wrought in him, and a spiritual faculty imparted, by which he could "see the kingdom of God." He remained for the evening service and meeting in the schoolroom, and was much impressed with what he witnessed. Instead of going away, he stayed with me till after midnight, when he found peace with God (as he said) in the church where we had been praying. Then he ordered his horse and rode home; but before he set out, he exacted a promise from me that I would not mention his conversion to any one. I consented to this, on the condition that he announced the change which had been wrought in him, from his pulpit on the following Sunday.

A few days afterwards my friend came to me in a great rage, and charged me with announcing his conversion all over the town. I told him that I was not sure enough of it myself to say anything about it, and that I had not spoken to a single person on the subject. Still he seemed to doubt me, for he said his brother had been with him, and had told him that it was known all over the town that he had been to Baldhu, and that he was converted. Upon inquiry, I found out that my servant, who sat up till after midnight to get his horse, had overheard our conversation, and was the offending party.

I am always afraid of persons who are ashamed to acknowledge their conversion. My friend, I am sorry to say, made no announcement, but went on preaching as if he had always been the same, and consequently never came out to be of any use or help in the work. His testimony was indistinct also, and without any power. He became a very popular preacher afterwards, which was his great ambition, for he cared more for a large congregation than for winning souls.

Soon after this, I fell across another of my old friends in the street. He tried to avoid me, but I went up and shook hands with him. At first he would not look at me, and said he was afraid of me because I had changed my views. I assured him that I had not changed anything, but that I had myself been changed. As he was listening, I went on to tell him that I had long tried to make myself good enough for God's acceptance, but finding that Christ would not receive reformed characters, I came to Him as a poor lost sinner, and He saved me. Seeing that he continued attentive, I was proceeding to make my meaning plainer, when he turned round, and looking sternly at me, said, "If I understand you, I am to cry for mercy as 'a common sinner.'"

"Yes," I replied, being very pleased to find that he had understood me so well.

"Then," he said, "I will do no such thing." With this, he turned away and departed. When he saw that I was following him, he said, "I desire you will not speak to me any more. I do not agree with you."

One morning, a short time after, I was praying and meditating in the church, when it came to my mind forcibly that I must go to this man's parish. I rose from my knees forthwith, saying to myself that I would go; but immediately the thought came to me, "This suggestion is not from God, for He must know that my horse has lost two shoes, and could not go all that distance." However, I returned home, and went to the stable to inquire, when, to my surprise, I found that my man had taken the horse out very early in the morning, and had got him properly shod. "He is all right for a long journey, master," he said, "if you want to go."

"Well," I said, "put on the saddle, and be ready in half-an-hour." I went in to prepare, and started in due time. On the way I was thinking what I would say, and how I would begin the conversation, for as yet I did not know the particular message I was to take.

When I arrived at my friend's gate, I saw the marks of his horse's feet, as if he had just gone out. However, I rode up to the front door, and rang the bell. His wife appeared, and said that her husband had gone out, and would not be back before six o'clock; she added, "You look disappointed"; and so I was, for I thought the Lord had sent me with some message to him. The lady kindly asked me to put up my horse, saying, "Perhaps he may return sooner; you had better rest a little." I thanked her, and doing so, went in.

As soon as we were seated, the lady said, "I have been wishing to see you for a long time; we have started more than once to visit you, when my husband's courage has failed him, and we have returned. He says that he loves you still; but, somehow, he is very much afraid of you."

Then she went on to tell me that when they were removing from their late parish to where they now were, having sent all their furniture on, they were driving in their own carriage; and that coming along over a bleak and desolate moor, the horse took fright at something, they knew not what, and ran away. Because it could not get along fast enough from its imaginary object of fear, it began to kick, and breaking the carriage in pieces, made its escape, leaving her and her husband on the ground. He was not much hurt, and soon rose, and came to help her. She was severely bruised, and her leg was broken besides. He managed to drag her gently to the side of the road, where there was a little bank, and, collecting some of the broken pieces of the carriage, he placed them round her for protection, and hurried off in order to get assistance. He had to go two miles, and was absent nearly three hours. During that time she suffered great pain, but it came to her mind all at once that her sins were pardoned; she was exceedingly happy, and could not help thanking and praising God. In this state her husband found her when he returned, and on hearing her talk, became very unhappy, because he thought that besides her leg, her head was broken too; and that she was going out of her mind. She assured him over and over again, that she was wonderfully well, and really happy; but he could not bear to hear her talk like that, and said that he should go mad also, if she did not stop.

During the six weeks she was laid up, he continually brought doctors and clergymen to talk her out of her delusion, as he thought it, but without avail. Her happiness continued for several months, and then gradually died away. She asked me, "Can you tell me the meaning of this?" I was deeply interested with her experience, and told her that I had read of a similar one only a few days before.

My heart now began to cheer up, for I saw why I had been sent to this place. I at once pointed her to passages of Scripture, where we are told that we have forgiveness of sins through the blood of Jesus, and I put Christ crucified before her as the object of faith. I told her, that as certainly as the blood of Jesus had been shed, there was mercy and forgiveness for her. I said, "I believe it, and have forgiveness: and you may have it too; not because you feel happy, but because Jesus died." She did believe, and we rejoiced together.

She exclaimed, "Oh that the Lord would change my husband's heart, and bring you here for a revival!"

"Very well," I said, "let us ask Him," and we did so. I then rode home praising God.

Before leaving, I promised to come again on the following Wednesday. I kept my word, and had an interview with her husband; but it was not encouraging. He said he could not agree to ask for mercy as a sinner, because he had been baptized. Some months afterwards, his man-servant came to me on horseback at three o'clock in the morning, to say that his master was very bad, and would I come as soon as possible and see him. I asked, "What is the matter?" "Oh, bless the Lord," said the man, "it's all about his soul!" "That is right," I replied, thanking God; "I will go with you at once," and immediately I saddled my horse, and rode back with him.

I found my friend was under deep conviction, and in the greatest misery; he now thought that he was a most "*uncommon sinner*," and that there was no mercy for him, there could not be any! After a time he acknowledged the power of God to forgive sin, and declared that he believed in Christ, and I was led to say, "he that believeth hath everlasting life." Upon this text he found peace, and we all praised God together.

The Sunday following, he asked the congregation to thank God with him for having saved his soul; and in his sermon told them something of his experience. Subsequently his church became the centre of a work of God, as Mr. Aitken's church and mine were in our respective neighbourhoods.

The power of the Lord overshadowed the place, and there was as usual a simultaneous melting of hearts all over the parish, and a running together of the people to hear the Word, and what is better to obey it. Then followed a true Cornish revival with full manifestations, and Mr. Aitken came to preach. The fire was burning and shining before; but when this mighty man stirred it, it rose to a tremendous height. The excitement of the parson and people was intense, and hundreds of souls were added to the Church, who had been brought from the death of sin into the life of righteousness, which all the previous preaching on Baptism and the Lord's Supper had failed to produce.

CHAPTER XVIII.

A Visit to Veryan.

1853.

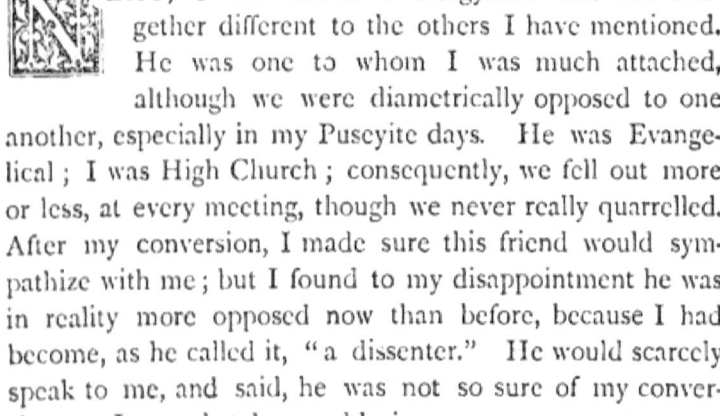

NEXT, I will tell of a clergyman who was altogether different to the others I have mentioned. He was one to whom I was much attached, although we were diametrically opposed to one another, especially in my Puseyite days. He was Evangelical; I was High Church; consequently, we fell out more or less, at every meeting, though we never really quarrelled. After my conversion, I made sure this friend would sympathize with me; but I found to my disappointment he was in reality more opposed now than before, because I had become, as he called it, "a dissenter." He would scarcely speak to me, and said, he was not so sure of my conversion as I was, that he would give me seven years to prove it, and then pronounce.

I said, "You are an old bachelor, and know nothing about the treatment of babies; we do not put our babies out on the lawn for seven days before we decide whether they are born or not!"

He could not resist joining in the laugh against his inexperience in this respect, although he was not over-pleased.

With all his head-knowledge of Gospel truth, he had not seen anything of the work of the Spirit, and moreover, like too many others, could not distinguish between death and grave-clothes. Because I announced some sacramental views after my conversion, he fancied that I must be dead still; whereas these were only the grave-clothes in which I used to be wrapped. We shall speak more of this hereafter.

One day, he came to me and said, "I have been thinking for some time that I should like to come to your church one Sunday, and see your work."

I agreed to this with thanks, as the first sign of sympathy I had found in him, and said, "Shall I go and take your services in exchange?"

"Oh no, certainly not; I wish you to be present in your own church. I will preach in the morning; and in the evening I will be there to see and hear you." We soon fixed upon the day.

He came to dinner with us the previous Saturday, but before he would sit down he must needs go into the Church, and adjust the height of the pulpit, and see that all other things were to his taste. He asked me if I would remove the candlesticks from the communion table, and let him preach in a black gown. These were all matters of indifference to me now, so I readily acceded to his wishes. Having completed his arrangements, we spent a very pleasant evening together, talking over the work in the place, and then went to the weekly prayer-meeting; but he took no part. On Sunday morning the service was conducted at his request, in the usual manner, excepting that he stood away in the eastern corner of the north side of the table, "scrootching" away like a Papist, as the people described it. They had been accustomed to see me stand at the western or outside corner of the north side. He was much amused at this criticism.

Then he went into the vestry, having asked for an interlude on the organ before the last verse of the Psalms (for we sang the metrical version in those days), and while this was being played he came sailing out again, and swept up the steps into the pulpit. He gave us an excellent sermon—preached, as the Cornish say, "to a form," that is with a manuscript before him; though he did not look at it much. He showed it to me afterwards; it certainly was a curious thing, done in cyphers and hieroglyphics of his own; again and again there appeared a figure with two horns and a tail; this, he told me, stood for Satan; there were also many other striking signs. He preached with far more animation than he was wont, and towards the end of his sermon seemed to forget his manuscript altogether, and leaned over the front of the pulpit, gesticulating with his hands, and looking at the people. They got very excited, and followed every sentence with some response, till he became excited also. When he came down from the pulpit, he said that he had never preached with such help before; he had quite enjoyed his own sermon, and that now he thought he understood the secret of what I called being "converted."

He came in the afternoon to the catechising of the children, and expressed himself very pleased with their behaviour, and readiness in answering questions.

In the evening, he sat in a part of the church where he could see the congregation, and the preacher, and so make his desired observations. The service was, perhaps, a little more animated than usual, and the sermon may have been the same. After this was over, he went with me into the schoolroom, where he heard the people pray, and also thank God for the morning sermon. Several souls were brought in that evening.

About ten o'clock at night we returned home, when my friend declared he had never known a day like this in all his ministry, and never heard of such things as he had seen. "Your congregation," he said, "is like the waves of the sea, and mine like a glassy mill-pond. Now I must have you come and preach in my church. I wonder what the effect will be."

I agreed, and we fixed upon the second Sunday, as he wanted a week to announce my coming.

I was quite eager for the time, and when Saturday arrived, I set off, intending to stay for several days. On Sunday morning the church was filled from end to end, the people being on the tip-toe of expectation. Many anxious ones remained after the sermon to be spoken with, about their souls. The church was scarcely cleared, before the men came to ring the bells for the afternoon service. This time, the passages, chancel, pulpit-stairs, and every available corner were crowded, and the congregation certainly did not look like a "mill-pond," but more like "the waves of the sea."

At the close of this service, the people begged for another in the evening.

The vicar said, "Oh, that is impossible, for I dine at six o'clock."

"But," I involuntarily added, "do not mind the dinner; I can come, if you like."

He gave me such a look! I continued, "I have had dinner enough for to-day. I can take the service alone, if you are agreeable."

"But we have no lamps for the church. It cannot be."

I was silenced now, and gave up the point; when the churchwarden came forward and said he would be responsible for lighting the church.

The vicar at last consented, on condition that he was allowed to have his dinner in peace. As the time approached, however, he put off that important meal, and joined me in a cup of tea, after which we went together to the third service.

This time it was as much as we could do to get in, and when we did succeed a most striking sight presented itself. The whole church was lighted from the pews. Some of the wealthier people had lamps, but the others had candles, one two, or more in their respective compartments. From the pulpit it looked more like a market scene than a church congregation. I had liberty in preaching, and the people were greatly moved, some of them greatly agitated—indeed, so much so, that the vicar thought he would not have another service in the church, and accordingly announced that the Monday evening meeting would be held in a building which he named, in a village about two miles off. This was a large barn-like structure, where they cured fish in the season, but at other times it was unoccupied.

The next day happened to be very wet, and, added to this, in the evening it began to blow as well. Notwithstanding this inclemency, when we arrived at the "fish-cellar," as it was called, we found it crammed with people, the women and children occupying the ground, and sitting there on straw, which had been provided for the occasion, the men and boys were sitting on the cross-beams of the roof. The heat in the place was stifling beyond all description, for besides being densely crowded below and above, the wooden shutters were shut, on account of the wind and rain, the people's wet clothes were steaming, and there was a strong smell of stale fish. At first we felt as if it would be impossible to bear it, but after a little time we became used to the disagreeables, and had other things to think about.

I gave out a hymn, and after a short prayer commenced the address, speaking as loud as I could, that all the congregation might hear me. During the sermon, the responses were most vociferous and hearty, and the attention very encouraging. After speaking for about thirty minutes, I observed a tall, fine-looking fisherman, in large high boots, who had come in late. He was standing in the little vacant space before the table, on which were placed two candles and a glass of water. I saw, as the address went on, that though he was very quiet, his breast was heaving with emotion, as if something was passing in his mind. All at once, without a moment's notice, he fell on the ground, and bellowed out a loud prayer for "God's mercy—I want God's mercy!" Besides upsetting the table—candles, water, and all—which went down with a great crash, he fell on one or two women, who screamed, in their fright and consternation, as only women can.

If this had been a preconcerted signal, it could not have been more effectual, for there was instantly a simultaneous as well as an universal outcry. The whole place was filled with a confused din of voices; some were praying, some singing, some shouting, and others exhorting, and that at the top of their voices, in order to be heard. In the midst of this I began to sing a hymn, hoping to restore order, and many joined me; but it only added more sound to the uproar.

The good vicar was overwhelmed with fear and dismay, as well he might be, at this tumultuous scene. It was bad enough to stand and look at the waves of the sea; but when they rose and broke, as it were, on the shore where he was standing, and surrounded him, it was altogether too much. He made for the door, and, waiting there, beckoned me to him. When I came he suddenly opened it, and drew me out, saying, "There will be no peace till you are out of this place." The extreme change from the hot cellar into the cold and pitiless wind and rain was so great, that we fled precipitately to the cottage which stood opposite. Happily, the door was on the latch, and we went in. I felt about in the dark for a chair, but not finding one, sat on the table, listening to the noise and din of the meeting.

The vicar vainly thought that the tumult would subside as soon as I was gone, for he said that I "made as much noise, if not more, than any of them!" He went back into the storm to get my hat and coat, and also the inevitable umbrella, without which no one can get on in Cornwall. He was a long time absent, during which a man with heavy boots came into the dark cottage where I was sitting, and tumbling down on a seat somewhere, heaved a heavy sigh. He evidently did not suspect that any one was there. After sighing and groaning several times, he said to himself, "What shall I do? what shall I do? The man is right, sure enough; he is right, I'm sure on it—that he is."

I disguised my voice, and asked, "What man?"

"Oh," he said, "are you there, neighbour? Couldn't yer get in? Why, I mean the man what's been speaking inside."

"What did he say?"

"Why, said he, 'the devil's no fool!' and of course he ain't. He has hooks in all his baits, and I have swallowed lots o' them. Oh, what shall I do? what shall I do?"

Then I heard him shuffling to his knees, groaning and praying. I sat still on the table, saying, "Amen! amen!" every now and then, to his prayer, till he became terribly in earnest, and at last got into a state which the Cornish call "wrastling in prayer." In this condition he was quite past heeding any one's presence. I helped and guided him to the Crucified One, and then he found peace, and began to praise God. On coming to himself, he recognized my voice. "Why, you are the very man," he cried, and putting his great heavy arms round my neck, he nearly strangled me! The vicar (who I did not know was in the room), here interposed, and got my release.

"Here you are," he said, "at it again; and they are getting worse and worse in the barn—what ever is to be done? We cannot go home through this rain, and the carriage will not be here for at least an hour. What am I to do?"

I said, "Let us go then to the barn for a short time, just to see how they are getting on."

After some hesitation, he went in with me, and found the people praying and rejoicing; but, as I expected, far too much absorbed to observe our presence.

After a time, some lads noticed me and cried out lustily, "The parson is here! The parson is here!" and in a moment we were surrounded by a number of happy people, who were so demonstrative that they made the poor vicar tremble (as he told me afterwards) with a strange fear.

They said, "You will come again to-morrow?"

"Certainly," I replied.

"Oh, no," rejoined the vicar; "on no account. One night of this work is quite enough—more than enough."

I was very loth to give up; but a man said, "Never mind, we will carry it on. This revival will not stop for a week or fortnight, for certain."

This was terrifying news for the vicar, who turned, and looking at me with astonishment, said, reproachfully, "How did you do it?"

I replied, "This is not my work. I did not begin it, neither can I stop it; nor would I, even if I could. I dare not. I have known persons brought under heavy judgments for hindering a revival. Take my advice, and do not hinder this. Let these men go on; they know what they are about."

Soon the carriage came, and we returned to the vicarage;

but the dear man was much put out, and evidently very sorry that he had asked me to come and disturb his millpond. Indeed, he said as much; so I concluded my visit the next morning.

Going through the village, I heard that the meeting on the previous evening was continued till two o'clock in the morning, and that it was announced there would be one in the chapel that evening. As the Church refused the blessing, there were others who were happy to receive it.

I returned home sooner than I was expected, and told my people, at the evening meeting, the things I had seen and heard; and they "glorified God."

CHAPTER XIX.

A Mission in the "Shires."

1853.

AT the time of which I am writing, twenty-six or twenty-seven years ago, special services for preaching were not called by the name of "Missions." I think that word has been derived from some Roman Catholic perverts, who made aggressive efforts in London, which they called "Catholic Missions." From them it has been adopted by some who love to copy Rome and Romish phrases. Strange infatuation, by which these Romanizers in vain court a Church which despises them, and gives them neither place nor quarter! However, the word is now well understood, and its meaning is plainer than any definitions of mine could make it.

My first journey to "foreign parts" (as the Cornish call it) was to a town in Devonshire, where I stopped three or four days. The day I arrived I preached in the church, because it was the regular evening service; special services were not then known, unless it was for some Missionary Society, or other such advocacy. The idea of preaching to awaken souls, was considered very strange and fanatical. The church I preached in had high pews, which prevented my seeing the occupants. I was told that it was full, and certainly there were faces visible here and there; but the whole congregation was so still, that the dropping of the proverbial "pin" might have been heard. It was all very chilling and dead, no "Amens!" or "Glory!" as in Cornwall; indeed, the stillness had such an effect upon me, that I found it difficult to get on. After making two or three hard appeals, and meeting with nothing but silence for a response, I concluded, and came away much disappointed and disheartened. However, the next morning, the vicar showed me some beads, feathers, and flowers which had been left in the pews of the church. So I found that the shots had hit somewhere, or something.

Walking through the town in the course of the day, a tall mason, with a large whitewash brush in his hand, came running after me (not to whitewash me) but to ask the question, which he did most eagerly, "Are you the man that preached last night?"

I said, "Yes, I am."

"Oh," he replied, "will you preach to-night?"

I answered him somewhat doubtfully, "I suppose not," for the vicar did not know what excuse there could be for my preaching a second time.

He continued, "Will you come to my house and preach this evening? I have a good large room at your service, and can promise you a congregation."

I assented; so we fixed the time, and made all other necessary arrangements. On coming down in the evening, I found my mason friend had invited his neighbours, and finding more had promised to come than his room would hold, he had opened the folding doors between two rooms upstairs, taken down three large bedsteads, and having borrowed forms and chairs, he was able to accommodate seventy people. As many as this came, and more, for men and women stood on the stairs and landing besides.

We sang heartily, and after prayer I felt a little more at home than I had done on the previous evening; but it was not up to Cornwall yet! In my address I had liberty and power to hold the people, and we had some conversions that evening, and the following one also. My mason friend was greatly cheered and revived, and from this time began preaching himself, carrying on meetings in various cottages and farm places.

From there, I went on into Dorsetshire, and arrived at the vicarage to which I was going, rather late on Saturday night, very tired; so much so, that I was glad to go to bed as soon as possible. On Sunday morning I went to church and preached to a large congregation, the words which God gave me. On coming out, the vicar's wife said, "If I had sat up all night telling you about the people, you could not have preached more appropriately; indeed, I am sure that some of them will think that I told you what to say."

It was so, for this same lady was charged with telling me to put before some of the congregation things which her husband dared not! In the evening the church was crammed to excess, and the people were most attentive and eager. Some of them could scarcely restrain their feelings, so powerfully did the Word come home to them. At the conclusion of the service, I announced that I had come there to preach every night for the week, and would visit them during the day. Accordingly in the morning I called at several cottages, in one of which King George the Third used to attend a prayer-meeting with the country people.

In the afternoon I went to the convict prison at Portland. It was sad to look upon the prisoners clanking about in their chains, many of whom were employed in making a road to the sea. I could not help saying to the chaplain, who was walking with me, "What a picture is that! It is exactly how Satan employs unbelievers to make their own road to hell. As such, they are condemned already, because they do not believe in Christ; and for the same reason, their sins not being pardoned, they are bound in chains."

"Well," said the chaplain drily, "that seems all clear and scriptural. Would you like to speak to them?"

"Yes," I said, "I should."

He then made a sign to the warder, who commanded that the convicts should give attention, and the order was at once obeyed.

Standing on the bank, I spoke to them as they were assembled before me; but instead of telling them of the devil and chains, as the chaplain expected, I spoke of God's love to sinners, and said that "chastisement and sorrows were not sent in anger, but in kindness. God is angry when the wicked are allowed to go on unpunished; but when punished in this world, it is not for expiation of sin (for only the blood of Jesus can do that), but for the purpose of awakening and humbling the transgressor, that he may with contrite heart return to the Lord, who alone is able to deliver us from sin and from Satan's power. 'It is good,' said the Psalmist, 'that I have been afflicted: before I was afflicted I went astray, but now have I kept Thy word.'"

Many of the men were so affected, that they sobbed aloud, and I could scarcely refrain from doing the same thing myself. After this I prayed that the word spoken might be blessed to those who had heard it, and then took my leave. It was not easy to dismiss this sad scene from my mind, nor have I ever lost the impression it made upon me.

We had a very good time that evening in the church, and there was much power and blessing. At the close of the service, I gave out that I would preach again the following evening, and having no opportunity for an after-meeting, the word preached was left with prayer for a blessing on it.

The next morning there came an unexpected, as well as a most abrupt, opposition to the work; and no wonder, for it was not likely that Satan would permit it to go on smoothly. A vicar from the neighbourhood, who had formerly been a military man, and had still the commanding manner of such, presented himself, and tried to terrify my good and kind friend, the vicar. He told him that he had heard a great deal about me; that I was just like Starkie,* and preached the same doctrines; and that he was deputed by other clergymen to come and ask that my preaching might be stopped. Then he went on to say that I was nothing less than a Jesuit in disguise; and turning to me, he said, "Sir, you know you are!" I replied, begging his pardon, "I can assure you I am not. You must be altogether misinformed." But he said, again turning round, and sternly looking at me, "You know I am not mistaken or misinformed; your countenance betrays you!" I smiled at this, not knowing how my countenance looked. He was quite satisfied with himself, and rather more so because he thought he had succeeded in extracting a promise from the vicar that the services in question should be stopped.

This officer-clergyman then went away, saying that he was quite convinced in his mind that I was a Jesuit, and nothing should ever dissuade him; this interview had confirmed his thoughts on the subject. My dear good friend was so afraid of that loud, overbearing man, that he consented to give up the services after that night.

Presently another clergyman, evidently in concert with

---

* A clergyman who had associated himself with H. J. Prince and some others, and founded the "Agapemone" at Spaxton, near Bridgewater.

the former, called on the same errand. His more gentle manner and plausible words had greater effect, so that the vicar more than half decided to have no service, even on *that* evening.

Before he had fully made up his mind, it so happened that there came on a tremendous thunder-storm, accompanied with hail and vivid flashes of lightning. This was considered by him quite providential, and an indication that God wished the services stopped. When the sexton came over to the vicarage, a little before the service time, the vicar said, "Don't ring the bell for church to-night; it is of no use: no one can possibly come out this weather!"

"Why, sir," said the sexton, "the church have been crammed full this half-hour. It's no use ringing the bell, sure, for we ain't got no room for no more people."

"Now, that is remarkable," said the vicar. "I do think, after all, the Lord would have us go on. What do you think?" he said, turning to me.

I replied, "Without doubt I think so. I cannot suppose that the Lord would send such men, in such a tone, to stop His work."

"Well, then," said the vicar, "we will go on till the end of the week."

But this could not be; for in the morning, as soon as he had decided to stop the services, I sat down and wrote to a cousin of mine, in the neighbourhood (and the letter had gone), to get me the parish church for the next evening, and said, "I would come to her on a visit for a few days, as my preaching in this place was brought to an end."

I spoke that evening, and announced that I would do so again on Thursday. On the following day I went on this promised visit to another part of the county, and was not long in the company of my cousin, before I found out that she had been brought up in Evangelical doctrines, and

hated Puseyism; but that she had never been converted
In the evening, we went to the Minster Church, the use
of which she had obtained for me. There, I preached
from the words, "Behold, I stand at the door and knock."
(I did not know then, as I do now, that this is a text for
believers.) Accommodating it for my purpose, I made out
that many people assented to evangelical doctrines, without
yielding to them: that is, they heard the knocking, but
did not open the door and receive the Saviour; therefore,
they remained unsaved; and if they died like that, would
be lost for ever!

When I first ascended the pulpit, which stood outside of
a high chancel screen, I looked towards the nave, and saw
it filled with high pews, which, as I thought, were for the
most part empty; whereas, I could see that the choir and
chancel, which was brightly lighted, was full of choir-men
and boys, besides many people; so instead of turning my
back upon the many in the lighted chancel, and addressing
myself to the unseen few in the large dark nave, I turned
round in the pulpit, and, looking through the screen,
preached to those I could see. The people in the nave,
however, were most attentive to hear; and after the sermon
came up and asked me why I had turned my back on them,
for they could not hear all I said. Evidently they had
heard something which had interested them. Seeing so
many were anxious, we invited those who wished for further
help, or instruction, to come home with us. Many did so,
and we held a kind of after-meeting, in which my cousin
and several others found peace.

I could not promise to stay there any longer, having
settled to return on Thursday to resume services in the
church previously referred to. Accordingly I went back to
a neighbouring town, where my good vicar had appointed to
meet me. He did so, and, without delay, commenced

telling me, that he had had a long talk with some of his brother clergymen, and had given his word that the services were positively to be discontinued after that night; he also told me he had taken my place by the coach, and that I was to start for Exeter the next morning, on my way home. Then he went on to say that he found it would be dangerous to keep me any longer, for he should have the whole neighbourhood up about it. In his timidity, he would rather let the work stop, than be embroiled with the neighbourhood!

The evening service was crowded, and the people were very disappointed that I was not allowed to remain. However, I told them it could not be, and that I must go— so took leave of them.

The next morning we rose early, and breakfasted at six o'clock, then drove out to the turnpike road, to meet the coach at an appointed corner, at seven. It arrived in due time, piled up high into the air with passengers and luggage; but having an inside place secured for me, we were not dismayed at the outside appearance. The coachman got off the box, and, instead of opening the coach door as we expected, put some money into my hand, and, with a grinning countenance, said, "There's your money, sir. Sorry to say can't take you to-day; hain't got a crevice of room anywhere. Good morning, sir." In a moment more he was up on his box, with reins in hand. "Take you to-morrow, sir, same time. Good morning." And off he went! Imagine our surprise at being left on the roadside in this unceremonious way. My good little vicar was most indignant at being thus treated. "I'll make him pay for that," he said. "I'll punish him—it's against the law." And then, as if a new thought had suddenly come to him, he said, "Ah, I know what we will do! Jump into the carriage again"; and putting my luggage in, he got up, and drove me to the next town. He said, "We will take a post-chaise, and make the coach people pay for it; that's it—that's what we will do."

I suggested that I did not think we could do that, having received the money back.

"Ah, that's nothing," he said; "that's nothing. We will take a post-chaise."

This scheme was prevented; for on arriving at the hotel, there was not a carriage of any kind to be had. "Are you sure of that?" said the vicar (as if all the world was in league with the coach proprietor). "Are you quite sure?"

"You had better come and see for yourself," said the ostler, in a surly tone.

We went into the yard, and found the coach-houses quite empty.

"That's very remarkable," said the vicar; "but these people are connected with that coach—it changes horses here. We will go to the next inn."

There they did not let out carriages at all!

"Well now," said the vicar, "this is very remarkable," and was silent.

"Perhaps the Lord does not mean me to go to-day," I said meekly.

"It seems so, certainly. I must say it is very remarkable."

I suggested that I would stay at the inn till the next morning, as there was no means of getting on. "Shall I do so?"

"Oh, no; certainly not—certainly not," said the kind man. "Not at all—not at all. We will go back again."

"But," I said, "what will they think when they see me?"

Poor dear man, like many others he was dreadfully

frightened at the thought of "what will 'they' think?" As if "they" did not go on thinking whether one gives them occasion or not.

In due course, we arrived again in sight of the vicarage gate, and there we saw the vicar's wife, with her hands up in astonishment. She exclaimed, "What! are you come back?"

"Yes, we are indeed!" said the vicar, and he was going to tell her how it was, but she was too impatient to listen, having, as she thought, something more important to communicate. She said, "After you went away this morning, the weather being so fine, I thought that I would go into the village, and see some of the people who were at church last evening. In passing by widow S.'s cottage, on my way to another, I saw her door and window open, and heard her praying very earnestly, 'Lord, bring him back!—bring him back!' I thought she was praying about her husband, who had recently died; and that I would go in and try to comfort her. So I knelt down by her side, and repeated the words, 'I shall go to him, but he shall not return to me,' when she turned round and said, 'Oh, I don't mean that!' and then, as if she grudged every breath which was spent in other words, she went on repeating, 'Lord, bring him back! Lord, bring him back!'

"'Who do you mean?' I said, 'what can you mean?'

"She went on, 'O Lord, I saw him go away. I saw them take him away. Lord, bring him back!—bring him back!'

"I again said, 'Who do you mean?'

"She took no heed, but went on, 'O Lord, when I opened the window I saw him coming out of the vicarage gate. Lord, bring him back!—do bring him back!'

"At last I understood that she was praying for *you* to be brought back. Then I said to her, 'Dear woman, do get up from your knees, and let me talk to you.' No, she would not get up.

"'No, I can't get up. Lord, bring him back! bring him back!'

"'It cannot be,' I said; 'he is on the coach by this time—a long way off.' The woman became frantic at the thought. 'Oh, what shall I do? what shall I do? Lord, bring him back!'

"Seeing that I could do nothing in the matter, I went to call on some other people, and coming back found the widow still on her knees, urging the same petition without stopping."

"Well, that is remarkable," interposed the vicar.

Without a moment's pause, I set off to show myself to the widow.

"Now, there you are," she said; "the Lord has sent you back. I lay awake best part of the night, thinking of some questions I wished to ask you; and when I saw you go away like that, so early in the morning, it gave me quite a turn. I thought I should be lost for ever!"

Her questions concerned her soul's condition. On my putting Christ and His salvation before her for her acceptance, she found peace; and afterwards became a good helper in the parish. There were some other anxious ones she urged me to visit, which I did. On referring to my letters, written at the time, I find a record of five persons who professed to find peace that morning.

In the evening, we had a kind of service in the schoolroom, with as many as we could get together, and spent a very happy time in prayer and praise.

The next morning I started for home, which I reached late on Saturday night, or rather early on Sunday morning, and appeared quite unexpectedly among my people again. I gave them an account of the state of things in the "shires." This, my first experience of "foreign missions," was not encouraging.

Ever since my conversion, I had been over head and ears in conversion work, and, as a loyal young convert, thought at that time there was nothing else in the world to live, or to work for! How surprised I was when I found that this was not by any means the first thing in the minds of my Evangelical brethren; and more so still when I saw that even preaching for the salvation of souls was put aside altogether, if it did not fit in with the stated service-day of the week, or public opinion. If people came to church, or better still, to the communion table, they were considered quite satisfactory enough, even though they were dead in trespasses and sins. I did not, of course, expect anything from my own neighbours, for I knew them of old; but from accredited "standard bearers," I did expect something and got nothing.

While I was still feeling sore and disappointed, intending not to go out on such errands any more, I found myself promised to another mission in a most unexpected manner; but this did not happen to be out of Cornwall, and therefore prospered better, as we shall see.

CHAPTER XX.

A Stranger from London.

1853.

 LADY in London, reading in the Cornish newspapers about our revivals, became much interested, and having a strong desire to witness such a movement personally, proposed a visit to her uncle in Truro, who had sent her those papers. Being accepted, she came down—a long way in those days, when railway communication was not so complete as it is now.

This same lady was present at my church on Sunday morning; and expressing a wish to attend the afternoon service, we gladly welcomed her to the parsonage. In course of conversation, she spoke of churches in London where the Gospel was preached in its fulness; and I naturally asked her whether they had "after-meetings." She said, she did not know what I meant.

"Prayer-meetings, for conversion work, I mean."

"What is that?" she inquired. "Is not conversion God's work?"

"Yes," I answered, "indeed it is; but so is the harvest yonder in the corn-fields: it is all God's work, but men have to plough the ground and sow the seed."

"Oh, is that what you call revival work? I have read

of it; and, to tell the truth, I have come all the way from London to see it."

She evidently had an idea that revivals were something like thunder-storms, which come of themselves, no one knows how or why; or something that is vented, like an occasional eruption of Mount Vesuvius.

I said, "Revivals—that is, the refreshening of believers and the awakening of sinners—ought to take place wherever the Gospel is preached in faith and power."

She could not understand it, and said, "It is not so in churches, is it?"

"Yes," I replied, "in churches as well as in cottages, halls, and chapels too."

"I am sure Mr. —— in London preaches a full Gospel, but I have never heard of a revival there; indeed, I feel convinced they would not allow it."

"Is he converted?" I asked.

She smiled at the question, and said, "I suppose he is."

"I mean, does he preach about the forgiveness of sins? and, more than this, does he expect people to have forgiveness?"

She said she could not understand my Cornish way of talking—"They do not speak like that in London."

"Your sins are pardoned," I said, by way of explanation, in order to get her to comprehend my meaning from her own experience. "Your sins are pardoned." She got very confused. "You know," I continued, "that it is a happy day when Jesus takes our sins away." This only made matters worse. She became greatly embarrassed. While we spoke of London and Gospel preaching she was free enough; but the moment I made a personal application of the subject, she was altogether bewildered.

At last, with a kind of forced effort, she said, "I have been a child of God for eleven years."

"Thank God!" I said, much relieved; "that is what I

mean. You have been converted and pardoned for eleven years. It is all right, then. I did not intend to perplex you, and am sorry I did not convey my meaning in a better manner."

But I could not smooth down her ruffled feathers so easily, and was glad when the five minutes' bell began ringing to summon us to church. We got ready, and went. It happened to be a children's service, and our subject that afternoon was Joseph's reconciliation with his brethren. Three questions, among others, were asked and dwelt upon.

First, "Was Joseph reconciled with his brethren while they were self-convicted before him, and condemned themselves as verily guilty concerning their brother?"—"No."

Second, "Was he reconciled when he feasted with them, and made merry?"—"No."

Third, "When, then, was he reconciled?"—"When they surrendered themselves, and all the eleven were prostrate at his feet, like the eleven sheaves which bowed to Joseph's sheaf in the harvest field; then he made himself known to them, and forgave them. It is not when a soul is under condemnation, nor yet when it is happy, that it is saved; but when it is actually, once for all, surrendered to Christ for salvation, then it is He makes himself known to them, even as Joseph did to his brethren."

The lady went away. I did not ascertain who she was, nor where she came from; I was not much taken with her, nor was she with me. Hers was evidently a kind of religion which I had not met with before, and did not care to meet with again.

The next day I went for a few hours' rest and change to the sea-side at Perran, but there was a burden of prayer on my soul. I could not thank God for that unknown lady, but I could pray for mercy for her. The impression on my mind was very clear: I felt that she was not saved. The day following the burden was heavier still, and I was on my knees praying for her for several hours in the day. In the evening I was quite in distress. The next day I was most anxious for her, and could do nothing but pray, even with tears. This lasted till the following day (Thursday), when I happened to go into the drawing-room for something, and there I observed a strange Bible lying on the table. I remembered that I had seen that same book in the lady's hand on Sunday. I took it up, and saw a name, and on making inquiry of the servants I found out that she came in Mr. ———'s carriage on Sunday.

This was enough. I wrote a note immediately, and sent the Bible, saying that I was greatly burdened for her soul, and should much like to see her. She sent me a kind letter in reply, appointing the following Monday for my visit.

On that day I called, and found her very kind, and seemingly thankful for the interest I expressed in her welfare. I said that she had nothing really to thank me for, for I could not help myself; the burden had been laid upon me. Then I asked her if she would tell me how she became a child of God.

She did so readily, and told me that once she was in the world, and as fond of dancing and pleasure as others with whom she associated; that in the midst of her gaiety she was called to the death-bed of a cousin, who was just such a lover of pleasure as herself. Her cousin said, "Oh, Mary, give up the world for my sake. I am lost! Oh, Mary, give it up!" Soon she died, poor girl, just awakened enough to see and feel herself hopelessly lost—a dying worldling. No one was near to point her to the Saviour, so she departed as she had liked to live, without salvation. Mary wept at the remembrance of that solemn scene, and said she could never forget it.

"Well," I said, "and what did you do then?"

She answered firmly, "I knelt down then and there, by the side of the bed where my poor cousin had just died, and I called God to witness that I would give up the world. I did so; and have never had any inclination to go back into its gaieties and pleasures since. I began from that time to pray, and read my Bible, and go to church; and I love these things now better than I did the things of the world before."

At the time of this change, she was led to a church where Evangelical truth was preached simply and plainly; and thus became distinctly enlightened as to the way of salvation. She fully assented and consented to what she heard, and therefore became a very earnest disciple, enthusiastic about the sovereignty of God and the doctrines of grace, and all such matters. She understood the meaning of the Levitical types and offerings; could speak of dispensational truth and prophecy; was very zealous about missions to the heathen, and was also earnestly devoted to many charitable works at home.

There was, however, one little suspicious thing in the midst of all this manifest goodness. She had not much patience with elementary Gospel sermons, or much interest in, or sympathy with, efforts made to bring in perishing souls; she loved rather to be fed with high doctrines, and the mysteries of grace with its deeper teachings. There are some men who love to preach exclusively about these things, even before mixed congregations, addressing them as if they were all real Christians.

It is surprising how many people there are just like Mary, who seem to care more for doctrines than for God Himself—more for favourite truths than for souls. A simple elementary Gospel address, with some clear illustrations, was just the very thing which Mary wanted for her own soul's good, more than anything; but, unfortunately, this was the thing against which she was prejudiced, for she abhorred "anecdotal sermons."

After hearing her story, I said, "It is very interesting; but there is one great deficiency in it. You have not told me anything about Christ; have you nothing to say abou the blood of Jesus, and about your sins? Have you had no real transaction with God about them?"

She said she "did not know what I meant."

"Did you never come as a sinner, and obtain the forgiveness of your sins?"

"No," she replied; "that is what I do not understand about *your* teaching."

I showed her, as plainly as I could, that she had not told me about conversion, but reformation. "You have only turned over a new leaf, and kept your resolutions prayerfully and well for eleven years; but this is not turning back the old leaves of your past life, and getting them washed in the blood of the Lamb. 'He that covers his sins' in this way, 'can never prosper.' If a man owes a debt for which he is very sorry, and determines that in future he will pay for everything he gets—this will not pay his past debts."

She went on to justify herself, and said, "that she knew a great many good Christian people, and that none of them had ever suspected her as I did."

I endeavoured to assure her that I was dreadfully alarmed about her condition, and was certain that if she died like that, there would be no more hope for her salvation than for her cousin's. This seemed to rouse her hostility, and I saw that I had lost influence. However, I could not blame myself, for I had only said what I felt to be true. I returned home and prayed for more wisdom. All that night I could not sleep, and most of it was spent in pleading with God. I felt as if a restless bird was flying about the room, and something was saying, "She will be lost for ever." I urged my petition again and again.

The next day I called, and found this lady quite broken down, and ready to pray and listen to my teaching. I was most thankful, and greatly relieved after the night's restlessness. I had much happiness in pointing out the way of salvation as an experimental thing. She knew, before I did, the doctrine of the Atonement, but she had had no experience of its real efficacy. Now that her eyes were opened, she was in right earnest to know the reality of sins forgiven. Soon she found this, though not yet the joy of deliverance; she knew the peace and shelter of the sprinkled blood (Exod. xii. 13), but not yet the joy and liberty of being on the rock on the other side of the Red Sea (Exod. xv. 2). I was sure that it would all come in due time, and therefore was able to take comfort, and also to comfort her.

I saw a good deal of her at that time, and one day she told me that a relation of hers, a clergyman, was coming to have it out with me for saying that she was not converted before.

"Certainly," I replied, "I shall be happy to meet him, and hope you will be in the room."

When the dreaded man arrived, we were introduced to one another.

"Well," he said, "you are a very different-looking man to what I imagined. I have heard a deal about you. So you are a Puseyite turned Evangelical, eh? I have often heard of people going the other way, but must say I have never met a man who had come in this direction." He then asked about the results of my ministry.

I told him what was the effect in my church and parish, and that the same signs followed the preaching of the Gospel wherever I went.

"I wish," he said, "you would come and preach in my parish. You know a great friend of mine at Veryan, and have preached in his pulpit. Will you do the same for me?"

"Oh, yes," I said, "certainly, with pleasure."

"Now, look at me, for I am a man of business: when will you come? Name your day."

I looked at my pocket-book, and fixed upon a certain Monday.

Then he arranged that we should have a kind of missionary meeting, "in course of which," he said, "you can preach as much Gospel as you like. If it goes well, we will have a lecture the next evening on 'Heart Conversion,' and another the evening following, on something else. He was "quite sure no one would come to hear a sermon only. It must be a missionary meeting, or something of the kind, to bring the people out."

On the day appointed, the barn where we were assembled was well filled, and seeing that the people were interested, the vicar gave out, "Mr. Haslam will lecture to-morrow evening on Heart Conversion."

The next evening, when we arrived, we found the barn quite full, and numbers standing outside; besides, there were many more whom we passed on the road. So it was determined that we should go into the church and have a short service. The edifice was soon lighted, and filled, and after a few collects and hymns (for they had a hymn-book in that church), I went up into the pulpit, and preached upon the absolute necessity of conversion—no salvation without it. As to "heart conversion," what is conversion at all if the heart is not touched? Then I treated my subject from another point of view. "Every converted person here knows what heart conversion is; and if any one does not, it is clear he is not converted. If he dies in that state, he will be lost for ever!" I concluded the sermon with prayer; and while I was praying in the pulpit, one after another of the people in the pews began to cry aloud for mercy. My friend Mary likened it to a battle-field, and me to a surgeon going from one wounded one to another to help them.

At eleven o'clock we closed the service, promising to hold another the next day.

On Wednesday morning Mary awoke from her sleep with a voice saying to her, "Behold the Lamb of God, which taketh away the sin of the world."

"Then all my sins are gone. He has borne them. He 'Himself bore our sins in His own body on the tree.'"

She was filled with joy unspeakable, and came to breakfast rejoicing. The lady of the house was in tears, the servants were troubled, and the vicar alternately glad and sorry, for he was not sure whether it was excitement or the work of God, and did not know what to make of it. However, in the evening he broke down in his reading-desk in the middle of the sermon, and burst out, "Lord, save me!" In an instant the whole congregation was up, and the people everywhere either crying for mercy, or rejoicing. The power of the Lord was present to heal them, and many souls were saved that night; and besides these, there were others who were troubled.

Amongst this number was the young squire of the parish. He was afterwards decidedly converted to God, and took great interest in the work. When twitted on the bench by his brother magistrates about the revival, he stood his ground manfully, and gave good testimony. He continues to this day a bold champion for the truth as it is in Jesus.

CHAPTER XXI.

Golant Mission.

1854.

IT is a good plan to strike while the iron is hot; and as the people at Golant were in an interested and receptive state, I put off other things which had been appointed, and made arrangements to return to the battle-field as soon as possible. My people were much excited to hear what I was able to tell them of my three days' visit, and they wished me "God speed" for my next venture, praying most heartily for great blessing.

Accordingly, on the following Monday I went back to Golant, and found the place (an unusually quiet country village), together with the whole neighbourhood round, including two or three small towns, all astir. As a rule, in order to insure success in a mission, there needs preparation, visitation, and prayer; and I have observed that when there has been no preparation in the way of public announcements of services, the people have not come out, and the mission has been a failure. Where there has been a regular system of visitation, without prayer, the congregations have been abundant, but the services have been dry and hard; but in places where preparation and visitation have been made with much prayer, there has ever been a most unmistakable blessing. So much for human agencies, which are necessary to us, though God is not bound to them.

There had been no preparation for the mission I am about to tell of, no visitation, nor any special prayer; and yet it pleased the Lord to give in this little village such an outpouring of His Spirit and demonstration of His power as is rarely known. There was a great running together of the people, notwithstanding the difficulties of access to the church. Some had to come several miles from the towns by road, some by sea, and others across a tidal river where mud abounded; and after landing, they had to climb a steep hill. None of these things, however, deterred or discouraged them; they came, and they would come, in spite of everything which was urged at other times as an excuse for staying away, even on dark nights. It was the day of the Lord's power, and He made them willing; so much so, that in some places work was suspended, and people came even three times a day.

On the Monday evening, when I arrived, I found that the church would scarcely hold the people who had gathered to hear the Word of God. It was a time of much blessing, and we remained there hard at work till eleven o'clock, when, having four miles to go in order to get home, I closed the service, offering to meet any anxious souls there at half-past ten the next morning. This I did, and was surprised to find a number of persons waiting, even at this early hour. There were too many to speak to individually, so I addressed them collectively, giving the ordinary instruction to seeking souls. In the afternoon we had a still larger number, and in the evening a crowded congregation; in this way the work continued, with three services a day throughout the week, accompanied with remarkable conversions every day.

Among the number of those who attended were a surgeon, his wife and brother, and the wife of a respectable yeoman. These, together with several more from the village on the other side of the river, were converted to God. Their rector was amazed to see them so changed, and wondered by what process this was accomplished. He attended an afternoon service, and was astonished to see so many people present on a week-day. Afterwards introducing himself, he asked me very politely, "What is the secret of all this?" He said, "I have heard you preach, and certainly do not agree with most part of what you said, nor do I see anything either in your manner or matter which can account for this effect and work amongst the people. I must say, I cannot ask you to my pulpit, but I should much like a talk with you. Will you come over to luncheon with me?"

I liked the candour and gentlemanly bearing of the man, and wished to go, but could not fix a time while I was so much occupied; so I promised I would write, and offer him a visit when I had more leisure.

In addition to the three services in church, we had another in the morning at seven o'clock, in the town where I slept. There we gathered the anxious ones who had been at the church the night before, and had come away early on account of the distance. The little town was all in a commotion, and the vicar in this place was beginning to get furious about my holding this meeting in his parish; his daughter, in particular, went about warning the people against attending it. Some young men hired a four-oared boat to come to the evening service, intending to disturb the congregation. They arrived in good time, but, for all that, they were too late to get a seat. One young man, the ringleader of the party, instead of causing a disturbance, stood still and listened most attentively. I preached that evening from the words, "And the door was shut," referring to the ark, and the awful desolation and doom of those who were shut out. All the time I was preaching, I could see this same man standing before the pulpit, with his elbow leaning on the end of a high pew. He maintained this position throughout the service, and at the end of the sermon was still there, rigid and stiff, looking at the pulpit as if in a trance. He would not move or speak; there he stood, till we feared he had gone out of his mind. His companions were awed, and took him away as well as they could, but did not embark on their return journey till after midnight, and then the tide was against them.

Soon after they had started, the wind rose, and there came on a great storm; the thunder was loud, and the flashes of lightning awful. The wind became so strong and violent, that, in spite of all their efforts, the boat was stranded; they managed, however, to get out and pull it out of the water, and took refuge for a time under overhanging rocks on the shore. The young man continued as one stunned, and said nothing. There they remained till between four and five o'clock in the morning, when the storm abated, and they were able to set out again. At last they succeeded in reaching home.

While these unfortunate young men were battling with the elements, we went home by land and had a night's rest, though it was but a short one. I rose and went to my meeting at seven o'clock, and on arriving found the room quite full, there being only one chair unoccupied. As I stood to speak, this seat remained vacant, so I beckoned a young man who was standing at the door to come and take it. He looked worn and sad, and I thought I recognized in him the same young man I had noticed the previous night, and who, I was told, was the ringleader of the party who came in the boat with the purpose of disturbing the meeting. He sat down, sighing heavily several times.

Almost directly a man came forward and whispered to me, "You have a wolf near you—take care!"

"All right," I said: "he is tame enough now; there is no more bite in him."

"Yes, yes," said the young man, overhearing us, "no more wolf. O God, change me to a lamb!"

Poor fellow! he was in great trouble all day, and fainted away several times before he found peace, which he did very clearly. He came to the evening meeting, shouting "Hallelujah!" and stirred us all greatly. Several others of the same party were also converted.

The news of this made some of the town's people furious; and, being the fifth of November, they consoled themselves by making a straw effigy to represent me. They put on it a sheet in place of a surplice, with a paper mitre on its head, and, setting it on a donkey, carried it through the town, accompanied by a crowd of men and boys, who shouted at the top of their voices, "Here goes the Puseyite revivalist! Here goes the Puseyite revivalist! Hurrah! Hurrah!" In this complimentary sport the curate and one of the churchwardens took part.

That same night this churchwarden (who, I should say, had been one of the boating party two nights before) had a dream. He dreamt that his house was full of people, just like the church he had been in; all the rooms, the staircase, and even his own bedroom, were filled with people standing. There was a tremendous storm of wind and rain; the thunder rolled, and the lightning flashed. In the midst of this a voice said to him, "This is all about you, you sinner!" He awoke up out of his sleep in a terrible fright, and began to cry to the Lord to have mercy on his soul.

I was sent for before five o'clock in the morning to come and see him, for his friends said that they thought he would go out of his mind. Instead of this, he came to his right mind, for the Lord heard and answered his prayer, and brought him from darkness into light, and from the power of sin and Satan unto God. He went with me to the early morning meeting; there we had the two chief leaders of the riotous party in a changed condition, for which we heartily thanked God.

Their friend, the curate, was very excited and angry about this, and did not quite know who to blame. He said that he would write to the Bishop and tell him what was going on; and I believe he did not fail to carry out this intention. As there were many who, from various causes, were unable to go four miles to an evening service, I managed to secure the Town Hall for a course of lectures on the "Pilgrim's Progress." The curate came to the first, and, after hearing the lecture, stood up to speak, and gave vent to his feelings by saying a great many very angry things. The people were so indignant, that I could scarcely restrain them from laying hands on him to turn him out.

Some of the old forms and seats in the Town Hall (which was not accustomed to be so crowded) broke down with the weight of people. The vicar's daughter suggested that most likely they should hear next that "the forms and seats *were converted*, for she had been told already that they were *broken down*." This little straw will show which way the wind blew in that quarter, and what was the drift of this lady's mind.

My friend with whom I was staying was evidently much perplexed, and found himself let in for far more than he had calculated when he invited me. He certainly would never have asked me had he foreseen such an upset as there was everywhere, especially in the town in which he lived, and the country parish of which he was vicar.

At last he made up his mind to take me with him to consult a clerical neighbour, upon whose judgment he greatly relied. On our way a sudden thought of misgiving came over him; he all at once turned to me and said, "I say, my friend, I'll be done with you altogether if you say Mr. ——— is not converted!"

"Then," I replied, "you may be sure I will not say it."

"But suppose you think so?"

"Well, I must confess I think so already, and not without good reason (at least, to my mind), for he has taken no interest whatever in this remarkable work of God, nor has he shown the least sympathy in the spiritual welfare of many of his parishioners, who have received blessing at the meetings. His High Church neighbour, who does not profess to be converted, could not help coming over to ask about it, while your friend has never been near, nor even sent to make inquiry. Besides this, one of his own people told me that he was much put out, and very angry with you for asking me."

"Ah," said my friend, "we are not all revivalists like you, remember."

"Well," I said, "let me hope you are a deal better than I am."

He seemed very uneasy at taking me on after this conversation; but as he had written to say we were coming, he thought we must go forward. In order to ease his mind, I made an agreement with him that during luncheon I would tell about the conversion of one of Mr. ———'s parishioners, and said, "While I do so, you watch his face. If he is at all interested, I will conclude that I am wrong, and that he is converted; but if he is not, I will leave you to judge for yourself. I must say, I cannot understand a converted man not interested in the conversion of others, even if it does nothing more than remind him of his own."

My friend agreed to this, and seemed somewhat relieved in his mind.

On our arrival, Mr. —— received us courteously, and asked after the family—indeed, about everything he could think of but the work.

My friend, after a little pause, said, "Have you not heard of the revival?"

"Revival!" he said, calmly. "What is that?"

"The special services in my church."

"What services?"

This evidently was enough. He went out of the room to try and hurry the luncheon. My friend looked very thoughtful, and said nothing, but was clearly beginning to suspect that the judgment I had formed was not far wrong.

In course of the luncheon I told my story, but not without being interrupted over and over again by the host's attentions, and importunities to "take more vegetables." "Have you any salt?" "Will you take some bread?" "Will you not take a glass of wine?" It was quite evident he wished the story at an end.

My friend said, "That is one of *your* parishioners he is talking about."

"I suspected so," he replied. "All I can say is, that if Mr. Haslam had only known that man as long as I have, he would never speak of him as he does. This is not the first profession he has made. He has been reformed and changed several times before this, and has always become worse afterwards."

"That is just the very thing Haslam says," said my friend—"that some reformations are all flesh, and not the work of God; and, as such, can never stand. I believe the man to be converted by God this time."

"We will see—we will see," said our host, quietly helping himself to a glass of wine. "For my own part, I don't believe in these things."

My friend and I exchanged looks. I was silent, but he

continued, "I am bound to say that *I* was never converted before, nor yet my wife, my daughter, or my sister."

"What!" said the vicar, starting, "you mean your sister Mary? Well, that is enough! I don't wish to hear another word about your conversions after that! I can only say that if I were half as good as Mrs. S——, I should be well satisfied."

"Well, now," replied my friend, "do come over and see her, and hear what she has to say about it herself."

"No, thank you," he replied; "I have no desire to interfere in such matters."

There the conversation stopped, leaving a wall of separation between the two clerical brothers, who had together professed to be Evangelical, and cordially hated sacramental religion. They had also professed to believe in salvation by *faith only;* but for all this they never urged upon their people to perform any acts of faith—they only expected them to receive the doctrine. I found that such people opposed me and my work a great deal more than even High Church men.

My friend and I returned home, and he told his wife and sister the result of our visit. They said that they were not surprised, for they had made up their minds on the subject, and were quite sure that Mr. —— had no personal experience, though he was so intelligent about the doctrine of salvation by faith.

The work, in the meantime, went on and spread. Some of the people came over from Mr. ——'s parish to ask me to come and preach to them in a large sail-loft, which they had prepared for the purpose. My friend would not consent to my going, and I was obliged to give them a refusal. The next day they sent again, not to ask me to preach, but if I would just come over to visit a sick man who was anxious about his soul. My friend hesitated at this also. I said,

"Why do you object to my going to see the poor fellow? You took me to the vicarage to talk to the vicar himself; surely you can let me go and do the same thing to one of his parishioners."

"No," he said, "I cannot; that is quite a different thing."

Seeing that he was unwilling, and that it would displease him, I gave it up, and went to the messengers and said, "I cannot go."

They were not satisfied, and asked "if the ladies would please to go;" meaning my late dear wife and Mrs. S. (Mary), whom they had seen working in the after-meetings.

My friend did not see any objection to the ladies going, and the men seemed better pleased than if I had gone. They visited the sick man the next day, and after that were asked "just to come and speak to a few people up here"— that was, in the adjoining sail-loft. On entering this place, to their astonishment they saw about three hundred people sitting quietly waiting.

"What is this?" asked my wife.

The man said, "I only asked a few, but all those people are come. Do give them just a word." She had never yet ventured on addressing a large company like that, and Mary was shocked at the idea; but still, they were afraid to refuse; so they mounted the carpenter's bench, which was placed there with two chairs on it; and after a hymn and prayer, Mrs. H. gave an address, which Mary told me afterwards "was far better than anything I ever preached." They had an after-meeting, and some conversions, and promised to come over again. Thus the work spread to another part, and I had to go there also.

Poor Mr. —— was very excited about this, and said that he "thought it most ungentlemanly." I dare say it was, and that I was somewhat uncouth; but I never stop to consider prejudices and fancies when the Lord's work is in the way.

It was a widespread and remarkable awakening, and one not without much opposition and jealousy. I happened to say from the pulpit, that at one time before I knew the truth I used to be quite a popular man: people liked me, and clergymen let me preach in their pulpits; but now that I had something to tell for the good of souls, they seemed to agree to keep me out. Very few were so bold as the vicar of this parish, who had not only invited me, but stood by me also.

A neighbouring clergyman, who was an important man—a prebendary, and what not—wrote to the vicar to ask if it was true that I had said in the pulpit that my clerical brethren scouted me, and would not let me preach for them.

The vicar very wisely handed the indignant prebendary's letter over to me to answer, which I did. In my reply, I took the opportunity to put in some Gospel teaching, which was supposed to be very irrelevant matter, and counted evasive. I did not deny that I had said something to the effect of which he complained, but I pleaded in extenuation that I was justified in doing so. He was more enraged by my letter than by the report he had heard, and threatened to publish the correspondence. This he did, with a letter to his parishioners, in which he warned them against revivals in general, and me in particular. He told them that I was "infatuated;" that I had "usurped the judgment seat of Christ;" that I was "the accuser of the brethren;" that I "acted the devil's part now, and was to be his companion hereafter." I thought of giving more choice extracts from this publication, but on second thoughts I consider it better to pass it over.

CHAPTER XXII.

The High Church Rector.

1854.

LET bygones be bygones. I am thankful to say times are changed, but the letter referred to in the last chapter, though expressing the sentiments of one man, yet showed the feeling of many others. I do not complain of it, for I must say I rather like the outspoken opposition of the natural heart; it is far better, and much less trying, than smiling indifference or hollow assent.

The work which began in this part went on and spread. The refusal of the clergy to take it up sent it to the chapels, where it was continued for miles round. For this reason I was charged then, and have been since, with encouraging Dissent, but the accusation sits very lightly on me, for I know what I would rather have. Nothing would please me so well as to have the clergy converted, and taking up the work; but if they will not, then I would rather that the Dissenters had the benefit, than that it should die out and be lost. Dissent makes division, but it is necessary for vitality, under present circumstances, and counteracts the great evil of spiritual death. The light of God ought to be in the

Church of England, for it is the Lord's candlestick in this land; but when the truth is not represented, and the Church is dark, it is a mercy that God has been pleased to raise up witnesses for Himself in other bodies.

The Calvinist, with a needless bitterness, holds up God's sovereignty, as if man's will were not free; the Arminian is equally energetic for man's responsibility, as if God were not sovereign; and the Quaker is a witness for the work of the Spirit. These, and several others, each maintain their particular doctrine. They are raised up to show respectively their own portion of the light, because the Church, which has in her formularies all these great truths, is remiss in her duty. The full blaze of light which ought to be emitted from her to all sides, is shed upon her in detail from others; and her members are too often lighted from without, and not from within.

In many parishes there was no light, and no life or testimony in the Church; and had it not been for the chapels, men and women might have perished in ignorance and error.

Imperfect and erroneous as was some of the Gospel which was preached in chapels and rooms, there was more vitality in it, and also more saving power, than in the refined and critical teaching which emanated from many of the accredited and accepted preachers of the land. Where the Church was rising up into energetic action, in too many cases it had a sectarian, and not a catholic object—that is to say, it was aiming to make Churchmen and communicants, or members of guilds, instead of proclaiming the Gospel for the salvation of souls.

The sovereignty of God, the responsibility of man, and the work of the Holy Ghost, were frequently altogether overlooked, although *this* is the true catholic teaching. In this I comprehend not only the bringing of souls from the power of Satan to God, that they may receive the forgiveness of sins, but also that believers might go on to have "an inheritance among them that are sanctified by faith in Christ Jesus." Churchism, with its sacramentalism, is as sectarian as any form of Dissent, Romanism included; for it falls short of God's object, as declared in the Word.

When the work at Golant church abated, I had more time for looking about; so I proffered a visit to the High Church rector, who had asked me to come over and tell him the secret of my success. He readily fixed upon a day, so I went over to luncheon; after which we began to talk. The curate, who was present, and who had heard some ranters shouting and screaming in the "shires," kept on every now and then putting in a word of caution to restrain the rector from admitting too much; for little by little he was yielding to me. I spoke of letting down the nets for a draught, and catching men, not to smother and kill them in some Church system, or by some erroneous teaching, but to keep them alive. "This," I said, "is the meaning of the word in the original;" and we looked it out in the Greek. It was very interesting. We then talked over the difference between the Church system and that of the Bible. The one, I said, makes apostolic succession and the sacraments the channel of salvation; the other the Word of God, as applied by the Holy Ghost.

We had a great battle on this point, two against one; but having the Word of God on my side, I stood by my experience. I had myself been on the other side, and was then ten times more zealous and earnest than these two were. I said, "I used to preach salvation by Church and sacraments once, but I was not saved that way. I used also to teach that the new birth was by Baptism; but I was not born again when I was baptized. *Were you?* Are you quite sure that, with all your faith in Baptismal Regeneration, you are born again of the Spirit? Are you satisfied that you are now saved because you are in the Church?"

They were dumb. So I went on to say, "I have no party or sectarian object in my work; my only desire is to bring souls to Christ Himself for salvation. I used, as a priest, to think I was mediator between Christ and the sinner, and that I had received by delegation some power for this purpose; but now that I have been over the ground experimentally, I would as soon blaspheme God in your presence, as dare to absolve a sinner, or come between Christ and him. My orders are to bring them from the power of Satan to God, and to Christ crucified, for forgiveness of sins."

At this point, the rector brought out a printed sermon by Dr. Pusey, on Justification by Faith, which he had been carefully reading. I asked him to read it to me. The first few pages contained statements of the doctrine in New Testament words, with a fair exposition of them; but when the author came to his own thoughts about the subject, he said that Baptism was the *cause* of justification. Here I challenged the statement, and said, "Have you any references there—any ' stars ' or ' daggers ' to that?"

"Yes," he answered, "references to the Fathers."

I replied, that "the Fathers were not inspired. There is no such thing as ' Justification by Baptism ' in the Scriptures; it is by faith only, as you will see in the fifth chapter of the Epistle to the Romans."

"Yes," he said, "that is just what Dr. Pusey means—Faith, as shown in Baptism."

"Then," I said, "according to that, in your Baptism you were justified by Faith; and as a consequence you have peace with God, and have access into grace, and rejoice in the hope of the glory of God. You will see that St. Paul connects this experience with what he calls Justification by Faith. Evidently he did not expect so much from Baptism as you do, or for a certainty he would have baptized every one he could reach; but, instead of this, he thanked God that he had only baptized a few persons whom he named (1 Cor. i. 14—17). He had gone about for three years, teaching the Ephesian Christians, even with tears, and he called them to witness, not that he had administered the sacraments, and done priestly work among them, but that he had ceased not to teach, and to preach, 'repentance toward God and faith toward our Lord Jesus Christ'" (Acts xx. 21).

My two High Church friends were not convinced, though they could not answer me. It was a question in their minds who was right, Dr. Pusey, or this "Fanatical Revivalist."

"Come," I said, "there is your man-servant outside in the garden; he was converted two weeks ago; and though he cannot read, I feel sure he knows more about this experience than the author of that learned sermon. Let us call him in, and read a few pages."

We did, and told him to sit down while we read a little while.

The rector began, and, as he went on, Sam's face lit up with joy, until the rector came to the sacramental passages; then any one could see Sam's interest was gone. He became very restless, and at last interrupting, said, respectfully, "If you please, sir, is there much more of that?"

"Why, Sam," said his master, "don't you like it?"

"No, sir," he said; "that man ain't converted at all!"

"Well, that is strange," said the rector; "I saw his interest went off just at the very point where you took exception to the sermon. You and Sam understand something that I do not know."

Thus our sermon-reading concluded, and, besides this, my witness had given his testimony.

I had stayed already two hours longer than I intended, and was tired of talking. The rector asked me to remain, and dine with him, and promised that he would send me to church in the evening in time for the service. I agreed to this; so he kindly took me upstairs to wash and rest. Coming into the room with me, he shut the door, and said in confidence,

"I know you are right; my mother taught me all this when I was young!"

"Then," I said, "we had better kneel down and pray about it."

We did so. In his prayer he entreated very earnestly that the scales might fall from his eyes, and that these truths which he loved when he was young might be brought to him again.

He was only praying for truth, and not for pardon and salvation; so I pointed this out to him.

"Yes—yes," he said; "Lord, save me! Lord, save me! Pardon me!"

I believe he found peace before he came down; but it is more difficult to pronounce in the case of educated, than in that of uneducated people. In the latter, the transition from darkness to light and life is often very manifest; whereas in the case of the educated, the effect is not so clear.

However, he came down to dinner, and it was not long before he roused the anger and contempt of his wife and curate, by saying, "I am converted." They tried hard to laugh him out of it, and asked him which of the chapels he would join? They suggested he had better be a Bryanite; Mr. Haslam is king of the Bryanites; and so on!

I was happy to hear all this, and could not help telling them so: first, because the rector was counted worthy of such taunts; and, secondly, because their natural enmity was raised. I said that I hoped that they would both be converted also, and that very soon.

When I was leaving for my service, the rector, in bidding me good-bye, said, that he "was sorry he could not go with me; but would I come and preach in his pulpit on Sunday?" I promised that I would.

On the way, Sam, who was driving me to church, became much excited, and seemed beside himself for joy. Putting up his arms all of a sudden, with reins and whip in either hand, in the act of praising God, he frightened the horse, so that it ran away at full speed.

"Oh, never mind—never mind!" he said, "don't be frightened! No doubt the old devil 'ud like to upset both on us; but I am sure the dear Lord will take care of us: don't fear."

Certainly there was need, for the horse went headlong down a long narrow hill, and if anything else had been on the road, we must have come into disastrous collision. We were, however, carried safely down, and reached the church in good time.

Sam's joy, I need scarcely say, was all about the master's conversion, and the fact that I was to preach in their church on Sunday—two circumstances he did not fail to announce to every one he met.

He put up his horse, and stayed for the service. In the after-meeting, when he prayed, he sent up his prayer with a thanksgiving for these two things, which set the congregation praising God also.

Thus the revival, which began on one side of the river, passed over to the other, and brought out people from another town, and also villages beyond. There was a great awakening in that part of the country. The curate found peace on the Sunday, and many more; but not the rector's wife. She continued her opposition most vigorously.

The wisdom of the serpent is seen in capturing the wife first; but still I am sure in this case that the serpent's wisdom was outwisdomed, for her persecution made her husband pray and work all the more earnestly.

People in these days did not regard "missions" so complacently as they do now. The very idea of preaching night after night, not for some Missionary Society, or for collections, but simply for the conversion of souls and the salvation of sinners, seemed to cast a slur upon ordinary preachers, as if they did not aim at such a thing; and upon people generally, as if we meant to imply that they needed it. Most certainly they did.

I believe ordinary preachers in the churches of that neighbourhood did not expect conversions; and most of the people were unconverted. I could not help telling them so, which only roused their wrath so much the more.

From this place I returned home; for my prolonged absence, I found, was likely to bring me into trouble. Other clergymen might go away for months, travelling or salmon fishing; but if I was absent for a few weeks, I was supposed to be neglecting my parish. On my return, I had much to tell, and did not expect to be invited out again in a hurry; for very few clergymen would willingly desire to be drawn into such a whirlwind of storm and trouble, as my visits usually involved.

CHAPTER XXIII.

A Mission in Staffordshire.

1854.

THE work at Baldhu, which had been going on almost incessantly for three years, was now beginning to flag; that is to say, there was not that ardent and eager attendance at the services and meetings, to which we had been accustomed in the revival time. We had had occasional lulls like this before, but they did not last more than a few weeks; and then the "swallows" returned, and the bright hot summer of work came again with its loud songs and pleasant fruits. This dulness was continuing longer than usual; the crowded congregations were falling off; strangers did not come from a distance; and people at home were not so lively. However, the classes were continued, as also the services at the church, and the number of communicants did not decrease. Still any one could see that the revival was over. It was rather discouraging to me, and a cause of triumph to some outsiders; but we were occasionally cheered by work amongst visitors, and with sick-bed cases.

The majority of the people were complacently waiting for another tide of revival; this was their custom, but it sat very uneasily upon me. I did not like it, nor agree to it; but at that time I knew not what else to do, but wait as others did. I said that we looked like vessels which had come so far up the river with the tide; and now that it had turned we were stranded and fast in the mud. Sometimes I changed the figure to one not so ignoble, and likened ourselves to the stately vessels anchored in Falmouth harbour, which were there because the wind was contrary. We were wind-bound too, and dependent on circumstances; but my idea of true religion was that we ought not to be like this. I rather took for our type the great steamers which are propelled by powerful engines, and come in and go out, and proceed on their voyage without regard to wind or tide. We ought to be constrained, I said, from within by the love of God, and thus be enabled to show the power of grace by riding over all obstacles and triumphing in the midst of discouragements. "He giveth songs in the night." Any bird can sing in the sunshine.

The self-restraint and self-control I had exercised in my churchy days, and which I supposed was derived from sacraments, I found wanting in my new work. We required something with authority, such as church and priest supply. I could not, however, conscientiously go back to that legal system, nor did I think there was any need, for I was sure there was something somewhere to be had, which should and would supply our want, if I could but discover it. It appeared to me that my people, without this, were subject to impulse, and consequently in bondage to their feelings.

In this time of lull I found that the steadfastness of some was shaken; but I had known others, who had gone further back than these, return at a revival time with new vigour. In this way, some of the Cornish people professed to be converted scores of times.

While ruminating on these things and praying over

them, I was surprised by receiving a letter pressing me very much to come at once and preach in a parish in Staffordshire, near Birmingham. Mr. Aitken had been on a mission in the north, and on his return had stopped a night at this place, and preached one of his alarming and awakening sermons. The effect was so great that the people, together with their clergyman (a curate in sole charge) were in much trouble and anxiety about their souls; there was a gloom hanging over them, as if they had been sentenced to some dreadful doom, and did not know what to do, or how to avert it.

It is a good thing to wound, but it should be with the object of making whole; it is a blessed thing to show sinners their lost condition, but only for the purpose of getting them to lay hold of the great salvation which is provided for such.

In his perplexity the curate went to see the Bishop (Lonsdale) of Lichfield. When his lordship had ascertained the cause of the trouble, he took up a pamphlet which was lying on the table, and said, "If you cannot get Mr. Aitken back, send for this gentleman, and pay his expenses." "This gentleman," meant the author of the pamphlet, which his lordship held in his hand, namely, myself; "his name and address are here," said the Bishop; "take the book and read it carefully; he seems to have both knowledge and experience in such matters."

I was written to forthwith, and the letter urged me to "come at once." In compliance, I started off that night, and reaching the place on Saturday afternoon, opened a mission the same evening without further notice. On Sunday I preached three times, and went to the schoolroom for the after-meeting. There we had a scene which, for noise and confusion, was quite Cornish. Men and women cried aloud for mercy, while some believers who were there shouted for joy. The curate in charge was completely bewildered, but felt he could do nothing; and seeing, as he remarked, that I appeared to understand it all, and know what I was about, he thought he had better remain still, till the noisy meeting was over. That same night, before he retired, he gave his heart to God.

The work went on in this place with the force as of an explosion; just as if hungry desires had been pent up a long time, and now they had vent and opportunity to be satisfied. The church was crowded every day, even in the week; and we were kept in the schoolroom night after night till twelve and one o'clock.

The town was a dark, smoky, sulphury place, and the air filled with exhalations and iron filings from the various works. It was a dreadful atmosphere, and everything was black and dirty; the red fires from the furnaces around glared all night long, and presented an awful appearance. To come from the pure air and beautiful scenery of Cornwall into such a place as this, was most trying and uncomfortable; but the reward was great. The work was deeply interesting, and scores of men and women of all classes, besides five clergymen, professed to be converted that week.

The devil did not leave us alone; he was very angry, and raised up a great opposition. The rector of the old church, who used to be most benevolent and smiling, suddenly changed, and made it his business to call on the curate in charge of the church, to tell him that he was quite sure that his friend the vicar (who was away at the time in ill health) would never have sanctioned this excitement. The curate said that the Bishop had bid him invite Mr. Haslam, and that he had done so, not knowing anything further about me or my work. The rector went off to write to the Bishop forthwith, and in the meantime ordered bills to be posted all over the town, warning people against "the Cornish fanaticism at St. James's," which, of course, had the effect of drawing out a greater concourse of people.

What with excessive work and bad air, by Friday evening I was quite exhausted. I came out of the pulpit to the vestry, and remembering that Cornish miners, in order to recover themselves after climbing ladders, often found it necessary to lie down flat on the ground, I thought I would try the same plan for a few moments while the people were going out to the schoolroom. I did so; and while I was in this position a clergyman came in and asked me if I was ill. "No," I said; "I am only resting for a short time."

"Very well," he said, "rest on; but listen to me. The Bishop has sent me here to see and hear you, and this is my report to his lordship." Opening out a paper he held in his hand, he read: "St. James's crammed to excess with a most orderly and devotional congregation; their attention to the sermon marked and rivetted; sermon from St. Luke xv., verse 2, 'This Man receiveth sinners, and eateth with them.' The exposition of chapter most vivid and instructive; never heard better, or so good; the application fervent and pointed; altogether, most edifying service." "There, that is my report, so you need not be afraid of anything you hear. I will tell the Bishop all about it. Thank you very much for what I have heard. God bless you. Good-night!"

"Oh," I said, springing up from the ground, "do not go yet! the best part is to come. You have only seen me let down the nets; come now and see them pulled up."

"What is that?" he said. "Where am I to come?"

"To the schoolroom," I replied, divesting myself of my gown and bands, and putting on my coat with all haste. "Come with me!"

He seemed a little afraid, and asked many questions. When we reached the place we could scarcely get in, and the noise certainly was tremendous.

"What is all this confusion about?" he asked. "I think I had better not go in to-night."

"Oh, come in! come in!" I said; "do not fear." But somehow he slipped off in the dark, and I did not see him again. When I entered, almost the first thing I noticed was the two curates of the parish church, taking notes. However, I did not heed them, or ask to see what they had written; for I would always rather have real work, though with a noise, than orderly, respectable stillness, and spiritual death.

On Saturday I rested, but was very unwell all day, and did not know how I should be able to work on Sunday. When the morning arrived, my strength and voice were gone; it was impossible to preach. The people met together and had a prayer-meeting before the service, asking the Lord to restore me. The curate was so much cheered, that he came to me and said, "If you only get up and try, we feel sure you will be able to preach." I got up, but had to go to bed again, for I was very ill.

Just before eleven o'clock a visitor arrived—a very queer-looking little man, in a black suit of Quaker cut, and a college cap without a tassel, with the corners of the square board rounded off. Standing by my bed-side in this costume, he said that he was a convert of Mr. Aitken's, and had come all the way from Birmingham to hear me. "Moreover," he said, "I am a herbal doctor. Please let me feel your pulse."

He did so, and looking grave, sounded my lungs, put his ear to my chest, and then asked, "What is the matter with your left lung?"

I replied, "I don't know. Three doctors told me, more than fourteen years ago, that it was all gone."

"Well," he said, "you stay quietly in bed till I come again at half-past eleven."

When he returned, he bade me get up and dress, and then gave me a cupful of something very hot with cayenne, at the same time telling me that I should be quite strong enough to preach by twelve o'clock.

So I was. I preached that morning, and again in the afternoon; after that I went to bed till six o'clock, when I took another dose, and in the strength of it preached a long, loud sermon to a crowded congregation; after which I attended the after-meeting, and was there till twelve o'clock at night. I then set off to the station, accompanied by at least two hundred people, and left by the one o'clock train for Birmingham, to the house of my new friend the herbal doctor. He nursed me like a mother, and let me go on my way home to Cornwall the next day.

I never heard any more of the rector of the parish, or of the Bishop, but was frequently cheered by letters saying that the work thus begun was going on week after week in the same place. Some years after, when I was passing, I stopped there for a few days, and gave them "a lift," as they called it; and I then saw with half a glance that they had become practised workers—that both clergymen and people were fitted to missionize the whole country side.

One's great object in this mission work is not only to save souls, but to encourage believers to do their part; that so the effect of a mission may be continued and extended. God has a twofold blessing for us. He says "I will *bless thee*, and *make thee a blessing;*" and it is well to remember that the benefits we receive are not so much to be kept for self, as to be imparted and transmitted to others, even as they were transmitted to us.

CHAPTER XXIV.

Sanctification.

HEN I returned from the far-off mission in Staffordshire, whether from over-fatigue or other causes, I was much depressed in mind as well as body, and quite out of heart with the Church of England. It is true I found the converted people in Staffordshire were not so leavened with Dissent as in Cornwall, and that there was some attachment to the Church; but still I could see that Churchmen there, as elsewhere, distrusted spirituality, and preferred to work on their own ecclesiastical or sacramental lines; they chose to draw water to quench their thirst, rather than to ask, and receive (directly from Christ) the living water.

If a bishop accidentally invited me, or if a clergyman cordially did so, they were marked exceptions. I felt myself to be obnoxious to the majority of my clerical brethren who professed to represent the Church; but, somehow, I was convinced that, as a converted clergyman, I represented the Church of England more truly than they, and that the principles of the Reformation were the principles I was working upon. This was trial from outside, which, however trying to flesh and blood, is by no means so bad as misgiving from within.

I was discouraged also about the work in which I had been engaged; for there was evidently an imperfection about it. I observed that some people over whom I rejoiced as converted, went back to their former worldliness, which perplexed and troubled me more than I can describe. I knew from my own experience, that CONVERSION was necessary to salvation and a new life; but when people professed to be saved, and did not live a new life, I was sure there was something wrong. My dear friend, Mr. Aitken, said, "My brother, this work is the Lord's; you must go to Him and ask what is wrong. Lie on your face before Him, till He shows you His will about the matter!"

This I did; for, shutting myself up in the church, I cried to the Lord till I felt that an answer would come in due time.

Soon after, I was led to preach from the text, "Through this Man is preached unto you the forgiveness of sins; and by Him all that believe are justified from all things" (Acts xiii. 38, 39). This opened my eyes to see that the proclamation was twofold—that through Christ Jesus, pardon was offered to any and every sinner as such, and moreover, that by the same Christ Jesus, every believer—that is, every one who had received the forgiveness of his sins—was justified from all things.

Those who know how old familiar texts flash upon the mind with new meaning, will understand my surprise. God was speaking to me in answer to my inquiry. I had been preaching forgiveness and salvation through the bloodshedding and death of Christ; and confining myself to this, as if salvation were all. I now saw that I had not preached about Justification to believers, as fully as I had dwelt on the subject of pardon to sinners; indeed, that I had preached to believers the same Gospel which I preached to them before they were converted; that is, that Christ died for their sins, but not the "yea rather, that is risen again." No wonder they did not stand, if their standing-place before God their Father was not simply and plainly put before them. Believers having been brought from death unto life, from the cross to the resurrection-side of Christ's grave, should be led to the Throne of Grace, where Christ sits at the right hand of God, making intercession for them. Once enlightened on the subject, it was easy to see that this truth was set forth all through the Bible.

For instance, when the prodigal son received pardon, immediately his father called the servants and said unto them, "Bring forth the best robe and put it on him, and put a ring on his hand and shoes on his feet." Here, besides pardon, is standing—union—strength; and over and beyond these, the feast of rejoicing.

When the children of Israel were brought out of Egypt, it was not that they should escape from bondage only, but that they should be led, and even carried, by God through the wilderness. Moses illustrated this in a simple yet comprehensive figure, when he wrote, "As an eagle stirreth up her nest, fluttereth over her young, spreadeth abroad her wings, taketh them, beareth them on her wings: so the Lord alone did lead him, and there was no strange god with him" (Deut. xxxii. 11, 12).

The thousands who perished in the wilderness were persons of whom it may be said that they professed to come up out of Egypt, and did so in act; but God, who looks upon the heart, saw that they were still lingering in that place; for when they were in trouble, they said, "Would God that we had died in the land of Egypt! or would God we had died in this wilderness! . . . Let us make a captain, and let us return into Egypt" (Num. xiv. 2—4).

This is one secret of the "going back" which I have noticed. People came out as converted, whose hearts were still entangled in the things of this world, or in some besetments with which they were fettered. Those who are really converted should come out, as Caleb and Joshua did. They left Egypt behind them altogether, and finally, in their trials and troubles in the wilderness, they looked for deliverance, not in going back, but in going forward, assured that if lions were before, there were dragons behind.

Another lesson which we may learn from these two, is, that they compared difficulties and giants, not with themselves, but with the Lord. It was true that they were not able to conquer their enemies or take their cities, but, as they said, "the Lord is able to give us the victory." In this I saw how Joshua trusted God, also how God wrought a great deliverance.

I urged the people to consider that we were not created and redeemed to be saved, but saved to glorify God in our lives; but I grieve to say, this teaching did not meet with the acceptance I hoped for. I wondered at their slowness of heart to believe in the "risen" Christ, and was sure that this was reason enough for their instability; and I felt that there would be nothing else while they continued to receive only a part of the Gospel instead of the whole.

One thing leads to another. While I was thus making discoveries, my attention was drawn to a hymn which spoke of "Jordan's stream," and "death's cold flood," as if they were the same thing. Now, I had always regarded Jordan as death; but the question in my mind was—What is all that fighting and conquering in the land of Canaan, if Canaan represents heaven? I observed, moreover, that the Israelites were on the defensive in the wilderness, and on the aggressive on the other side of Jordan; that they were led by the cloud on the one, and by a living Person on the other; that they were daily sustained with manna, as children, on the one side, and ate the old corn of the land, as men of Israel, on the other, besides sowing and reaping for themselves. These striking marks of contrast excited much inquiry, and not obtaining, with sufficient definiteness, the satisfaction I sought, I went to the Lord about this, as before. I confessed my shortcomings, and the defectiveness of my teaching, and pleaded earnestly, "Lord, what wouldst Thou have me to do? What I know not, teach Thou me!"

Then I was brought into the deepest distress and perplexity of soul, to think that after my experience of conversion, and all I had done for the conversion of others, I was still such a vile, self-condemned sinner. I even began to think that I had never been converted; it appeared to me that my whole life was nothing but intense selfishness; that I availed myself of the blood of Christ for my salvation and happiness, and led others to do the same, rejoicing with them in thus making use of God for the purpose of getting quit of hell and gaining heaven. It was a clear case of making God serve me, instead of my serving Him. Many other things came to my mind, by which I knew there was an immense gap between my experience and the Word of God. I can see it all now; but at the time it was very dark and grievous.

When I had been under conviction before, at the time of my conversion, it was, as it were, with my eyes shut; but now they were open: then I saw my sins, and the penalty which was due to them; now I saw my unrighteousness, and the corruption of my nature. I felt as if I were two persons, and that there was a law in my members warring against the law of my mind, the flesh contending against the Spirit. "O wretched man that I am! who shall deliver me from the body of this death?" For a whole week I was in great distress of mind, especially during the last three days.

On Sunday morning, as I was going to the early Communion, my soul was set at liberty. I felt as if a great cloud was lifted up; the light shone into my soul; and I had deliverance. I was exceedingly happy in the knowledge that the risen Christ Himself was my help—that He, who had hidden His presence in a pillar of cloud and fire, now was Himself present in Person, my omnipotent Friend and Leader!

This was quite a new experience, and one I had not known before. I thought that I had not even heard or read of it, and therefore began to suspect whether it was a temptation. I determined to be wise, and not commit myself too soon, so made up my mind that I would not refer to it in the pulpit. But at the close of the service a stranger came into the vestry to thank me for my sermon; and when we were alone he put the question to me, "How long have you known Sanctification?"

I replied, "Do I know it now?"

"Yes," he said, "you preached it experimentally this morning; and I shall be very much surprised if you have not some inquiries on the subject before the day is out."

I felt reproved before this stranger's steady gaze, and confessed that I had received the blessing that very morning; but thinking that it might be a temptation, I had determined to say nothing about it.

He said, "That was a temptation from the devil, sure enough, to hinder you; for the Lord spoke on this subject through your sermon as clearly as ever I have heard. Do not be afraid, but go on and tell others."

So in the evening I preached on Sanctification, and we had an after-meeting in the schoolroom. Many believers stayed behind to ask questions upon the subject of my sermon. I do not remember how I replied to them; but imperfect as my statements must have been, it nevertheless led others to desire to enter into the experience of this same blessing.

The following morning, I happened to take up a tract by John Fletcher, of Madeley, in which I read, that at a breakfast party on the occasion of a wedding, to which he was invited, just in the middle of idle and frivolous conversation which was going on, he was constrained to rise up and say, " I have three times had an experience of joy and liberty, which I believe to be Sanctification, and it has passed away; now that it has returned again, I take this opportunity to testify." The company were all struck with amazement; the power of God was present; and the festive gathering was turned into a meeting for prayer and praise. I took warning from this tract never to withhold my testimony on this subject.

Soon after this, I was holding an afternoon Bible class in another part of the parish; we were going through St. Luke's gospel, and had come to the fifth chapter; I said with reference to the miraculous draught of fishes, that the fish had been swimming about in their native element in all quietness and freedom, till they came in contact with a net, and it came in contact with them. Observe, I said, three things: 1. They are caught in the net. 2. They are drawn out of their native element. 3. They are laid in the boat, at the feet of Christ. So it is, where people are caught in the Gospel net—this is conviction; they are drawn out of the state in which they were—this is conversion; but they are not yet in the state in which they should be, this is why it is so hard to hold them: they ought to be drawn to Christ Himself, for this is the ultimate object of catching souls; the one thing needful is to be brought to the feet of Christ.

I intentionally abstained from using the word "Sanctification," though I was endeavouring to typify the experience of it, and to contrast it with conversion. As I went on speaking, a woman in the small assembly put up her hands and began to shout and praise God, "That is Sanctification!" she cried; "I have it! I know it! Praise the Lord!" There was a great stir in the class; some cried, and some asked questions. One woman, who was more advanced in general knowledge and experience than most of the others, declared, that she did not believe in Sanctification, for she had known so many who professed to have it, and had lost it. "Lost what?" I said, "you cannot lose an experience; the joy of it may depart, and certainly does where people rest on their feelings instead of the fact, on the effect, instead of the cause." She confused the sanctification of the believer, with the effect it produced on him. The Spirit which works sanctification in our souls, can keep us in it, if we continue to look to Him, instead of looking at His work. I said to her, what I have said ever since to all who are inclined to argue on the subject: Believers too often dispute about Sanctification, in the same manner as the unconverted do on the subject of Justification. It is not worth while for those who *know*, to contend with those who only *think*. I told her to go home and pray about it, and ask the Lord if He had anything more to give, to let her have it.

She was sullen, and hard to persuade; but after a little more conversation and prayer, she consented to lay aside her prejudice and do as I had told her. She did so, and came again the next morning to see me. Fortunately, I was not in my house, but shut up, as my custom was, in the church for meditation and prayer. She followed me thither, but being engaged with my Master, I answered no knocks or taps, whether at the doors or windows; even on this occasion I did not respond, although I heard some one walking round and round the church, and knocking impatiently for admittance. When I came out, I heard that Hannah —— had called, and wished very much to see me; for she wanted (to use her own expression) "to hug the dear head of him, if she could catch him." She was happy beyond expression, for she had had a dream; and what is more, she said that she had entered into the "second blessing."

In her dream she saw a well of water as clear as crystal; it was beautiful, and the clean pebbles at the bottom quite glistened with brightness, so that she could count them. "There, there," she said, "What does any one want clearer and cleaner than that?" As she looked into this clear well, my voice said to her, "Throw a pebble into it," when she did so; in an instant the water became thick and dirty. "Ah," said my voice again, "The water of grace is always clear as crystal, but the well in which it is—that is your heart—is most unclean. The Lord can give you a clean heart, and renew a right spirit within you" (Ps. li. 10). She woke up from her sleep, and immediately began to pray, asking the Lord for a clean heart, until she obtained it.

Some may say, "But what did she obtain?" This question is seldom if ever asked by persons who know the experience of this blessing; but to those who do not, it is very difficult to convey an idea of what it is by definitions. Let it be enough to understand that there is something desirable to be had, which may be obtained by doing as this woman did. "As in water face answereth to face, so the heart of man to man" (Prov. xxvii. 19). Those who know it, understand one another and rejoice together. There is no such mutual sympathy and joy as that which brethren have who are partakers of this higher blessing.

After this, Hannah became a restful, peaceful soul; and many others, with her, found that quiet confidence which can only belong to those who can and do trust a risen and living Christ.

It was quite a new era in the work, and called out fresh energies; but like every new thing, it absorbed too much attention, to the exclusion of the simple Gospel for the unsaved. "Christ died for our sins," is only part of the Gospel, though a very important part. "Christ rose again the third day according to the Scriptures" (1 Cor. xv. 3, 4), is also a part, which should not be omitted in its due time and place. These two important truths, I am sure, are needful for scriptural work, and they should both be systematically preached.

CHAPTER XXV.

The Believer's Hope.

1854.

IT was indeed a great mistake to supersede the preaching of the truth as it is in Jesus for the forgiveness of sins, with the higher subject of the risen Christ. In the freshness of this new-found truth, and thinking that the want of it was the secret of our depression, I was urged on to press it upon the people, and took in connection with it the life and walk of the believer. I exhorted my hearers to pray with me, that God would cleanse our hearts, and even our very thoughts, "by the inspiration of His Holy Spirit, that we might perfectly love Him, and worthily magnify His name." This suited some of the earnest and devoted people; but the majority did not think Sanctification essential to salvation—salvation was all they wanted and all they cared for; nothing else, they said, was necessary.

It was a time of bright light and dull darkness. I was very happy—also disappointed. It was as if the influence God had given me in the parish, and on the people as a whole, was being taken away, and that I was not to be the leader any more. I did not see this at the time, nor indeed did I wish to do so, for I thought I had found in this place my life-work and my sphere of labour. I had even selected a piece of ground in the churchyard for the final resting-place of the weary body.

One day a Christian friend came on a visit, and we had much sympathy and communion together, and discussed all these subjects. He begged me to be patient with the people, as God had been with me, and exhorted me not to scold or discourage them, but rather to lead them out of the low standard of truth in which they lived to a higher and deeper one. His visit was a great comfort at this juncture, and encouraged me very much; but before leaving he plunged me into another gulf of difficulty. At the railway station, as he was going away, he said to me, "Brother, do you believe the Lord is coming again?"

"Certainly," I replied.

"What will He come for, do you think?"

"Why," I said, "to judge the quick and the dead, of course." Seeing he was not satisfied, I added, "What else would you have me say?"

He replied quietly, "I thought you would say that; but there is not time to speak about it now. Good-bye! good-bye!" And so saying, he stepped into the train, and was soon out of sight. I was left behind, wondering what he could mean.

One morning the postman brought me a packet of tracts on the Second Coming; but somehow I did not connect this with my friend's question. I merely thought that they were some "Plymouth" effusions, and put them aside. Then a stranger came to church, and, in conversation after the service, asked me if I would read a little book, and give him my opinion of it. It was called "Jesus Comes Quickly." But even this did not enlighten me. I told him that I thought the writer considered the end of the world very near, but that I did not care to dwell on such gloomy subjects while we had the brightness of a present Saviour before us. Thus I went on a little longer, till one morning I awoke with a strong impression on my mind that I ought to read those tracts which had been sent me. I therefore rose earlier than usual, and taking up the packet, went into the church to consider them. The first one I read was on Prophecies concerning the Lord Jesus, in which the writer modestly stated that it was reasonable to suppose that those predictions which had not yet been accomplished would certainly be so; and that, as literally and distinctly as those which had been fulfilled. If the prophecies concerning the Lord's humiliation were fully accomplished—and they did literally pierce His hands and feet, stood staring and looking at Him, parted His garments among them, and cast lots for His vesture; if He actually had His death with the wicked and His grave with the rich—(what impenetrable enigmas these must have been in the old time! The very angels desired to look into these things, and could not see them)—if, then, these were so absolutely fulfilled, we may expect other distinct prophecies to be so, at least as fully and clearly. He who came in "weakness" shall come in "power;" He who came "lowly, and riding upon an ass," shall come "in the clouds of heaven;" and "His feet shall stand upon the Mount of Olives." These are the words of Scripture.

The tracts spoke of the Lord's coming for His saints, and then with them, to deliver His people the Jews, and eventually to convert the Gentiles.

1. He said in John xiv., "I go to prepare a place for you," and "I will come again and receive you unto Myself." This departure of the Lord referred, not to His death, but to His ascension into heaven, where He is now engaged making intercession, and whence He will come to change our vile bodies, and take us to Himself, that we may be ever with

the Lord. I was as one awaking from a dream when my eyes were open to see these things. I had had an idea that the Jews were all done with, and that there was nothing more to come but the last Judgment. But now I saw that the Jews were to return to their own land; that Jerusalem was to be rebuilt, and even to be besieged by a great army! (I had thought that this was all over long ago); that in the midst of the terrible siege the Lord would come, and by His appearing convert the people, a whole nation in a day, and deliver them by the destruction of their enemies; that there was to be a restitution of all things, and a Millennial reign (Zech. xiv. ; Rev. xx.).

Altogether I had come into a new region of thought, and wondered where I had been all my life, that I had never seen these things. How could I have misunderstood or overlooked such clear and plain Scripture words? It was surprising. I gave up all engagements that day, and applied myself to investigating texts, and read over again the tracts which had been sent me; they were well selected, and referred all statements to the Bible itself for verification.

Before I saw the Christian hope, I had, instead of it, some idea about dying and going to heaven, "where the wicked cease from troubling, and the weary are at rest." As to my body, I expected that it would rise at the last day —that great day of doom, when the trumpet would sound, and there would be a simultaneous resurrection of all, good and bad. I expected that, as a saved one, I should then enter into a higher glory than that of the intermediate state. I had no idea of expecting Christ as a Bridegroom, or of looking forward with hope and joyful anticipation to His coming, as an event which might be expected at any moment. I thought the coming of the Lord, the Judgment, and "the end of things created," were one and the same thing; and as

I was sure they were not likely to happen in my time, I did not bestow much consideration on them. Such a "coming" was not an object of hope, but of dread and wonder, according to the common tradition which I had received. Like too many others, I confused together the judgment of believers for their works (2 Cor. v. 10), the judgment of the quick or living nations (Matt. xxv. 31—46), and the judgment of the wicked dead at the solemn "great white throne" (Rev. xx. 12). I had not the remotest idea that these three judgments referred to three classes of persons, and were distinctly separate from one another. I was profoundly in the dark about the believer's hope, and therefore confused in my ignorance—the Parousia, the Apocalypse, and the Epiphaneia. In short, the coming of the Lord at any time, to take up His saints, and to reward them according to their works, was not the object of my hope. I was looking rather for a Judge than a Bridegroom.

I felt now that I had possession of a secret which very few would believe, and I could not help seeing the startled or suspicious look with which people regarded me, when I ventured to utter it. I saw and felt another thing, that whenever I referred to prophetic subjects in preaching, I lost hold of the people, and their attention was gone. I was perplexed; for I wondered that God did not help me in this, as He did in the Gospel truth which I proclaimed. I could not doubt these truths; for the more I read the Word of God, and particularly the prophetic parts, the more firmly convinced I was about them. For some passages could have no other signification than that, which they literally declared. The Christian hope, that Christ was coming, in person, to take us to Himself to live with Him for ever, was a most cheering prospect, and brought the Saviour Himself more vividly before the mind.

To think that soon (and no one knows how soon) I shall

see Him, and be like Him, stirred me up to consider what manner of person I ought to be, who had such a hope as this. Instead of death and hell, heaven and judgment, it was Christ in His coming glory which filled my mind. I began to lose faith and interest in hymns which referred to Christ as the Judge of all; for, as a Christian, I was looking for a Bridegroom, and not a Judge. Nor could I follow the prayers of people who spoke of a judgment to come; for I believed that Christ had been judged and punished for us, that we might not come into the Judgment (John v. 24).

Perhaps the time was not then come for the people to receive this truth. The midnight cry, "Behold the Bridegroom cometh!" was not yet gone forth to them, and therefore they slumbered on in their indifference to this teaching. I felt I was separated from the people, and that they were drifting away from me. I had a truth which they would not receive. There was unrest, and the work did not go on smoothly or happily as before.

A vessel which is constructed to stand upon three feet cannot stand upon one, or even upon two, without being propped up. When propped and stayed up, it will stand, to be sure, in some way; but there is effort and agency superadded, which would be needless if the vessel were allowed to rest by itself, upon its own feet. So it is with the Christian. He is intended to rest in Christ, in a threefold way: as the object of Faith, and Love, and Hope. No man can really and truly rest upon one, or even two, of these without taking from God's word, or adding to it. In ordinary life he cannot be happy if he does not trust, and love, and hope. Imagine a man who can trust no one; how harassed and distressed he is with suspicions! Or suppose he is trustful; yet if he does not love anybody or anything, his present life is marred by an insipid and dull selfishness. Or take one who is trustful even to credulity; but suppose he has no hope, his future is black, and dark with forebodings, in trying to look into the terrible clouds of darkness which stand before him.

So much for man in his finite life. But when we remember that he is created for infinity and eternity, and has life which is to endure for ever, how much more needful is it for him to have these three Christian graces combined—faith, charity, and hope! By this I mean, Christ the object of Faith, for salvation; Christ Himself the object of Love, for devotion and service; and Christ in His coming glory, the object of Hope, for separation from the world.

A man must have the first, or he is not saved at all; for there is no Saviour and no salvation but in Christ, whether it be from the penalty, or from the power of sin. "This is a faithful saying, and worthy of all acceptation, that Christ Jesus came into the world," and is here still, "to save sinners" (1 Tim. i. 15). He is the only one who can, and does save; and, moreover, this honour He never gives to another.

Next, to a person who has Christ's work before him, surely nothing less than a personal Christ can be a sufficient incentive for the devotion of his life and energies.

Then again, if Christ is the object of faith and love, a believer cannot be satisfied with anything less for the object of hope; and therefore Christ, in His coming glory, is set before him for this purpose.

I can see all this plainly enough now, but there was a time when I could not do so.

CHAPTER XXVI.

The Removal.

1855.

WHEN I was on the eve of leaving Perranzabuloe, and before I knew that I was to go, I felt there was a gulf between the people and myself. Whatever else they held, they were quite ignorant of ecclesiastical antiquities, Church history, and Catholic truth; what is more, they were unwilling to learn about such matters.

Now I began to feel that another gulf was opening between my present people and myself. It was not as before, about ecclesiastical things; but on another score altogether. I wanted them to believe in a living Saviour: they were trying to content themselves with salvation instead. I wanted them to trust the Giver: they preferred to rejoice in the gift. I longed to lead them on to trust Christ as the object of faith, and from this to go on to devote themselves to His service, for very love of Him—to be loosed from the present world, by the hope of the Lord's coming. I could not get the people to receive this teaching, though it was God's truth, and could be verified by the Word.

I confess that this threefold truth was not so satisfying

to my own soul as I expected it would be. I remembered that I had not learned it from men or books, but experimentally, by God's teaching, in answer to prayer. I could not imagine what was wanting, and did not discover, for several years after, that the mere knowledge of a truth by itself, even though it is about Christ, cannot deliver. It is not the truth of Christ that delivers, but the Christ of the truth. In itself, it is but an instrument in the hand of the Spirit; and our expectation should be not from it, but from the Divine Person, whose it is.

I have found out that the power is Christ Himself; that where He is really the object of faith, He keeps the believer in peace; and that if there is no peace, it is only because there is a deficiency of trust: that He, as the object of love, constrains us to work for His Father's glory; and that He, as the object of hope, can and does separate us from the world and its entanglements, by drawing our affections to things above and beyond the present. Not having discovered this simple yet important truth, I was restless; and from God's Word came down to read the words and thoughts of men. I fell in with the "Life of Madame Guyon." Here I found much sympathy, but somehow not that peace I was looking for. Then I read the writings of the Port Royal school, the Jansenists, Butler's "Lives of the Saints," and other such books. These diverted my mind, employed and interested it; but I cannot say they satisfied me. I was craving for something which I had not found yet, and had to wait three years or more before I did so.

About this time I was invited to go to a parish in Plymouth, to a church where sacramental teaching was the rule. The incumbent was evidently as much dissatisfied with the state of his congregation as I was with mine. He wanted something new, and I thought that I did likewise.

Accordingly I went and preached in his pulpit, and the word spoken produced a marked sensation. My sermon brought to the vicar's mind many truths he had heard and loved in early days, and for this reason he urged me to stay and preach again. Then, to my surprise, he invited me to leave Cornwall and come to Plymouth, in order to take a district in his parish, that I might help him occasionally in his church. This was altogether such an unsought-for thing, and so unexpected, that I took time to consider. The next day I told him that I could not entertain his proposition, and that for three reasons :—

1. I said, "I am sure that the Bishop would not consent."

2. "I have a debt laid on me by my patron for nearly £3,000, which I spent in building the church for him."

3. "I am responsible for a debt of £300 as security."

He still urged it, and said he would go and see the Bishop, and speak with him on the subject. In his zeal he set off that very morning. The Bishop at first said flatly, "No;" and then, upon further inquiry, recalled the word, and said, "You may try it if you will." He returned in the evening with this information, which surprised me greatly. But what made me wonder still more, was the receipt of two letters the next morning by the same post—one from London and the other from Paris, releasing me from the responsibility of the two debts; and this without any request on my part. The three difficulties, which were like mountains before me only three days before, were now removed. I did not know what to say, and therefore determined, in all haste, to go home and consider the step.

When I had related these astonishing circumstances to my dear wife, we agreed to go together to consult with Mr. Aitken. On arriving I said to him, "You must please to sit still and hear all before you speak." Then I told him of the invitation to go to Plymouth, the result of the preaching, the unexpected proposal to remove hither, the Bishop's answer, and the remission of the £3,300. "Now," I continued, "what do you say?"

"You must go, my brother," he replied; "for you will never make Catholics of the Cornish people: the Methodist mind is far too deeply rooted in them."

Our friend's decision was firm; and so there remained nothing for us to do but to follow it. The novelty of the proposition, and the surprising circumstances connected with it were exciting, and took away our thoughts for the time from the place which was to be left. When the decision was given and accepted, then Baldhu seemed to lift up its voice, and urge its claims. Certainly it was a strong tie which bound us to this place; but nevertheless, on our return home, I wrote to the Bishop, and proposed to resign my present incumbency, in order that I might take a district in Plymouth. He replied in due course, that he would accept my resignation. After I was thus pledged, my wife's mind veered from her consent to go; and Mr. Aitken changed his tone also, and said that the text had come to him, "Cast thyself down," and that I was tempting God. Yet all the steps I had taken had been in prayer, and had been even taken reluctantly, for I was much attached to Baldhu.

For nearly three months I was torn with distractions; sometimes hope lifted up the mist from the horizon, and then let it down again. I did not know what to do; the work at home had come to a stand; but there was one thing, my successor was not yet appointed, nor had I signed my resignation; therefore every now and then the thought came over me, that I would stay. Then a letter came from Plymouth, urging me to come away at once, "for the iron was hot for striking." Sometimes people came in and said, "You had better go;" then others would come and say, "You will do no good if you go." It was desolating, as well as distracting beyond description.

I had a family of six children and three servants; it was a great expense to move there; and yet, if God was calling, it was quite as easy for Him to move eleven people as one; and I had ten claims upon Him. At last, suspense was over; for my successor was appointed, and the day fixed for our going. I signed my resignation, having to pay four pounds ten shillings for it; then, suspense was changed into unmitigated sorrow.

I had designed and built that church and house, and had seen them rise; had made the garden, and had had many happy and wonderful days in this place. I found it had taken a deep root in my heart, and therefore it was like tearing one up altogether to go away. But it was done now, and the friends who had advised me not to resign, seemed to have their triumph; and those who advised to go, were discouraged and grieved at my sorrowful state. My dear wife cheered up when she saw me down, and rose to the occasion; she began to pack up as if delighted at going, and went about everything most cheerfully.

I told the people that I could not bear a leave-taking, but there would be a service in the church, and Holy Communion, at seven o'clock on the morning we were to leave. Many came, but the majority could not sum up the courage to do so. I put my resignation on the offertory plate, and gave it to God with many tears. A kind neighbour came to officiate for me, so that I did not take any part in the service; being exceedingly dejected and overwhelmed with sorrow. It was chiefly for fear, lest I was doing that which God would not have me do, and taking my family out from a comfortable home, I knew not whither, or to what discomforts.

One thing I certainly saw plainly enough, that my affections were too deeply rooted in earthly things. I had no idea till then, that that place of my own creation had taken such a hold upon me. It was well to be loose from that, and free for my Master's service.

After breakfast we left the old place; many people stood weeping by the roadsides; some ventured to speak, and others only thrust their hands into the carriage windows for a hearty grasp, without saying a word. It was indeed a sorrowful day, the remembrance of which even now makes my heart sink, though it is more than twenty-five years since.

In the evening we arrived at the house of some friends, who had kindy invited us to break our journey, and remain the night with them; and in the morning we proceeded on our way to Plymouth. When we reached the house, we found our furniture unpacked, and distributed in the various rooms, and the table spread ready for us to take some refreshment. The word "WELCOME" was done in flowers over the door, besides many other demonstrations of kindness; but I am afraid we were all too sorrowful at the time to show our appreciation of, or to enjoy them.

We never settled in that house, and did not care to unpack anything more than necessary, or hang up the pictures or texts.

My work did not prosper here, for I found I was unequally yoked with strangers, and accordingly felt dry and wretched.

I sent my resignation of Baldhu to Bishop Phillpotts, and with it my nomination and other necessary papers, saying that I would wait on his lordship for institution on a certain day.

At the appointed time I went to him, when to my great surprise, he very calmly said he could not appoint me to that district. I could not understand this, for as I told him, I had only resigned conditionally, and reminded him that I had asked his permission to resign, for the purpose of taking this district.

"How can I conscientiously appoint or license you to anything in my diocese?" he said, looking me full in the face, and then in his courteous way he laid his commands on me to stay to luncheon, saying he would be obliged "if I would do him this honour;" he bade me walk in the garden, as he was busy, and would be occupied till luncheon.

I felt that I needed a little quiet and fresh air to get over this climax of my troubles—out of one living, and not into another; and that with a wife, six children, and three servants, with very little to live on. Here was a state of things! I had plenty to occupy my thoughts and prayers. I feared and mourned, above everything, lest God should be angry with me. "Oh, if I could only know this is the will of God, then I should not care a fig for all the bishops on the bench, and would not ask one of them for anything!"

I was soon roused from my reverie, by the presence of Miss C. P., the Bishop's daughter, who had come out at her father's request to show me the garden and the view. I had known this lady slightly for several years, and so she was not altogether a stranger to me, or I to her. She talked so cheerfully and pleasantly, that it came to my mind, "Perhaps, after all, the Bishop is only trying me. He will not appoint me to this bare district, because he has something better with which he means to surprise me." This sanguine thought cheered me up greatly. At luncheon he was as kind and happy as if he had neither done anything dishonourable, nor had any intention of doing so; so that I felt quite sure something good was coming. I began to wonder at intervals, "What part of the diocese I was to be sent to?—Where is there a vacancy?" and so on.

The Bishop was as friendly to me as he used to be in other days. After the repast, he summoned me to his study again. "Now," I thought, "I shall hear where I am to go;" but instead of this, he said that he was "much engaged, and must take leave of me."

I was more than astonished at this, and said, "I can scarcely believe that you refuse to appoint me!"

"I do then, most positively."

"But I have a copy of my letter to your lordship, and your answer."

"Then you may urge your claim by law, if you please."

"No, indeed, my lord, I do not think I will do that." And then, after a short pause, I said, "You have done for me what I could not dare do for myself, though I have often been tempted to do it."

"And pray, what is that?" he inquired.

"To give up parochial ministration, that I may be free to preach wherever I am led."

"Could you do that?"

"I could not do it conscientiously myself; but now that you have stripped me of harness, I will put on no more."

The Bishop made his bow, and I made mine; and that was the end of our interview.

In my unconverted days I used to be an ardent and enthusiastic admirer of this man; his charges, his speeches, and especially his withering, sarcastic letters to Lord John Russell and others, who came under his tremendous lash, to my mind made him a great hero. His straightforward manner also commanded my respect, for, generally speaking, I had found bishops very smooth and two-sided, or rather *both-sided;* but in his case there was no mistake.

It used to be a proud time for me when this Bishop came into Cornwall, and I was permitted to accompany him, and to act as his chaplain at the consecration of a church or burial ground, or to attend him when he went to a Confirmation. Sometimes I had the happy privilege of rowing him in a boat on the sea. He seemed to take such an affectionate and intelligent interest in my parish and my church work. He asked various questions about my neighbours, just as if he lived among them and knew all their circumstances. He struck me as a wonderful man, and I was his champion upon all occasions in my unconverted days. Notwithstanding this, he was too honest to his own views to favour me after my conversion.

On my return home without a licence, I had but a poor account to give, and the future prospect looked very gloomy.

CHAPTER XXVII.

Plymouth.

1855.

 OCCASIONALLY preached in the parish church, and went to the daily Communion and the daily service. My spare time I occupied (it was like going back to brick-making in Egypt) in painting the church. I laboured for hours and hours to try and make this great chalk-pit of a place look somewhat ecclesiastical. All round the church I painted a diaper pattern, surmounted with a border, which went over the doors and under the windows. Then on the bare wall at the end I painted a life-sized figure of our Lord, as a Shepherd leading His sheep, taken from Overbeck's picture. This, together with a few other pictures of Christ, warmed up the building very well. Then for the chancel I had a most elaborate design.

First, there was a beautiful gilded pattern over the very lofty chancel arch, which I managed to reach by means of a ladder. Professional people need scaffolding and platforms, which I dispensed with, and accomplished the whole space in less time than it would take them to put up all their needful erections. Inside the chancel I had twelve niches, with tabernacle work above them, for the twelve apostles; and these were all duly represented after a true mediæval pattern.

The local newspaper made great fun of these paintings; and the reporter would have it, that "these lively saints looked very conscious of being put up there, and that they were constantly ' craning ' their necks to look at one another—as if they would inquire, 'I say, how do you like being there?'" My favourite figure, St. John, upon which I bestowed extra pains, the provoking man would have it, was St. Mary Magdalene, leering at the apostle next to *her*, or at the one opposite—it did not seem quite clear to him which; but her head was down on one side in a bewitching attitude.

In the middle of the great undertaking I was called away for a few weeks. During this time the reporter came again and again, but saw no progress; he therefore put an advertisement into his paper to this effect :—

"Stolen or strayed, a monkish priest, who paints apostles. He is not to be found. Any person or persons who can give information concerning this absent personage, will greatly oblige."

My preaching was not acceptable in this church, neither was my connection with it; and my apostles were no better appreciated, for they were soon after whitewashed over, and disappeared like a dream. Sometimes, in damp weather, they were still to be seen "craning" their necks as heretofore (much to the amusement of the chorister boys) though with a kind of veil upon them. Doubtless, in a future generation, when the plaster begins to blister, some antiquarian will discover this "wonderful mediæval fresco," and call the attention of the public to it.

My ideas and dreams about catholic advancement were thus brought to a calamitous end. This church to which I had come was one in high credit for much private and public devotion; but, alas! I found what I might easily have expected, that without spiritual vitality everything must be dry and dead! Dry and dead indeed it was. The conversation of these supposed ascetics was for the most part secular, and at the highest only ecclesiastical. Their worship, on which a great amount of pains and cost was bestowed, was but a form carefully prepared and carefully executed, as if critics were present; yet it did not, and could not, rise to spirituality. A lady presided at the organ, and had the teaching and training of the choir. Much of her own personal and religious character were imparted to the performances, which in tone and manner were admirable and precise. She made the boys understand the sense of the words they sang, till I have seen them even in tears during the singing. The "chaste old verger" (as our reporter called him), who headed the procession at least four times a day, up and down the church, was a very important and successful part of the machinery, and from him, up to the highest official, everything was carried out with exact precision.

But oh, how unsatisfying and disappointing it was!—to a degree which I was ashamed to own! How could I be so foolish, to give up a living, where there was vitality, though it was rough, for a superficial and artificial semblance of religion? In the book of Ecclesiastes we read, that "a living dog is better than a dead lion;" and though I had often quoted this saying, I never felt the truth of it so deeply as now. The dead lion and the dead elephant are quite immoveable things for a live dog to bark at or fret about. It was a hard and trying time to me in that place. I could not see my way, or understand at all what was the Lord's will towards me.

While in this state of mind I had a vivid dream. I

thought that the ornamental iron grating, which was for ventilating the space under the floor of the church, was all glowing with fire, as if a great furnace were raging there. I tried to cry "Fire!" but could not. Then I ran into the church, and saw it full of people reverently absorbed in their devotions. I tried again to give the alarm, and cry "Fire! fire!" but I could not utter a sound. When I looked up, I saw thin, long, waving strings of fire coming up among the people through the joints of the floor. I called attention to this, but no one else could see it. Then I became frantic in my gesticulation, and at last was able to tell some of the congregation of the great fire which was under them; but they looked at one another, smiling, and told me to go about my business—that I was mad! I woke out of my troubled sleep in a very agitated and perturbed state. Since that, whenever I have seen or heard of churches, where Church and Sacraments are preached, instead of Christ, as the one way of salvation, I long to warn the people of the fire raging underneath, and to show them the way of the Lord more perfectly.

One day, when I was feeling more desponding and wretched than before, a lady called, and said she wanted to speak to me—would I come to her house for this purpose? I went, and she was not long before she opened the conversation by charging me with being very uncharitable. "You say we are all unconverted."

I replied, "Of course, as children of Adam we are, till conversion takes place; there can be no mistake about that! But when did I say that you were unconverted? Is it not your own conscience that tells you that? When we preach to people as unconverted, those who are changed, and brought from death into life, know as well as possible that we do not mean them; and they pray for a blessing on the Word, that it may reach others, as it once reached them. They do not sit there and resent the charge, for they know what has passed between God and their souls, and are anxious for others to share the same blessing." She was silent; so I continued, "May I ask you the question, Are you converted? Can you tell me that you are?"

She replied, "I do not know what you mean."

"Well then, why do you suppose that I mean something uncharitable or bad?"

"Because I know very well it is not a good thing to be unconverted. But," she added, "it seems such an unkind thing to put us all down for 'lost,' while you suppose yourself to be saved."

"You may know more about this some day, perhaps; but in the meantime will you allow me to ask you one thing: Do you believe in the Lord Jesus Christ?"

She replied indignantly, "Of course I do. Now, this is the very want of charity I complain of—the idea of asking me such a question!"

She was one of the Rev. ———'s, (the confessor's) favourite devotees, and had been absolved by him for several years; the very idea of asking her if she believed in the Lord Jesus Christ, made her quite impatient, as well as indignant.

I said, "Do not be angry with me, but what do you believe about Him?"

"Believe everything, of course! I believe the creed."

"Yes, I do not doubt that, for a moment. But do you believe that Jesus died *for you*?"

"Why, yes, certainly: how could I do otherwise; He died for us all."

"That is not the point. I mean, do you believe that He died; and that you have *a personal interest* in His death?"

She hesitated, and then looking at me said, "Do you mean objectively, or subjectively?"

"May I ask what I am to understand by these words?"

"Dr. ——— taught me that, 'Christ died,' is objective, and that 'Christ died for me,' is subjective."

"Very good indeed," I answered, "I like that very much; it is quite true. But it is one thing to know about subjective faith, and quite another thing to have it. Now I will come back to my question. Do you believe that Christ died *for you*?"

"You evidently mean something that I do not understand," she said, in a perplexed manner.

Then looking at the crucifix on her table, I said, "What does that remind you of?"

"Oh, I pray before that every day, and ask the Lord to take my sins away."

"Then you do not think your sins are forgiven yet. How can you ask for forgiveness, and have it at the same time?"

"Do you mean to say then," she replied, with surprise, "that you have no sins?"

"Yes, I mean to say that my sins were atoned for, once for all, on the cross; and that, believing this, I have peace and remission of sins. My past sins are cast like a stone into the deep; and as to my daily sins of omission and commission, I do not take them to the cross like a Romanist, but to the throne of grace, where the risen and living Christ is now making intercession for me."

She was silent; and so was I, inwardly praying for her.

Presently she looked up and said, "I do thank Him for dying for me. Is that what you want me to say?"

"Thanksgiving is an indication of living faith. How can I believe that Jesus died for me, and not thank Him?"

"But   do thank Him, and it is very uncharitable of you to say,   not thank Him; we all thank Him!"

She was gone again, and I wondered whether I should ever bring her back!

"You remind me," I said, "of three ladies of good position, whom I met last year. They all professed to thank God for Christ's death; but yet they had no peace, and w not satisfied. Seeing they were in real earnest, I proposed to go over the General Thanksgiving in the Prayer-book with them. They did so, and thanked God for creation, preservation, and all the blessings of this life, but *above all*—then as I emphasized this 'above all,' they said, almost together, 'That is where we are wrong. We have not put the redeeming love of God as shown in Christ's death, *above all.*' These three ladies found peace and pardon that same evening."

"That has been my mistake too," said the lady interrupting me. "I have never put Jesus above all; but I do desire to do so, and that with all my heart."

"Then do so," I said, "and thank Him for His love in dying in your stead, and shedding His blood to wash your sins away."

"He *shall* have all my heart!" she exclaimed.

So saying, she knelt before the crucifix, and bowing gracefully and most reverently, she reproached herself for not putting Jesus first, and said, "Thou art worthy! Glory be to Thee, for Thy great love to me."

Then she rose from her knees, and once more turning to me, said, "Thank you so much! God bless you for your kindness and patience with me! I cannot tell you how much I thank you. Do you remember once preaching about Abraham offering up his son Isaac? You said, 'God the Father has done more than this for us; and yet how few cry to Him and say, "By this I know that Thou lovest me!"' I thought, and felt then, that you knew something which I should like to know; and I have been longing to speak to you ever since. Oh, I do thank you so much!"

"Dear friend, I cannot refuse your thanks, but I should like to see you thanking God more than you thank me."

I knew that she could sing and play, so, pointing to the piano, I asked her if she would sing a hymn.

"Yes," she said, "I will. What shall I sing?"

"Find 'When I survey the wondrous cross,'" I said.

She did not need to find the music, for she knew it without; so, sitting down, she began to sing, till the tears came into her eyes, and her voice broke down. "I never knew the meaning of these words before," she said; "'Sorrow and love flow mingled down.' How could I be so blind and ignorant? 'Love so amazing, so divine,' does 'demand my life, my soul, my all!' O Lord, take it!"

After this, I had a few parting words with her, and pointing to the crucifix I said, "Remember, Christ is not on the cross now. He died; that is past. He is risen, and has ascended up on high. The throne of grace is not the crucifix or the confessional, but where Christ sits—at the right hand of God; and we, as believers, may in heart and mind thither ascend, and with Him continually dwell. Have done, then, with this dead Popery; you know better now. Testify for the glory of God."

This lady's conversion vexed her husband greatly, and brought down the frowns and disapprobation of the reverend doctor; altogether, it did a deal of mischief in the camp. The "Sisters of Mercy" with whom she was connected were kept aloof from her contaminating influence, and soon afterwards were altogether removed from the place. There was one, however, a particularly hard-headed looking individual, who used to stare at me through her round spectacles whenever I met her, as if I were an ogre. I heard that she was a great mathematician. She looked like it; and evidently there was no fear entertained of her being converted. She and one other were left behind; but otherwise the house, which had been built at great cost, was empty. The lady was not allowed to speak to me any more; but I hope she continued to go to the true throne of grace, and not to the crucifix—to a living, not a dead Christ.

All this, doubtless, was intended to sicken me of my reverence for the Catholic theory. I was evidently under an infatuation on the subject, which, for the time, nothing could dispel. I had some poetic or imaginary fancy of spiritual catholicity before my mind, which I supposed was something better than the fleshly spirituality of Methodism, to which I had taken a great dislike; but where to find this Utopia, or how to embody it, I knew not. These specimens of catholic people I certainly had no sympathy with; nor had I any patience with their hollow devotion and their studied imitation of Popery. I plainly saw that light could have no fellowship with darkness, or life with death. I was more and more convinced that when a man has more sympathy with dead Catholics than with living Dissenters, he is not a living soul at all. There is no necessity to go to one extreme or the other. I believe the reformed Church of England (in her principles, at least) occupies the middle path between these two extremes, with the excellences of both, and the faults of neither. I think I was permitted to be thus unsettled in my mind, because I did not keep to my work with a single eye to God's glory.

CHAPTER XXVIII.

Devonport.

1855.

 WAS at this time invited to preach in a church in Devonport, where it pleased the Lord to give blessing to His word. With this exception, my work was, generally speaking, confined to individual cases. I will give an account of a few which present the most instruction and interest.

The first I will mention is that of one of the curates of the church in which I was asked to preach. At this time he was preparing for confession, and his self-examination had brought him to see and feel that he was a sinner. Under this course of preparation, the preaching of the Gospel had much effect upon him, and he came to tell me of his state. I was able to show him from the Word of God that he was in a worse condition than he supposed—that actually, by nature, we are lost sinners *now*. Under the operation of the Holy Spirit he was brought to feel this also, and was very miserable.

One day, while officiating at a funeral, the Lord spoke peace to his soul; so great was his joy, that, he said, he could scarcely refrain from shouting aloud in the middle of the service. After it was over he went about everywhere, telling of his conversion, and the Lord's dealings with his soul.

The result of this was that his fellow-curate (who was also preparing for confession) was awakened, and came to me in great distress of mind, declaring he "could not say he was converted," and that he was very unhappy. He acknowledged that he should not like to die as he was, and therefore knew he ought not to be satisfied to live in that state. However, when I got to close dealing with him about his soul, he said that though he could not say he *was saved*, he certainly thought that he was *being saved* by continual absolution and the sacrament. Upon this, I was enabled to show him that he did not go to the means of grace, or even to the Lord's table, because he was saved, but in order to be saved; and that he was working for life, and not from life. He gave up disputing, and was not long before he too found peace in believing.

The time was approaching for these two curates to go, as usual, to confession. They came together to ask me about it. I counselled them to go, by all means, to the reverend doctor, who usually received their confession, and to tell him in their own words how the Lord had convicted and converted them. I said that Bilney, one of the first martyrs of the Reformation, when he was converted, went immediately to make confession to Latimer, and by doing so he became the means of his conversion. "Go, by all means; you do not know what use the Lord may make of your testimony."

They went accordingly, but did not meet with the happy success of Bilney, for they were sent indignantly away one after the other for saying their sins were pardoned and their souls saved, and that by direct and personal faith in Christ, without the intervention of a priest. The reverend confessor, unlike the honest Latimer, said these young men had come to mock him.

Notwithstanding these instances of usefulness and encouragement, I continued to be very unhappy, for want of more general work, and felt as if God had cast me off. I can now see that this trying and perplexing dispensation through which I was passing, was not altogether such a barren desert as I felt it to be at the time. It was fraught with many lessons, which have stood by me ever since, though I must confess I never revert to this period without many unhappy memories.

I will record one more lesson which I was taught in this place, and then go on to other subjects.

One warm spring day, while I was sitting in my house with the doors and windows open, a gentleman came running into it in great haste, somewhat to my surprise, he being a perfect stranger to me, and I to him. Standing in the passage, and looking into the room where I was seated, he said, "Sir, are you a clergyman?"

I replied, "Yes, I am."

"For God's sake, come; follow me!"

So saying, he went away. I immediately took up my hat, and ran after him down the side of the square, and noticing the gate where he turned in, I walked leisurely to the same place, and found him in the passage of his house panting for breath. He had run so fast that he could not speak, but made a sign to me to go upstairs; then pointing to a door, he bade me go in. On doing so, I saw at once it was a sick-chamber, and found myself alone in the presence of a lady, who was sitting up in the bed. I bowed to her, and said, "Can I help you?"

She said, "Oh, no! it is too late!"

"Too late for what?"

"I am dying; I am lost—I am lost! It is too late—too late!"

"But Christ came, and is present, to save the lost."

"Oh, yes! I know all that. I taught it to others, but I never believed it myself. And now it is too late: I am lost!"

"Then believe it now! Why not 'now'?"

"Because it is too late!"

"While there is life there is hope! Lose no more time. 'God so loved the world, that He gave His only-begotten Son, that whosoever believeth on Him should not perish'" (John iii. 16).

"That is not for me. I know that text very well, but it will not do for me. I am lost! I am lost! It is too late!"

While I was speaking I saw her falling over the side of the bed. Springing forward, I put out my arm, and, with her head resting on it, and her despairing eyes looking into my face, she expired. I could scarcely believe it, when I saw that flush on her face fade away into the pallor of death. She was gone! I placed her poor head on the pillow, and rang the bell for assistance. Her mother and sister came in, saying, "Is it not dreadful?"

I said, "Look at her. She is gone. She said it was too late, and that she was lost for ever."

"Oh," exclaimed the mother, "it is most dreadful!—most dreadful!"

This poor young lady used to be a Sunday-school teacher and district visitor; but she was never converted, and she knew it. She had full head-knowledge, but no heart experience, and thus she died in unforgiven sins. Lost—for ever lost!

Notwithstanding this, and other solemn lessons which the Lord was teaching me at this time, I was still restless and unhappy. I felt as if my life, with its work, was cut off in the very beginning of its usefulness, and that there was no more for me to do. As the weather became hot with the advancing summer, I was more and more dejected in mind and body. I lived now among strangers, and had no settled occupation, nor could I apply myself to study.

One very hot and dusty afternoon, as I was slowly toiling up a steep hill, two women overtook me; and as they were passing, I heard one say to the other, in a very sad and disheartened tone, "I wish I had never been born;" and the other responded much in the same spirit, though I could not hear what she said. A fellow-feeling makes us wondrous kind, and has the effect of drawing out our sympathies. I followed these poor women, and when we were on the top of the hill, I spoke to them, and then added, "You seem very weary. Will you come in and take a cup of tea, and rest a little?" They thanked me, and consented. So I took them into the house, and asked for some tea. While it was being prepared, I said to them, "I overheard you talking on the road as you passed me. Do you really wish you had never been born?" The poor woman who had uttered these words burst into tears; and as soon as she could command her feelings sufficiently, she told me her sad tale of sorrow and trouble. She was a soldier's wife, as was also the other, and they were both in the same distress. "Well," I said, "trouble does not spring out of the ground; and we may be equally sure that God, who sends, or at least permits it, does so for *our good*. One thing is certain, that if we humble ourselves under the mighty hand of God, He can and will lift us up, for He has promised to do so. He will make all things work together for our good, if we trust Him. I then asked them if they had given their hearts to God.

One of them said, "Ah, that is what I ought to have

done long ago; I know a deal better than I do. I was brought up well, no mistake; but I was giddy, and went after the red-coats, and married an ungodly man, and now I am suffering for it."

"Dear woman," I said, "you may thank God for hedging up your path. He might have given you over to prosperity and a false happiness, or left you altogether. Thank God that it is not worse with you; and give Him your heart. Do you believe that the Lord Jesus died for you?" She would not speak. Then I turned to the other, who was also crying, and said, "Do you believe?"

"I did once," she said, in a dejected tone; "but I have gone back from everything."

By this time their tea was ready, so I refreshed them with it; and after that we resumed our conversation and united in prayer. They both gave their hearts to God. I found that they lived not far off, so I had the opportunity of seeing them from time to time, and was able to instruct and cheer them on their way. I can see now how God was speaking to me through these women; but somehow I did not hear or recognize His voice then.

About this time, my dear wife became very prostrate in health and spirits—so much so, that we felt anxious about her. I went to a famous physician, who was in the neighbourhood, and asked him to come and see her. He did so, and after careful examination, said that there was really nothing the matter more than that she was one of those persons who could not live in that limestone town in the summer. He said, "She will be perfectly well if you take her away into the country. You must do this at once, for the longer she remains here, the weaker she will be." He refused to take any fee, and said he would send a carriage at two o'clock, and that we must be ready to start by that time. This was more easily said than done; for where could I take the children, or how could I leave them at home? However, as the doctor was very peremptory, we prayed about it, and considered how we were to accomplish the task.

At this critical moment a friend arrived in his carriage, and said he had driven in from the country to bring some relatives of his to the train, and did not care to go back alone. "Would one of us, or both, take pity on him, and give him our company?" As soon as he heard of our position he greatly rejoiced, and said, "Come, all of you; I have plenty of room!" He took the invalid, with some of the children. I shut up the house, and followed with the others and the nurse, in the fly, which duly arrived at two o'clock. By five o'clock we were all out in the green fresh country, and our patient was already revived, and walking about the garden.

There happened to be a farm-house vacant, which we took, and removing some of the furniture, made it comfortable for the present. This we called "home" for a little time during my unsettled state.

CHAPTER XXIX.

A Mission to the North.

1855.

WHEN my family were all comfortably settled and surrounded by kind friends, I went off to the north of England, on a visit to a clergyman, who had invited me. He had already suffered for doing this on a previous occasion, in the diocese of Oxford; where the bishop took away his licence, because he had me to preach for him. The real cause of offence was, that there was a revival in the parish; and complaint was made to the bishop, that people were kept up till "all hours of the night, howling and praying." His lordship sent forthwith for my friend's licence; I advised him to send it, saying, "He will be sure to return it to you; but perhaps with a reprimand." Instead of this, the bishop kept it, and said that he would countersign his testimonials to go to another diocese. My friend was at first disgusted and disposed to rebel; but instead of this, he bore the treatment patiently; and went to another position and charge at G——, in the north of England.

Thither, nothing afraid, he invited me to come. In this part of the country I found a hearty lively people, something like the Cornish. Here I soon regained my spirits, and got to work in right earnest.

In this place a revival began at once; and every day we had people crying for mercy, very much in the way they did in Cornwall. Among others, there came to the church on Sunday afternoon, a tall Yorkshireman, in his working clothes. He stood under the gallery, in his shirt sleeves, with a clay pipe sticking out of his waistcoat pocket, and a little cap on his head. I fancy I can see him now, standing erect, looking earnestly at me while I was preaching, with his hand on one of the iron supports of the gallery. As the sermon proceeded he became deeply interested, and step by step drew nearer to the pulpit. He seemed to be altogether unconscious that he was not dressed for a Sunday congregation, or that he was the object of any special notice. After the sermon, he knelt down in the aisle, and there he remained. I was called out of the vestry to go to him, but could not get him to say a word. I prayed by his side, and after some time he groaned out an "Amen," then he got up, and went towards the door. I followed him, and saw that instead of going along the path, he made across the graves in the churchyard, to a particular one; and then he threw himself on the ground, in vehement and convulsive emotion. He said something about "Edward," but we could not distinguish what it was. The sexton said, that this was his son Edward's grave. Poor man! he was in great sorrow; but he kept it all to himself. He then went home, and shut himself up in his own room. His daughter could do nothing with him in his distress. We called several times to see him in the course of the evening, but in vain.

The next morning I called again, when his daughter told me that he had gone out early, and had not returned to breakfast. She appeared to be in a good deal of trouble, and said she had been to his mine to inquire for him, but that he was not there. All day long we searched for him. Some looked in the woods, half-expecting they might find his body on the ground, or hanging from a tree; while others inquired in every direction, with increasing anxiety, till the evening. Then, as we were returning home in despair and disappointment, whom should we see in the green lane between the vicarage and the church, but our friend. He was looking into the shrubs as if watching something; and when we came up to him, he turned to us with a radiant smile, and said, "The Lord is 'gude.'"

I said, "You are right, He is so."

"Yes, I am right, all right! thank God! Think of that! He saved me this day!"

"Are you coming to church to-night?"

"Oh yes, certainly I will be there."

"But," I said, "have you been home yet?"

"Oh yes, sir, thank you; my girl knows all about me."

That man was so manifestly changed, and so filled with the Spirit, that his old worldly companions were afraid of him. The publican of the inn he used to frequent, was particularly so, and said he was frightened to be in the same room with him.

There was a great stir among the people in this place; for the fear of the Lord had fallen on them, so that they were solemnized exceedingly, and many were converted.

The vicar being somewhat timid, began to be afraid of what was going on; and wrote to ask counsel of a clerical neighbour at C——, who answered his letter by inviting him to come over, and bring me with him. He said that he wanted me to preach in his church on the following Friday evening, adding, "I have already given notice, and also read parts of your letter in church. I am sure the people will come and hear this man; I expect a large congregation.

Be sure and bring him over; do not disappoint me on any account!"

Accordingly, on the Friday we appeared there, and in the evening I preached to a large and attentive assembly. Many were awakened, and some remained behind to be spoken with; others, who were too shy to do so, went home; and we heard the next morning that several had had no sleep or rest all night. Three men, whom we saw in the morning, had found peace. After this, we drove slowly back to G——, but a messenger had arrived before us, and said that I must come back again with him, for the bills were already out that I would preach on Sunday and following days at C——. The vicar was most reluctant to let me go, but under these circumstances, he at last consented; so I went back in the carriage the messenger had brought for that purpose.

At the Sunday morning service, the manner and tone of the people, and their eager attention, implied that something was going to happen. There was a deeply solemn feeling in the church, both morning and evening, which made it very easy to preach. In the course of my sermon, I know not why, I was led to speak about the endless misery of hell; and some who were present said I asserted, "That there was a great clock in hell, with a large dial, but no hands to mark the progress of time: it had a pendulum which swung sullenly and slowly from side to side, continually saying, 'Ever! never!' 'Ever! never!'"*

This seemed to make a profound sensation among the people: many stayed to the after-meeting—they would not go away until they had been spoken with. Among others, the churchwarden came to me in a very excited state, and said,

---

* Both Bridaine and Krummacher have expressed somewhat the same idea.

"What ever made you say, 'Now or never!—now or never!'?" He was like one beside himself with emotion when he thought of the pendulum which I had described. "Now or never!—now or never!" he kept on repeating to himself, till at last he went away. He was far too excited to talk of anything else, or to listen either.

Later on in the evening, we were sent for to come in all haste to his house. There we found him in great trouble of mind, and afraid to go to bed. After talking to him for a short time, he went on to say that he had a strange thing to tell us—"that that very morning he was lying in bed (he thought he was quite awake), and looking at a little picture of the crucifixion which was hanging over the fireplace. While doing so, he saw as plainly as possible some black figures of imps and devils walking along the mantelpiece with a ladder, which they placed against the wall, evidently for the purpose of removing this picture from its place. He watched them intently, and noticed that they seemed much troubled and perplexed as to how they were to accomplish their task. Some of the imps put their shoulders to the under side of the frame, while others went up the ladder; one, in particular, mounted to the top with great dexterity, to get the cord off the nail, but without success. Enraged at this, they made various other attempts, but all in vain, and at last gave up in despair, if not something worse; for by this time they appeared furious, and dashed the ladder down to the ground, as if it were the fault of it, and not of themselves. In rage and disappointment, they passed off the scene.

Presently the bedroom door opened, as he thought, and who should present himself but "Paul Pry" (that was the name he had given to a Dissenting preacher in the village, who was a portly man, and always went about with a thick umbrella under his arm)—the veritable Paul Pry, umbrella and all, standing at the door. He said to his visitor, "What do you want here?" The phantom pointed to the picture over the mantelpiece, and said, in a quiet, confiding way, "Now or never! Do you hear, man? Now or never!" The man was indignant at this untimely intrusion, and bade his visitor begone; but, for all that, he still stood at the door, and said, "Now or never!—now or never!" He got out of bed, and went towards the door, but the figure disappeared, saying, "Now or never!—now or never!"

Then he got into bed again, and all was still for a little while, when suddenly the door opened a second time, and the vicar appeared, just as Paul Pry had done, and came towards the bed, as if with a friendly and affectionate concern for his welfare, and said, "My dear fellow, be persuaded—it is 'now or never!'" Then, taking a seat at the corner of the bed, with his back leaning against the post, he went on talking, and saying, again and again, "Now or never!"

The poor churchwarden remonstrated in vain against being visited in this manner, and thought it very hard; but the vicar sat there, and persistently said, "Now or never!" He became very angry, and bade him go out of the room immediately; but the vicar said, "Now or never!"

"I will 'now' you," he said, "if you do not be off;" and so saying he rose up in his bed; while the vicar glided to the door, repeating, "Now or never!" and went away. The poor man, in great distress of mind, turned to his wife, and asked her what could be the meaning of all this; but she only cried, and said nothing.

Then, who should come next but Mr. F——, a quiet man of few words. He had thoughts, no doubt, but kept them all to himself. He came gliding into the room, as the vicar had done, sat on the same corner of the bed, leant against the same post, and in the quietest way possible repeated the same words, "Now or never!"

"Do you hear him?" said the poor distracted man to his wife—"do you hear him?"

"Hear him? Hear what? No! nonsense! What does he say?"

"My dear, there! listen!"

"Now or never!" said the quiet man.

"There, did you not hear that?"

"No," she said, "I can hear nothing," and began to cry more copiously.

He got up, and said he would take the poker and punish every one of them—that he would. The strange visitor made for the door, and, like all the rest, said, as he disappeared, "Now or never!"

The poor churchwarden continued in a most distracted state, and during the day met all his three visitors who had caused him so much anxiety—"Paul Pry," the vicar, and the quiet gentleman, none of whom looked at him or spoke to him as if anything had happened; but when he heard me say over and over again in the pulpit, "Now or never!" pointing, as it were, to the ghostly pendulum swinging there saying, "Ever!—never!" and inquiring of the people, "Do you see it? do you hear it?" it seemed to bring matters to a climax. He said he turned and looked at the wall to which I pointed, and almost expected to see that solemn clock.

I did not wait to hear more, but kneeling down, I begged him to close with the offer of salvation "now."

"No," he said, with a sigh, "I am afraid I have refused too long!"

"Don't say so! take it at once, 'now;' or perhaps it will be 'never' with you." A man does not often get such a plain warning as you have had. You had better take care what you are doing. 'Now!' why not 'now'?" He did accept salvation, and yielding himself to God, received forgiveness of his sins; and after that became a very different man.

He had, as may have been suspected from the above narrative, the besetment of drink, before his conversion, and it remained a trouble to him after. Conversion and forgiveness of sins do not put away present bad habits. Such a master habit as this requires a direct dealing with.

Zaccheus was a man who had been led astray by the love of money; when he was saved, he put his idol away from him at a stroke. This is the first thing to be done; and if it is done in the power of one's first love, it is a more easy task than afterwards. But it must be done with a firm and whole heart; not "Lord, *shall I give* the half of my goods to feed the poor?" but, "Lord, behold, the half of my goods *I do give.*" "Behold, Lord, I do give up the world, here, now." "Behold, Lord, I do here, and now, give up drink, and will totally abstain from it henceforth." This is the first step; and the next is not less important, and that is to carry out the determination in the Lord's power, and not in our own. The resolution and determination once made, must be given over to the Lord to be kept by Him; not by our own effort and energy, but with perfect distrust of self and in dependence upon Him to enable us to keep it. Without this, there is no security whatever for anything more than temporary success, too often succeeded by a sorrowful fall. The flesh is too strong for us, and even if it were not so, the devil is; these two together, besides the lax example of the world, are sure to overpower the weak one. Young Christians need to put away *at once* the sin, whatever it is, that "so easily besets" them, or they will be entangled by it. There is no real and thorough deliverance, except by renouncing sin, and self too, giving up and yielding to the Lord.

That soul was saved; but it was a miserable bondage of

fear in which he lived and died. He was brought home at last, like a wrecked ship into harbour, who might have come in with a good freight, a happy welcome, and an "abundant entrance."

The next day, Monday, we heard of other cases which were ordinary in their character, and therefore need not be detailed; but in the evening there was one which it will be instructive to mention.

It was that of a clergyman of private means, who came to this parish as a curate; but he had given up "taking duty," because, he said, "it was all humbug reading prayers, and all that." He drove a tandem, and smoked all day instead; nevertheless, he was the object of much and earnest prayer. He also happened to be at church the day I preached about the clock; and declared likewise that I said there was a clock in hell. The sermon had evidently made a great impression upon him. He came to church again the next day, and heard something else that he was unable to forget. After the service, as soon as I was free, he asked me to walk with him, to which I assented, though I was feeling very tired. We rambled on the beach, and talked about many things. I tried in vain to bring up the subject of my discourse. When I spoke about it, he was silent; and when I was silent, he went off into other matters. He talked about Jerusalem and the sands of the desert, and the partridges, which, he said, were of the same colour as the sand. Was it from looking at sand always that they became that colour? Do people become alike who look much at one another? Is that why husbands and wives so often resemble each other? and so on. These questions made an impression on me, so that they always come up to my memory in connection with that evening's walk. Certainly, the apostle says that, "Beholding the glory of the Lord, we are changed into the same image from glory to glory;" therefore there may be something in my companion's idea. But, however interesting the subject might be to consider, I was far too tired for anything else but real soul-to-soul work, and therefore proposed that we should return home. We did so; and when my friend left me at the vicarage door, he said abruptly, "Will you let me write to you?"

"Certainly," I replied.

"I will write to-night; but do not trouble to answer in person; send me a written reply."

I said I would. In a few minutes after I received a short note, the purport of which was, "How can I be saved?" It is a very simple question, yet one not so easily answered to a person who already knew the scriptural answer. However, I had a letter by me which Mr. Aitken had written to some one under similar circumstances; so, taking that for a model, I wrote according to promise, adapting and altering sentences to meet the present case. I sent the note, with a message that I would call in the morning. I did so, but found my friend was not at home. The landlady said, "Mr. F—— went out last night soon after he received a letter, and has not been home since." She became alarmed when she heard that we had not seen him. We too were taken by surprise, and did not know which way to go in search of him, or what to do. Presently we met the clerk of the church, who inquired if we had seen anything of Mr. F——; he had called the night before for the keys of the church, and had not returned them; so he (the clerk) could not get into the church to ring the bell or admit the congregation.

This threw some light on the matter; so we went immediately to the church, and with the vicar's keys entered by the vestry door. Looking about in all directions, we found our friend on his knees in the nave, where he had been all night. I went up to him, and, as he did not speak, I asked if I might pray with him.

He said, "Yes."

"What shall I pray for?"

"I don't know."

"Shall I ask the Lord to come down from heaven again and die on the cross for you?"

"No."

"Do you believe that He has done that?"

"Yes, I do."

"You do believe that He has died for *you*—for *you*?" I inquired, laying the emphasis on *you*—"for you, as if you were the only person for whom He died?"

"Yes; I believe He died for me."

"Do you thank Him for it?"

"No, I do not; I do not feel anything."

"That may be; but do you not think you ought to thank Him for what He did for you?"

He did not reply.

"How can you feel anything till you have it? or how can He give you any feelings till you thank Him for what He has already done for you? Make some acknowledgment."

"Thank you," he replied; and without another word he rose from his knees and went away.

The bell was rung, the people assembled, and we had the service; but he did not remain.

Again he disappeared for the whole day, until the evening, when he came into the vestry, and said, "Will you let me read prayers this evening?" To this the vicar gladly assented; so he put on the surplice for the first time after several months, and went into church with us.

The fact of his reading prayers again, and more especially the manner in which he did it, attracted attention.

The earnest tone and meaning he threw into the words of the prayers, and more particularly into the psalm, penetrated much deeper. One lady knelt down and began to pray for herself in the pew; others were riveted as by the power of the Spirit. All through the sermon, I felt that the Lord was working among the people, and at the close they were loth to go. Many more remained in the after-meeting than we could speak to; manifest was the power of the Spirit, and much good was done.

There was great joy in the little village that night, and for several days following the Lord wrought among the people. Many lasting mementos remain of this week's ministry, and of the weeks which followed.

Our reticent friend was changed indeed, and immediately gave up the tandem and the pipes. I do not think he has ever smoked since; he has had something better to do.

Smoking is an idle custom, and too often enslaves its votaries; and even if it does not become a dominant habit, it certainly teaches no lesson of self-denial. A Christian man needs not to seek relief in any such way. It is said to be very soothing when a man is in any trouble or anxiety; if so, in this respect it may be said to be next door to the beer-barrel, or to the use of spirits. If one man may soothe his feelings with this narcotic, another may stimulate them, when he is low and cheerless, with alcohol. The Apostle James says, "Is any merry, let him sing psalms." He does not say, Is any afflicted or low, let him smoke and drink! No; "let him pray," and depend upon God. Many a lesson which might be learned from God on our knees, is let slip altogether because we think there is no harm in relieving ourselves by self-indulgence. The flesh is a monster which is never appeased, much less subdued, by gratification.

Our friend put away the smoking, and sold his pipes of various kinds, which must have cost a considerable sum, for he realized eighty pounds by them. With this amount, and some addition, he was able to put stained glass windows into the already beautiful church in which he received his blessing. This suitable thank-offering was a lasting memorial of his gratitude, besides being an example to others, not only to give their hearts to God, but also to give up their besetments, whatever they might be, and in doing so be free for God's service.

This young man soon after was removed to a more arduous sphere, and carried great blessing thither; as he did also when he went from thence to a yet more influential and important place. Though now laid aside by ill health, he sends tracts and writes letters to many, and so continues to be, in the hand of the Lord, the means of winning souls; and in addition to this, sets an example of a holy and godly life.

Another little incident I must notice here. While I was still working in this place, I received a letter from home, telling me that they were all well, and very happy in the country, but that they wanted me back again, and thought I had been away quite long enough. Besides this, it was time to be getting summer things, for which they would want at least ten pounds. I had no money to send; and though I might have asked many kind friends, I felt a difficulty about it. I do not think it was pride. I had put myself and all my affairs into God's hands; and though I was not ashamed to tell our circumstances to any one who asked me, I made it a rule not to mention my troubles or wants to any but the Lord. I read the cheerful parts of my letter at breakfast, and kept the other till I went upstairs. There, I spread the letter on the bed at which I knelt, and read to the Lord the part that troubled me. I was praying about it, when there came a knock at the door, and before I had time to say "Come in," my friend F—— entered. Seeing me on my knees, he apologized for intruding, and in his shy way put a ten-pound note into my hand, saying, "I am ashamed it is not more; but will you accept that?" With this, he made for the door; but I detained him, in order to show him the part of my letter I had not read in the morning. I said, "I was just reading it to the Lord; and look, while I was still on my knees, He has sent you with the answer. It is the exact sum I want, so do not apologize for it. I thank God and thank you. I will send this off at once."

CHAPTER XXX.

Tregoney.

1855.

IT was time now to be returning southward and homeward; which I did by several stages, stopping to preach in various places on the way. At length, I reached the village in Cornwall, where my family were lodging in the farmhouse I have already mentioned.

Here, the two clergymen were rather afraid of me, and avoided asking me to preach in the church. They had both been converted (or, at least, so they said) more than a year; but instead of working for God, they were bent on Romanizing. One of them said that there was no salvation in the Church of England; and the other showed me a sealed letter he had in his desk, which, he said, he "dared not open." It was from a brother of his, who went to Rome, and contained his reasons for so doing. "Ah," he said, "if I open that letter, I feel sure that I shall have to go too." This fascinating dread was upon him till he really did go, six months afterwards. I tried to deter these men from the erroneous step they were contemplating, by getting them into active work for the Lord. Sometimes I preached in this church, but more often in the open air. I am sorry to say my friends were but half-hearted in their co-operation, so that after a few weeks I left, and went to the west.

On my way thither, a clergyman, who happened to be inside the coach, gave me his card, and then came outside for the purpose of talking with me. He asked me if I would take charge of his church and parish for six weeks. I said I would, but could not do so for a week or two. We agreed as to time, and on the promised Saturday I arrived at the place.

I walked there from a neighbouring town, having several calls to make on the way, and left my luggage to follow by the van. In the evening, about eight o'clock, I went down to meet this conveyance, and tell the man where to deliver me bag. I found a crowd of people in front of the inn where the van stopped, and heard the driver say, in reply to some question, "I've not got him, but I've got his bag." "Where is he?" said a voice. "I don't know," one said, "but I saw a queer little chap go into Mrs. M——'s house." "That's the place," said the driver; "that's where I'm a-going to take his bag. Come on, and let's see if he'll have it."

I went in and out among the crowd, as it was dark, asking questions, and found out that they "would like to duck the fellow if they could catch him;" they "did not want any such Revivalist chap as that amongst them," and so forth. They were greatly excited, and wondered which road he was likely to come, for they would go to meet him. Some one asked, "What is he like?" One answered, "Oh, he is a rum-looking little fellow that stoops. I should know him again anywhere." Hearing this, I held up my head like a soldier, in order to look as large as possible, and waited about till they dispersed.

Then I joined a young man, and, talking with him,

ascertained what it was all about. I passed the house where I was to lodge, for I saw that the people were watching the door. I came back among them, and, pointing to the door, said, "Is that where he stops?"

"Yes," one replied, "he is there. The man brought his bag and left it; he is there, sure enough."

I said, "Let us go in and see him; come along—come!"

So saying, I made for the door and knocked, beckoning to the others to follow me; but they would not do so. As soon as the door was opened I went in, and the landlady speedily closed it after me, saying, "I am glad you are come. How did you manage to get here? I have sent word to the constable to look out for you, and he is still watching somewhere."

"Why," I asked, "what is it all about? What is the matter?"

"Why, some of the lads here say, that if they could catch you, they would give you a good ducking in the pond."

"Indeed!" I said. "Then I don't think I will give them that pleasure to-night." So, sitting down by the fire, I made myself comfortable, and after supper went to bed.

In the morning, while at breakfast, I saw a number of men playing in the open space in front of the house. Some were tossing pence, some playing at ball and other games, while many were standing about smoking, with their hands in their pockets.

"There, that's the way they spend their Sundays in this place," said the landlady.

After watching them from the window for a little time, I put on my hat and went out, and told them "it was time to go home and get ready for church; that would be far better," I said, "than playing like this on Sunday. It is a disgrace to men like you—married men, too, with families! It would be bad enough if you were a parcel of boys. I am quite ashamed of you!"

They slunk away one by one, and I walked down the street to look about me, and to see the schoolroom, where there was no school; but I intended to have a prayer-meeting there in the evening, after the service. I put up a notice to this effect, and then came back to my lodgings, till it was near church-time, when I set out, arrayed in my gown and bands, for the sacred edifice.

On the way there I observed stones flying past me in every direction; but I walked on, till at last I was struck on the cheek with a patch of muddy clay which was thrown at me. There was an universal shout of laughter when the men and boys saw that I had been hit. I put my hand to the place, and found that the pat of clay was sticking to my cheek, so I pressed it there, hoping, by the help of my whiskers, that it would remain. I said to the crowd, who were laughing at me, "That was not a bad shot. Now, if you come to church you shall see it there; I will keep it on as long as I can." So saying, I walked on amidst the jeers of the people.

When I arrived at the vestry, the clerk was in great trouble when he knew what had happened. He said, "Do let me wash the mud off, sir."

"Oh, no," I replied, "I mean to show that all day, if I can."

During the morning service, at which there were about fifty people present, I succeeded in keeping on my mud-patch, and returned to dinner with the same.

In the afternoon I said that I would have a service for children, as there was no Sunday school, to which about twenty came. Before addressing them, seeing that they were intently looking at the patch on my cheek, I told them how it came there, and that I intended to keep it on all through the evening service.

This news spread over the whole place, and the consequence was that such numbers of people came out of curiosity, that the church was filled to overflowing. I preached without any reference to what had taken place, and succeeded in gaining the attention of the people; so that after the service I said I would have a prayer-meeting in the schoolroom. We had the place crammed, and not a few found peace. I announced that I would preach again the next evening.

A revival soon broke out in that place, and the crowds who came to the meetings were so great, that we had as many people outside the large schoolroom as there were in.

At the end of the six weeks the new vicar returned, and I was able to hand over the parish to him, with a full church, three Bible-classes, and a large Sunday-school. This I did, thanking God for the measure of success and blessing He had given to my efforts in that populous and wicked place.

After I had left I received a letter from some of the parishioners, asking me what I should like to have as a testimonial of their gratitude and regard; that they had had a penny collection amongst themselves, which amounted to several pounds, and now they were waiting to know what I should like!

I wrote to tell them that nothing would please me better than a service of plate for communion with the sick. They bought this, and had a suitable inscription engraved, and then placed it under a glass shade in the Town Hall, on a certain day for inspection. Hundreds of people came to see the result of their penny contribution. After this public exhibition, the communion service was sent to me with a letter, written by a leading man in the place, saying, "I was one of the instigators of the opposition to your work here; but the very first evening you spoke in the schoolroom I was outside listening, and was shot through the window. The word hit my heart like a hammer, without breaking a pane of glass. Scores and scores of people will bless God to all eternity that you ever came amongst us."

The revival in this proverbially wicked place, created such a stir that the newspapers took it up, and thought for once that I "was in the right place, and doing a good work!" The member for the borough sent me twenty-five pounds, "begging my acceptance of the trifle." Who asked him, or why he sent it, I do not know; but the Lord knew that we needed help. More than this, the vicar of the adjoining parish, who used to be very friendly with me in my unconverted days, but who had declared his opposition pretty freely since that time, sent me a letter one Sunday morning by private hand, to be delivered to me personally. This I duly received; but expecting that it was one of his usual letters, and also knowing that I had visited some persons in his parish who were anxious, I thought I would not open it till Monday, and so placed it on the mantel-piece. A friend who happened to come in, noticing it there, said, "I see you have a letter from the Prebendary; I dare say he is angry with you."

"I suppose he is," I said; "but it will keep till to-morrow; and I do not care to be troubled with his thoughts to-day."

"Oh, do let me open it," said my visitor; "I shall not be here to-morrow, and I should so like to hear what he has to say."

With my consent he opened it and read, "Dear old Haslam, you have done more good in that part of my parish where you are working, in a few weeks, than I have done for years. I enclose you a cheque for the amount of tithes coming from there. The Lord bless you more and more! Pray for me!"

It was a cheque for thirty-seven pounds. The next morning I went over to see my old friend newly-found, and to thank him in person for his generous gift. Poor man, I found him very low and depressed, and quite ready and willing that I should talk and pray with him. I sincerely hope that he became changed before I left the neighbourhood, but I never heard that he declared himself.

By this time, while I was still in Tregoney, Mr. Aitken had found his way to the village where my family were lodging, and he was preaching at the church with his usual power and effect. Night after night souls were awakened and saved. The vicar's wife was in a towering rage of opposition. Poor woman! she declared that she "would rather go to Rome than be converted;" and to Rome she went, but remained as worldly as ever.

It matters very little whether unconverted people join the Church of Rome or not; they are sure to be lost for ever if they die in their unconverted state: for nothing avails for eternal salvation but faith in the Lord Jesus Christ.

CHAPTER XXXI.

Secessions.

1856.

AFTER the mission which Mr. Aitken had held, people came out so decidedly, that the vicar and curate, who had all along kept aloof, doubting, fell back into a kind of revulsion, and began to read and lend Romish books. Eventually, they themselves decided to join the Church of Rome. Whether they were ever really converted or not, I cannot tell. I thought and hoped they were, but they seldom stood out on the Lord's side. They certainly had light, and may have had some experience. At any rate, they chose such a harlot as the Church of Rome for the object of their love, instead of Christ Himself.

I loved the curate. He was the man who had the unopened letter in his desk,* of which he harboured such a dread. Sad to say, he ended by falling away at last. Poor man ! he went over to Rome, and never held up his head any more. Evidently disappointed, and ashamed to come back, he lingered on for some months, and then died.

---

* See page 264.

Not long after his secession, we accidentally met in a quiet lane, in another part of the county, where I was walking for meditation. Perhaps he was led there for the same purpose. Meeting so unexpectedly, there was no opportunity to evade one another. I felt a trembling come over me at seeing him, and he was none the less moved. We held each other's hands in silence, till at last I said, "How are you? I love you still."

"I cannot stand it!" he said; and snatching his hand out of mine, he ran away.

I never saw him again, but mourned for him till he died. I cannot help thinking that he is safe, and that he died in a faith more scriptural than that of the Church of Rome.

Why do men secede, and break their own hearts, and the hearts of those who love them? Rome seems to cast a kind of spell upon the conscience, fascinating its victims much as the gaze of the serpent is said to hold a bird, till it falls into its power; or as a light attracts a moth, till it flies into it, to its own destruction. Such seceders mourn and dread the step; pray about it, think and think, till they are bewildered and harassed; and then, in a fit of desperation, go off to some Romish priest to be received. A man who had an honourable position, a work and responsibility, suddenly becomes a nonentity, barely welcomed, and certainly suspected.

Romish people compass sea and land to make proselytes; and after they have gained them, they are afraid of them, for their respective antecedents are so different, that it is impossible for them to think together. They get the submission of a poor deluded pervert, but he gets nothing in return from them but a fictitious salvation. They gain him: but he has lost the kind regard and sympathy of friends he had before, and with it all that once was dear to him; and he voluntarily forfeits all this upon the bare self-assertion of a system which claims his implicit obedience. The poor pervert is required to give over his will, his conscience, and his deepest feelings to the keeping of his so-called "priest" or to the Church, and is expected to go away unburdened and at peace. Some there are, it is true, who actually declare that they have peace by this means; but what peace it is, and of what kind, I know not.

Supposing that I was in debt and anxiety, and a man who had no money, but plenty of assurance and brass, came to me and sympathized in my trouble, saying, "Do not fear—trust me; I will bear your burden, and pay off your debt"—if the manner of the man was sufficiently assuring, it would lift up the cloud of anxiety and distress; but, for all that, the penniless man would not, and could not, pay my debt. I might fancy he had done or would do so; and then, when it was too late, the debt, with accumulated interest, would fall on me, to my overwhelming ruin, even though I had been ever so free from anxiety before. So it is with these deluded ones, who go to the priest instead of to Christ, and take his absolution instead of Christ's forgiveness.

Any one who carefully reads the Word of God may see that the Church of Rome has no such priesthood as she claims, nor power to forgive sins, as she professes to do. The whole supposition is based on a misunderstanding of the text, "Whose soever sins ye remit, they are remitted unto them; and whose soever sins ye retain, they are retained" (John xx. 23).

The disciples (some of them not apostles) who received this commission or privilege, never understood that they were by these words (men and women together) empowered to be absolving priests. Even the very apostles never knew that they had any such power; and it is certain they never exercised it. They were perfectly innocent of being priests after the Romish type, and never dreamed of offering a propitiatory sacrifice. They simply believed that Christ had completed the work of propitiation once for all; and that there is now no more sacrifice for sin—that Christ only can forgive sins. Therefore in the words of St. John we are told, that "if any man sin (apostles and people alike), we have an advocate with the Father, Jesus Christ the righteous; and He is the propitiation for our sins" (1 John ii. 1, 2).

The apostles and early Christians never understood that the power of the keys meant the exercise of mere priestly authority, neither was the doctrine known for several centuries after their time; therefore we may be sure that the peace which perverts have, if it professes to come from that source, is a delusion. No true remission or peace is, or can be given, but by direct and personal transaction with Christ Himself.

I am perfectly convinced that the Epistles to the Romans and the Galatians are the answer to all the pretences of the Church of Rome, and that a man who will not read and follow them deserves to be misled. God is perfectly justified and clear on this point.

During that winter six of my friends joined the Church of Rome. One I have already told about, who died, I am sure, from grief and disappointment.* Another became bigoted, and with a sullen, dogged pertinacity, set himself to work for Rome, looking very miserable all the time, although he used once to be happy in the Lord's work. The others, without exception, went back into the world, and made no secret of their conformity with it, its ways, and fashions.

---

* See page 271.

This was a time of trouble in more respects than one. These secessions to Rome brought great discredit upon the work, and especially on the effort to promote Catholic truth, and higher Church life. I found my own refuge and comfort was in working for God, and therefore went out on mission work whenever and wherever I could.

Early in the spring of this year I went on a mission to Worcestershire, and there the Lord vouchsafed a great blessing, which has more or less continued to this day; though I grieve to say the present vicar has no sympathy with it. The work is still carried on in an Iron Room, out of church hours, by people who continue to go to church.

The vicar of that time asked me to go and visit a farmer's wife, who was under deep conviction, and wished to see me. I did so, and as we approached the door (which was open) the first thing we heard was this individual saying, in a very high-pitched voice, "Confound——"

Seeing us, she suddenly stopped. "Go on with your text," said the vicar, quietly, "'Confounded be all they that serve graven images;' is that what you mean?"

"No," she replied; "come in, I am so wretched that I don't know what to do with myself; it has made me cross. Do come in and pray with me."

We at once consented; and on pointing her to Jesus, she found peace. Not content with praising God alone, she opened her house for a meeting for the people in the neighbourhood. This being situated on the confines of the parish, brought us into collision with the rector of the next parish. He was most indignant at our coming (as he said), "to entice his people away."

I tried my best to conciliate this gentleman, but nothing

would do, particularly when he heard that I was thinking of settling down in the district. This plan was however frustrated in an unexpected manner, and I was not permitted to remain there.

One day, when I was praying about the matter, a letter was put into my hand from a lady who had been asking the Lord for nearly six months that I might be appointed to her late husband's church. She had applied to Lord Palmerston, who was the patron, and though she had received no answer, yet she had continued to pray.

At last there came a courteous letter from his lordship, apologizing for having delayed his reply, adding that he "had mislaid the application of her nominee; if she would oblige him with the name and address of this person, the appointment should be made out immediately." She gave my name and address, and sent his letter on to me. I immediately wrote to his lordship, saying that I had not applied for the living, nor did I want it; but, for all that, I received by return of post the nomination; and actually, it was to go back to the diocese of Exeter! I did not think the Bishop would institute me, as I had committed a great many irregularities since his lordship had taken off my harness. But he did.

Somehow I was unwilling to go to this living, but was put into it in spite of myself. Here I had a good house, garden, and church, provided for me, with so much a year. I wondered whether God was tired of me! He had provided for me and my family during the past year wondrously, and I began to like "living by faith," and trusting in Him only. I have great doubts whether this appointment was altogether in accordance with God's will. Anyway, I had very little liberty or success in preaching, and could not settle down to work with any energy.

In the beginning of the summer, as usual, I had my

attack of hay fever, which completely incapacitated me, in this place of much grass. If I went to a town or the sea-side, it was well; but the moment I returned to the country I was ill again. Altogether, it was a dull and distressing time; but God was preparing me for a special work.

CHAPTER XXXII.

Hayle.

1857—8.

WHILE meditating upon my present position, and wondering what I was to do next, I received an invitation to take charge of a district in another part of the county, near the sea, which suited my health. Here there was a large population, which gave scope for energetic action; and, moreover, the people were careless and Godless, and, as such, were not pre-occupied with other systems. So I thought it was the very place in which I could begin to preach, and go on to prove the power of the Gospel.

With the invitation, I received an exaggerated account of the wickedness of the people, and was told that the thinking part of them leant towards infidelity, and that some of them were actually banded together in an infidel club. All this, however, did not deter me from going, but rather stirred me up so much the more to try my lance against this gigantic foe. I had learned before now to regard all difficulties in my work as the Lord's, and not mine; and that, though they might be greater than I could surmount, they were not too great for Him.

There were two large iron factories here, besides shipping. Many of the people employed were drawn from other parts of England, and were what the Cornish call "foreigners." They had no love for chapel services, or revivals, and no sympathy with Cornish views and customs; so not having a church to go to, they were left pretty much to themselves.

With this attractive sphere before me, I gave up my living and work in the country, and accepted the curacy at £120 a year, with a house rent free. My rector was a dry Churchman, who had no sympathy with me; but he seemed glad to get any one to come and work amongst such a rough, and in some respects unmanageable, set. He had bought a chapel from the Primitive Methodists for Divine service, and had erected schools for upwards of three hundred children. These he offered me as my ground of operation, promising, with a written guarantee, that if I succeeded, he would build me a church, and endow it with all the tithes of that portion of the parish.

Here was a field of labour which required much prayer and tact, as well as energetic action. In accordance with Scriptural teaching, "I determined to know nothing but Jesus Christ and Him crucified." I made up my mind that I would not begin by having temperance addresses for drunkards, or lectures on the Evidences of Christianity for the infidel, but simply with preaching the Gospel.

One thing that simplified my work very much was the fact, that the people were spiritually dead. I used to tell them, that in this free country every man is accounted innocent till he is proved to be guilty, but that in the Bible every man is guilty before God till he is pardoned, and dead till he is brought to life. In one sense it does not matter very much whether a man is an infidel, a drunkard, or anything else, if he is dead in trespasses and sins. It is of very little consequence in what coloured raiment a corpse is shrouded; it remains a corpse still.

Taking this position positively, I avoided much religious controversy, to the disappointment of many eager disputants, who longed to ventilate their views. I told them plainly, that whether they were right or wrong, my business was with the salvation of souls, and my one desire was to rescue the lost by bringing them to Christ.

Hitherto I had been to places where the Lord had previously prepared the hearts of the people, and therefore it had been my joy to see a revival spring up, as if spontaneously; that is, without the ordinary preparation by the people of the place. These were extraordinary manifestations of God's power and love; and they showed me what He could and would do. Now that I was somewhat more intelligent on the subject, He sent me forth to prepare and work for similar results.

Hayle was to all appearance a very barren soil, and the people I had to labour amongst were greater and mightier than myself. They already had possession of the ground, and were perfectly content with their own way. Moreover, they did not desire any change, and were ready even to resist and oppose every effort which was designed to ameliorate their condition, or to change their lives. In this undertaking I knew and understood that without prayer and dependence upon God to work in me and by me, my mission would be altogether unavailing. I therefore looked about, and found some Christians who consented to unite in pleading for an outpouring of the Holy Spirit. We agreed to pray in private, and also met together frequently during the week for united prayer. Finding that many of the petitions offered were vague and diffuse, I endeavoured to set before those assembled a definite object of prayer. I told them that the work was not ours but the Lord's, and that

He was willing and ready to accomplish it, but that He must be inquired of concerning the work of His hands. Also, in order that our prayers should be intelligent and united, I put before them the fact, that the people we had to work amongst were *lost;* not that they would be lost by-and-by if they died in their sins; but that they were actually *lost now.* It is true that many were quite ignorant of the way of salvation, and were also unconscious of the power of the enemy who held them captive; and besides, they loved their captivity too well; but all this would be overcome in a moment, when they were once enlightened by the Spirit (in answer to prayer) to see and feel themselves *lost.* No one could be more ignorant than the jailor at Philippi, but as soon as he was awakened he cried out, "What must I do to be saved?" (Acts xvi. 30).

I showed them that the work we had to do was clearly set forth in Scripture (Acts xxvi. 18), and that the order in which it was to be done was also made manifest. We must not begin with giving instruction as if the people were merely ignorant; but rather by awakening or opening their eyes to see that they were in a lost and ruined condition. Then they would appreciate being turned "from darkness to light, and from the power of Satan unto God, that they may receive forgiveness of sins" (Acts xxvi. 18). I strove earnestly to show them that until people had received forgiveness of sins, our work was not complete. We made this our definite aim, and prayed about it with clear expectation. Under the shadow and influence of this prayer, I began to preach to the people; not to believe, but to awake and see their lost condition; that is, to repent, that they might believe the Gospel.

At first there were very few people in my congregation, but by degrees more came, and listened attentively to the Word. After preaching for four or five Sundays, I asked the people during my sermon, what in the world they were made of; for I was surprised at them! They came and listened to God's truth, and yet did not yield themselves to Him. "Are you wood, or leather, or stone? What are your hearts made of, that God's love cannot touch or His Word break them?" I then invited the anxious to remain for an after-meeting, when I said that I would converse with them more familiarly; but they every one went away.

I returned to the vestry, feeling somewhat dejected, but still hoping for better days. As I opened the door to go home, two men ran away like frightened boys, but it was too dark for me to distinguish who they were.

The next morning it came to my mind that I must go round to the people and ask them what they were thinking about? I had done so from the pulpit; now I would go from house to house and do the same. I went first to the school, and finding that several children were absent, I took their names and determined to go after them, in the hope of reaching their parents.

The first house I called at was a mistake, and yet it was not. I knocked at the door, and said, "Does Mrs W—— live here?"

The woman who opened it said, "No, she lives next door."

I apologized for disturbing her, and was going away, when she said, "Will you not come in for a few minutes?"

I assented, and going in, took a seat. Then I asked her name, and whether she went to church.

She replied, "To be sure I do. Don't you see me there every Sunday?"

"Then," I said, "did you hear my question last evening?"

"Yes," she said, "but I was afraid, and ashamed to

stay behind. But I do wish to be saved; I have been wretched for more than a week."

It was very easy to lead to the Saviour of sinners one whose heart was so prepared. She soon found peace, and became one of my most useful and steadiest helpers.

Her neighbour, next door, was by no means so ready to receive the truth, and I had to supply another argument altogether. Eventually, she also found peace in believing; though not for some weeks.

From this house, I visited several others, and in all of them had serious dealing with individuals about their souls' salvation. Then I set off to see a man I had often observed in church; having noticed the anxious look with which he always regarded me during the sermon. I found him at home, and, on entering his house, he said, at once, "I know what you are come for. Wait a little, sir, please to sit down;" and, before I had time to say a word, he went upstairs. In a few minutes he returned, with a shilling in his hand. "There," he said, "there it is; that is my contribution for the Indian Mutiny Fund."

I thanked him for his offering, and promised that it should be given to the treasurer. "But," I added, "to tell the truth, I have not come about that, but to see you. I want to speak to you about your soul."

He sat down, looking, as I thought, most unhappy. Then he said,—"Last night my mate and I made up our minds to speak to you in the vestry; but, just as we were coming to the door, you opened it, and we ran away."

"Yes," I said, "I heard you."

"Well, after that, we came home, and prayed the Lord to send you to us: and here you are!"

"Thank God for the answer to prayer. Now then, what can I do for you?"

He told me that he was born of respectable parents in

Germany; but that, for his bad ways and habits, they had sent him to this country to work for his bread; that he had taken the pledge several times, and broken it again and again, though he had prayed and done all he could think of; but it was to no purpose.

"If you had stayed last night," I said, "I might have helped you. How did you come to break your pledge?"

"Oh," he said, "it came to my mind that when I signed, I was only thinking of beer and spirits, not wine; so I took some, and it flew to my head; and soon I was as bad as ever."

"Now," I said, "you have renounced wine and all; have you?"

"Yes, I have."

"Well then, will you give your heart to God also?"

In course of conversation it came out, that this man's first impressions were effected some years before, by a dream, or vision of Christ on the cross. He was passing by, but, somehow, turned to look at it; when, to his surprise, he saw that the eyes of the figure were looking at him. As he approached, the figure appeared to be standing on the ground, and beckoning, when a sudden fear came over him; he stopped, and the vision faded away. Ever since that time, he had felt that Jesus was the Friend he needed; and that nothing less would satisfy him.

Unfortunately, too many, like this man, stop at a critical point of their history; and, often, the crisis is not prolonged for them, as it was for him.

A long time ago there was a sinner arrested by a similar vision. He says, in a hymn which he wrote, giving a description of it—

> "I saw One hanging on a tree,
> In agony and blood,
> Who fixed His languid eyes on me
> As near the cross I stood."

He continues,

"My conscience felt and *owned its guilt;*"

and when he did so, he received a second look, which spoke forgiveness to him, as distinctly as the first look brought him under conviction.

I charged this man to make his surrender, and to own or acknowledge himself the sinner for whom Jesus died. On doing so, he obtained forgiveness and peace, and has since, by grace, been enabled to live a happy, consistent, and devoted life, and has been a blessing to many souls. No sooner had he found the Saviour, than immediately he began to plead for and with his friend James. I know not what passed between them; but that same evening he brought him to me with a heart prepared to receive Christ. We had only to point him to Jesus, and encourage him to thank God, when he realized the truth in his own experience.

So that Monday I rejoiced over five people brought to the Lord; and then the work began in real earnest. Every week after that, remarkable conversions took place, besides many ordinary ones. Some of these, including the one just mentioned, are described at length in tracts, and are also published in a volume entitled "Building from the Top, and other Stories;" but, notwithstanding this, a brief allusion to them in this narrative may not be out of place, being so particularly connected with the work here.

A woman called me into her cottage one morning as I was passing by, and told me of her son, a steady young man, though still unconverted, for whom she had prayed continually ever since his birth. She said, when he was a very little child, she heard him one night sobbing and praying in his room—"O Lord, save me up for a good boy!" She thought this was in answer to her supplication;

but as he grew up he became thoughtless and careless, like too many others of his age.

"Some five or six months ago," she said, "he had a dream or vision, and saw you so plainly that he pointed you out to me, among other clergymen, and said, 'Mother, that man is to be our minister one day: I saw him a little time ago, in a dream, as plainly as I see him now; I know that is the man.' We did not know who you were then, or where you came from, and never saw you again till you came lately to this parish to be our minister.

"Last night," continued the mother, "after he returned from church, my William was very unhappy and restless; and in the night I heard him crying and praying aloud for mercy, in great distress. He told me this morning, when I asked him about it, that he dreamt that the last day was come, and that the world was on fire: and he began immediately to try to pray, but could not; yet he went on trying till he heard some one laugh out at him, and say, 'Ho! ho! my boy, you are too late!—ho! ho!—too late! I have got you now—you are too late!' This frightened him so much that he woke up, and getting out of bed, began on his knees to pray in earnest for the Lord to have mercy on his soul."

Being much interested in the young man, I begged her to send him to me in the evening. She did so; and when he arrived I frankly told him what I had heard about him, and particularly about his distress and prayer the night before.

"Your mother has prayed for you for years; and when you were a little boy you prayed the Lord to save you: last night, again, you were constrained to cry for mercy. These are all tokens of God's good intentions and purposes towards you. Can you trust Him?"

As he hesitated (for so many like to feel something

before they make the venture of faith), I continued, "These tokens are better than feelings, for they are facts and sure signs by which you may know that the Lord is calling you."

We may well understand that it was not long before the Lord, who had so marvellously opened his eyes to see his sins, enabled him by the same Spirit to see Jesus as His Saviour, and to rejoice in the forgiveness of his sins. Then I asked him to sit down again, for I was curious to hear about the dream or vision which he had had some months before he ever saw me.

"William," I said, "did you ever see me before I came to this parish?"

"Yes," he replied, "I saw you once in a vision, more than six months ago!"

"Do you mind telling me about it?"

After a little hesitation, he answered, "I often dream things. One night I dreamt that I was walking on a wild barren common; there were many bare places where people had cut turf, and there were prickly furze-bushes about. I knew there were some old open mine-shafts there, for people sometimes fell into them in the night; but I was walking along without thinking of danger, and was not afraid, though it was dark, and I was alone. I don't know how long I went on like this, but next I found I was walking with you. I could see you very plainly, just as if it had not been dark, and you were talking about Jesus and His love to sinners. I liked your words very much, and was so taken up with them that I do not know when it became light; for now I could see the rough common, and a path, and we were walking in it. Going along this path, we came to a wall, and I could not go any further; but you walked on as if there were no wall. Presently you stopped, and, turning to me, said, 'Why don't you come on?'

"I answered, 'I cannot.'

"'Why not?'

"'Because there is a wall here.'

"'No,' you said, 'there is no wall—it is an open door.'

"I was surprised at your saying that, for I could feel the wall and see it.

"'What would you do if there was no wall? Do that. It is not a wall, but a door,' you said; 'walk on forward!'

"When I ventured forward I found your words were true. It was, indeed, an open way, leading into a beautiful garden. I was very happy, and said, 'Whose garden is this?'

"You answered, 'It is the Lord's, and you are to dress it and work in it.'

"Then I saw the Lord Himself. He came forward, and bidding me welcome, said that you should teach me for three years. Then I awoke."

From this extraordinary narration I gathered three things for myself.

First, that God intended me to come to this place.

Secondly, that I was to labour here for three years.

Thirdly, that I was to teach the people not to wait for feelings, but to act upon the Word of God.

This last intimation was so clearly signified by William's dream, that it came upon me with striking force. I had been speaking on this very subject more than once and had ventured so far as to say that I thought this delusion about waiting for feelings was from the devil, to hinder the work of God in the soul. It certainly did hinder us, very much; and, moreover, it was most distressing to see people, who were manifestly impressed under the power of a present God, waiting for Him; because they did not feel some token, which they had set their minds upon.

Day by day souls were being given in the Church, and

also in the cottage meetings; so that I could not help seeing that the Lord had begun to use me again. Some came to the meetings who had been awakened under the ordinary preaching of the Gospel; some because others brought them; and some out of curiosity. One of the latter cases I will mention.

A married woman, N. R——, heard people talking of the work which was going on. It seemed to her to be such a strange thing in connection with a Church minister, that she came to a cottage meeting to judge for herself, without the remotest idea of being converted. God's ways are not as ours; while she was listening, the Word reached her with power, so that she was convicted and converted, and came out of that cottage a rejoicing believer, lost in wonder, love, and praise. She was indeed strikingly and manifestly changed, and did not hide it. It was such a joy and surprise to her that she could not help telling every one. Out of the abundance of her heart her lips spoke to tell of the loving-kindness of the Lord.

CHAPTER XXXIII.

Bible Readings.

1858—9.

THE church (so-called) in which I now ministered had been built by persons who intended to accommodate the largest number of people for the smallest amount of money. It was scantily built, and almost square, with galleries on three sides. On the remaining one there used to be a pulpit, conspicuously placed in the middle of the wall. This important portion of the edifice was now removed to one side, to make room for a Communion table, the seats in front being arranged chancel-wise, facing one another, for the choir. This place was quite a damper to my ecclesiastical tastes; besides being ugly in the extreme.

I tried by putting ornamental scrolls over the windows, and by staining the glass in them, to make some improvement. I also painted a diaper pattern round the side walls; and upon the high blank wall behind the Communion table exercised all the skill I possessed, but fear it was somewhat in vain, though I laboured hard. The designs looked very well on paper, but when displayed on the wall gave no satisfaction; so one after another they disappeared, till my dissolving views, as they were called, ended in a large floriated cross of gold, with a monogram intertwined in it, on a dark background.

When once, however, the Lord began to bless the Word, and souls were awakened, despite all anti-ecclesiastical appearances, my heart was drawn towards the ugly place, and I loved it greatly. I could never have believed that my former tastes and tendencies could have been so completely changed as they were.

In those days it was a strange thing to hold an after-meeting in a church; it was never done, even by the few who had such meetings. Therefore, I took the anxious ones and others to my own house for the inquiry meeting, after the evening service. Having taken up the carpet in the drawing-room, we fitted it up with chairs and forms to accommodate ninety people, while half as many more occupied the hall, and often numbers stood outside the windows. In this house it pleased God to give us very many souls, who were brought in week by week for several months. I believe every room in that house, like the rooms at Baldhu Parsonage, was consecrated as the birthplace of one or more of God's children.

The number of those who attended the after-meeting became so great, that we found it necessary to go to the large schoolroom. This place will also be remembered in eternity, and many a soul will say of it, "I was born there!"

One night, when I returned home from a distant meeting, I was called to see a person in great distress of soul. As I went down the street at eleven o'clock, I was surprised to see lights in almost all the houses, and what was more, to hear voices in urgent and importunate prayer, as also the voice of thanksgiving. The whole street was alive, and indeed there was a most "joyful noise" on every side. I was praying or rejoicing in one house or another all through the night, which was one never to be forgotten.

A glorious work of salvation was going on without the extravagant noise and excitement we used to have in former years. I was exceedingly thankful for this also, and began next to consider what was to be done with these new converts. Besides inviting them to the church services, for which they needed no pressing, I urged them to read their Bibles at home, bidding them to mark any passages where they wished for explanation, that I might have something good and profitable to speak about when I visited them. Then I invited them to Bible-classes; instead of to experience meetings, which Cornish people rely upon so much. On these occasions I endeavoured to instruct the people from God's Word, and put Christ before them as the object of faith, hope, and love. After prayer I encouraged them to ask questions, which made these gatherings interesting and also instructive on the very points upon which they required information.

I found that these Bible-classes were a great blessing to those who attended them, but more than all, perhaps, to myself; watering other souls with the water of life I was more abundantly watered. The questions of the people drew my attention to distinctions and differences I had not noticed before, and helped to take off the coloured glasses through which I had hitherto read the Word.

I observed that the third, sixth, and twentieth chapters of St. John's Gospel had been held and interpreted by me in a way that I now saw to be altogether wrong. I had taken the first of these as bearing on Baptism, the second on the Holy Communion, and the third on Priestly Absolution.

I pondered much over these chapters, and marvelled how they could have been so diverted from their original and obvious meaning; and, more wonderful still, that countless millions in Christendom had so received them for many generations. It was a bold thing, and seemingly presumptuous to suppose that I was right and all Christendom wrong; but I soon found that mine was no new discovery, and that if millions who followed traditions without comparing them with the Bible, thought on one side, there were also millions who did read their Bibles, and thought on the other.

It was perfectly clear, moreover, that one obvious motive or policy had dictated the false application of the three chapters. It will be observed that *priest rule* is established in them; for, according to this teaching, no one can enter the kingdom of God without priestly operation in baptism; no one abide or be fed in it without the same in Holy Communion; nor any one receive absolution from sin, and final release from hell to heaven, apart from sacerdotal action.

On the other hand, I saw spiritual men, as sure as they were of their own existence that their new birth took place, not at baptism, but at their conversion. Therefore they were convinced that the third chapter of St. John, in which our Lord's conversation with Nicodemus is recorded, refers to that spiritual change which takes place at conversion, and not to baptism, which was not even instituted for two or three years afterwards (Matt. xxviii. 19).

Again, as to the sixth chapter. A spiritual man knows that he feeds continually on the body and blood of Christ, it is the "Bread which came down from heaven" for him. The Lord said, "He that eateth Me, even he shall live by Me" (John vi. 57). They know how they received spiritual life, and also how it is continually maintained; therefore they could not allow themselves to be carried away with such a palpable fiction as transubstantiation, or any other doctrine kindred to it. The sixth chapter does not refer to the Lord's Supper, but the Lord's Supper refers to the reality which is mentioned in it.

Lastly, as to the twentieth chapter of St. John, on the authority of which it is supposed and asserted that Christ left power with His Church and priests to forgive sins. Of this we may say, He has not delegated any such powers at all. When He gave commission to His disciples (not exclusively to the apostles), He said, "Lo, I am with you." Our power is not imparted to us *from* Him, but is *in* Him. We have no power at all, but in Him, and no grace but that which is in Christ Jesus (2 Tim. ii. 1). It is His presence, His real, promised presence by the Holy Ghost, which is spiritual power; and this is given directly to individuals by God Himself, and is not transmitted through other channels.

The Lord Jesus, on His resurrection day, said to His disciples, in the upper room—and, be it remembered, that all the eleven were not there (and some women may have been)—" Peace be unto you. Receive ye the Holy Ghost: Whose soever sins ye remit, they are remitted unto them; and whose soever sins ye retain, they are retained" (John xx. 23).

Is it possible or reasonable to suppose that our Lord intended by these words to constitute all that assembly absolving priests? The apostles and early Christians (both men and women) never thought so, either before or even after the day of Pentecost, when they were taught and led by the Holy Ghost. The apostles did not exercise any so-called priestly functions; they all preached the Gospel, and as ministers and witnesses, declared, through Jesus Christ, the forgiveness of sins. Their testimony was then, as such testimony ever will be, the savour of life or the savour of death. It was thus they remitted and retained sins; and yet not they, but God by them.

While I was thus ruminating, a book came into my hands which interested me greatly. This I read and re-read, and made an abstract of it. It was the "Life of Adelaide Newton." What struck me in it so much was, to find that this lady was able to hold spiritual communion with God by means of a Bible only. Is it possible, I thought, to have such close communion with God, apart from the Church and her ministrations? I do not hesitate to say that this was the means, under God, of stripping off some remains of my grave-clothes, and enabling me to walk in spiritual liberty, instead of legal and sacramental bondage.

Human reasoning would say, "What, then, is the use of ministry and sacraments? Let us dispense with them, and be independent of them altogether." This is no better than saying that we will continue in sin that grace may abound; and the same answer which the apostle gives will do for this also: "God forbid!"

It does not follow, because some people make too much of ministry and sacraments, making them absolutely necessary to salvation, that we should, on the other hand, disregard them. There is another and a happier alternative, and that is, to realize they were made for us, not we for them; therefore we should not be subject to them, but rather they should be subject to us, and be used by us, not in order to obtain God's grace and salvation, but to show that we have already done so. In our obedience to God's ordinances, we acknowledge our allegiance to Him, and our submission to His will.

For fear that my people should go off, as too many do, into disregard of the "means of grace," because sacramental people make too much of them, I began a class for exposition and explanation of the Prayer-book. I commenced by showing them that the Church of England is the Lord's candlestick in this country, not the candle, and certainly not the light, but the candlestick which the Lord set up here, possibly even as early as the days of the apostles, to show the true light, which is Christ. And though Romish corruptions supervened, it pleased God, at the time of the Reformation, to raise up men to deliver us from them, and to restore true Bible teaching.

Thus I endeavoured to show them, that the system of the Church of England was one which should commend itself to their regard, as quite agreeable to Scripture; and if it is not carried out according to its intention, that is not the fault of the system, but rather of those who administer it.

Next, as to worship.

The object of our assembling in the house of God is not, I said, so much to hear sermons, or get instruction, as in Bible, or other classes, but rather "to render thanks for the great benefits we have received at God's hands, to set forth His most worthy praise, to hear His most holy word, and to ask those things which are requisite and necessary as well for the body as the soul." That worship is devotion towards God; it consists more in giving than in getting. Some of the people were greatly interested when I pointed out to them, that the order of our Service was exactly the same as the order of their spiritual experience, in conviction, conversion, and Christian life.

For example, the Morning Service begins with a sentence such as, "To the Lord our God belong mercies and forgivenesses, though we have rebelled against Him;" then comes the Exhortation, which moves us to surrender ourselves; then the Confession, which is the act of surrender. Immediately after this is declared the Absolution and forgiveness of sins, "to all who truly repent, and unfeignedly believe the Gospel."

Then comes the Lord's Prayer, which leads us, at once,

into the place of children, accepted in the Beloved: then follow acts of thanksgiving—

"Open Thou my lips, and my mouth shall show forth Thy praise."

"Oh, come let us sing unto the Lord, let us heartily rejoice in the strength of our salvation."

These, and such-like explanations, helped to enlist the interest of the people; and whereas, before, they only used to endure the prayers, while waiting for the sermon, now they engaged in them intelligently, and even with more delight than in extempore prayer.

As to the Communion Service I bade them notice that it begins with the Lord's Prayer, in which we draw near to our Father, not as sinners, but as His children; asking for a clean heart and for grace to live according to His will; then, we approach the table, unworthy, indeed, to take even the crumbs under it, but trusting in His mercy. We do not go there to offer a sacrifice of Christ's body, but of our own, as a thanksgiving to God, offering and presenting ourselves—spirit, soul, and body—a living sacrifice to His service.

Every week we took some subject from the Prayer-book, noticing the special seasons in their order, such as Advent, Christmas, Epiphany, Lent, Easter, Ascension, and Whitsuntide, each with their respective teaching.

I was now happy in my work; but it did not, of course, go on as sweetly as the theory sets it forth. We made, however, as straight a course as we could, under contending winds and currents. The intelligent part of my congregation, however interested they were in the work outside the church and the worship within, nevertheless, had their misgivings and doubts, which they did not hide. They said: "This teaching seems all true and scriptural; but what will become of us if you go away, and another man comes who thinks otherwise? We have no security as in the chapels, that conversion work will go on, and living souls be fed and encouraged. Very few churches have such a work as the Lord is doing here!"

This, indeed, was the sad part of working in the Church of England then. Even still, there is much discouragement on this head; and too many living souls, who would not willingly go, are driven away from their own Church, to seek teaching in other communions; but they cannot take their children and servants to witness priestly ceremonials, or to hear sacramental, as opposed to spiritual teaching; neither can they conscientiously give countenance to these things, by going themselves.

However, I endeavoured to pacify the people by begging them to be thankful for present privileges, and to trust God to lead them for the future.

It is an awful thing to see and know that people come for bread, and get a stone; for fish, and they get a serpent; and for an egg, they are offered a scorpion (Luke xi. 11, 12). Exceedingly trying it is to be frowned upon by clerical brethren in the presence of Dissenters, who, to say the least, do know the difference between life and death. In one church we have the service elaborately rendered, and the sermon is nothing; in another the sermon is everything, and the service most slovenly; and, too often, souls remain unawakened, and perishing on all sides.

CHAPTER XXXIV.

The Work Continued.

1859.

WHILE I was at Hayle, I had so much to do among the people, and so many meetings, that I seldom had leisure to go out for preaching elsewhere; nor do I remember that I had many invitations to do so. Occasionally I went to preach at Penzance, where a good work was steadily progressing at St. Paul's Church; but otherwise, I seldom left my pulpit.

Everything was now going on in a way which satisfied me, after all my tossings to and fro. I was surrounded with a happy people, who were living and working for the Lord. All the week they were busy, and also on the watch for souls. On Sunday they came regularly to church, with an intelligent idea of worship, and joined heartily in the services of the day. At eight o'clock in the morning they assembled in large numbers for the Holy Communion; then we had the usual morning and evening services in the church, concluding with a prayer meeting. In the afternoon we had something else. There was the Sunday school for some of our workers; tract distribution for others: many went out to preach in the villages; and others went with me either to the sands, the common, or on board some ship, for an evangelistic service. The day of rest was not one of inactivity, but of useful and happy occupation for the Lord. Many a former Sabbath-breaker, now changed and rejoicing in God, was amongst us, delighting in the Christian privilege of working for the Master. It was a day that many of them looked forward to and spent with intense delight; and on Monday evening we met to tell what we had seen and heard of the Lord's goodness to ourselves and others.

Whenever the good ship "Cornwall" was in harbour, it was expected there would be a preaching on "board of her," under the well-known Bethel flag. The mate of this vessel had been a terribly wicked man, and a most daring blasphemer. It pleased God to convert his soul in a remarkable manner; and now nothing would do but he must work for God.

One Sunday, when he was at Cardiff, he heard that a vessel which had left that port on the previous Friday morning had gone down with all hands. He was greatly grieved about this; for one of the seamen of the vessel was in former times a friend and companion of his. He had prayed for his soul, but hitherto without any success, and this added to his grief. To his amazement, he saw his friend standing on the quay. "Hallo!" he said, "I am glad to see you. How is it you are here? Have you heard that your vessel has gone down with all hands?"

"Has she, indeed!" he exclaimed, bursting out into tears; "then it is all my fault, for I let her go short-handed. After we set sail I had words with the captain, so he dismissed me, and I came back in the pilot boat. It is all my fault!"

"This is the third time, then, that the Lord has given you your life," said Sam. "You had better call on Him to have mercy on your soul." So saying, he fell on his knees, and began to pray for him. His companion soon followed, crying aloud for mercy. Though a crowd of people quickly assembled and stood round, he took no heed, but continued his supplication until he obtained mercy, and could praise God.

Seeing that some of the bystanders were looking anxious, Sam invited them on board his ship and had a meeting, at which he told them how the Lord had saved his soul. Having received much encouragement that day, he determined, if possible, that he would get a Bethel flag, and hold services whenever and wherever he could.

On his arrival at Hayle from Cardiff, he went at once to see the wife of the owner of the ship, knowing that she took a great interest in the welfare of sailors. He told her his plans, and made his request for a Bethel flag, which this lady kindly and generously gave him permission to get.

On obtaining it, Sam came and asked me if I would preach at the first hoisting of it. This I consented to do, and on the following Sunday afternoon we had a large concourse of people on board, and also on the quay alongside. I gave out the hymn—

> "O God of Bethel, by whose hand
> Thy people still are fed."

While I was giving it out, Sam ran his flag up to the masthead in the shape of a ball. So it remained while we were singing; and during the prayer which followed; and when I gave out my text (Gen. xxviii. 19), "He called the name of that place Bethel," Sam pulled the halyard, and the flag, some eighteen or twenty feet long, flew out in all its grandeur. Before the sermon was finished, some of the people began to cry for mercy, and dear Sam was in an ecstasy of delight, and rejoiced aloud. Thus his flag was inaugurated with blessing from on high, and " Many is the time since," said Sam, " when souls have been blessed under it, both at Cardiff and at Hayle."

I have said nothing about the infidels I had to work amongst when I first came to this place. Some of them raged and opposed themselves against us for a time, but one by one the ringleaders of their party were brought to God, and eventually their club dwindled away. The history concerning some I have already published in tracts; but there is one case I feel I must insert here, for besides being a remarkable history, there is much teaching in it.

It is the story of a man who professed to be an infidel, and used to speak very freely of things which he said he did not believe. For instance, he boasted that he did not believe in God or the Bible, Christ or devil, heaven or hell; though I must say he seemed to believe in himself very considerably. It was very difficult to deal with a man who took his stand upon nothing but negatives. He was well known among his neighbours, dreaded by some and quite a mystery to others. He was continually to be seen about with a gun, especially on Sundays, when he was not ashamed to be thus desecrating God's holy day; on the contrary, he rather prided himself in not " shifting " his working-day clothes, when other people were dressed in their best.

It was sad to see a man of such intelligence and capacity defying public respect and opinion, and trampling upon every sense of right and propriety. There is generally a reason, if we can only discover it, why people outrage public opinion, and break out of the stream and path of their fellow-men.

One Sunday evening, however, after a day spent as usual, in idling about and shooting little birds, our friend John was observed by a woman standing outside a church, under the window nearest to the pulpit. He stood there, listening very attentively to the sermon, till it was over; and then, before the congregation could come out, he made off stealthily and hastily, to escape observation. But passing near the woman who had been watching him, she heard him say, with a look of distress on his countenance, "It's no use—the devil's sure to have me! It doesn't matter!"

This woman told me on Monday morning what she had seen and heard; so I determined to go at once and see the man. It was not his dinner-time yet; but I thought I would have a little conversation with his wife before he came home. To my surprise, however, I found him there. "What, not working to-day, John?" I said. "What's the matter?"

"I ain't very well," he answered. "I got no sleep last night; but I mean to work in the afternoon, for all that," he continued, with an air of determination and defiance.

"What's the matter? Have you got anything on your mind?" I inquired.

"Mind!" he repeated, as if in contempt at the thought. "There is not much that ever troubles my mind." He then went on to give me a long account of his bodily ailments.

"But do you never think about your soul, John?" I asked; "never think about another world and eternity?"

"Soul and eternity! I don't believe in either the one or the other of them!"

"Not believe you have a soul! Come, John, I am sure you know better than that." And I went on to speak of the joys of heaven and the bitter torments of hell; of the love of God, who willeth not the death of the sinner, but rather that he should turn and live; and then I proceeded to tell him of the atonement which Jesus Christ finished on the cross, and that now there is pardon for the vilest sinner through the efficacy of the blood which has been shed once for all.

"You know, John," I continued, "that I do not care to argue about these things. There is mercy for you, if you will have it. We can bring water to the horses, but we cannot make them drink. My business is to put the way of pardon and salvation plainly before you; and after that, if you reject it, it will be your own fault if you perish. Do you know how to get forgiveness of sins?"

He seemed very uneasy all the time I was speaking, and at length, after a pause, he looked me in the face with a hardened expression, and said, "There's no pardon for me—I know it."

"That cannot be," I said; "I do not believe it."

"No," he continued, "there's no pardon for me. I have known that for fourteen years."

I inwardly resolved to get this dreadful secret from him, which was driving him to such evident desperation. A few days afterwards an opportunity occurred, and I pressed upon him for his own sake to tell me, or some one else, what had happened fourteen years ago; and what special communication he had had with another world.

"Oh," he said, "I never told anybody; but I would as soon tell you as any one else. I had a dream once—do you ever have dreams? I have many things told me in dreams." Then he was silent; but I was more curious than ever now, and begged him to tell me what had happened. At last he began, "I dreamt that I was walking along a broad smooth road, where everything was most lovely; the weather was fine, and the scenery grand; there were beautiful gardens, churches, chapels, theatres, houses, and indeed everything you could think of. The people all seemed to be delighting in it, and as though they were out for a holiday. Some were walking, some singing, some dancing, and in one way or the other they all appeared to be enjoying themselves beyond bounds. Seeing a working man in a field close by, I called to him, and asked 'Where does this road lead to?' He answered, 'To hell, straight on; you cannot miss!' 'Hell!' I was surprised; 'Hell,' I said to myself, 'this is very different to what I thought. Is the way to hell as pleasant as this? and are people so unconcerned about it?' I was amazed; but though the man told me this pleasant road led to hell, I did not stop; I went on and on, seemingly as pleased as others were. However, it did not continue like this long, for soon I came to a rough part, all up and down, where the atmosphere was thick and sulphury, and it was almost dark. I did not like it, and wished very much to get out of the place, but I could not.

"Seeing some people in the distance, I went near to ask them the way out. They were busy with long rakes raking cinders about on the dry ground, and would not answer my urgent inquiries. As I approached them I saw that they did not look like 'humans,' and that every now and then fire appeared from under ground, over which they raked cinders to keep it out of sight. They were so absorbed in their work that they did not heed my question, though I pleaded more and more earnestly. At last, I observed that one of them ceased from his strange work, and looked at me; whereupon I addressed myself to him, begging him to show me the way out of the place." John added, "If I ever prayed in my life I prayed then; but he shook his head as if he pitied me, and said mournfully, 'The way you came in.' I replied, 'I cannot find it'; then again he shook his head, as if to say, 'You never will.' I was obliged to rise from my knees, for the ground was so hot, and in my despair I ran I know not whither. As I passed along in haste, I came to cracks in the ground full of fire; I stepped over them one after another, and ran on till I came to such a large chasm, that I could not jump over it. I turned and went in another direction, leaping and running, in a state of terror, till at last I came upon a sheet of glowing fire, into which I fell. Then I awoke. For fourteen years this has followed me; there is no hope for me!"

By this time he became very much excited and agitated: seizing his cap he ran out of the house, leaving his wife and myself in mute astonishment at his strange tale.

I went home pondering over the meaning of this dream, and was struck at the amount of truth in it. I thought— How fair are the promises of the world to begin with, and how delusive and disappointing they are at the end! Of course, Satan, the god of this world, will make the way of hell as bright and pleasing as he possibly can; and if people take outward circumstances and pleasing prospects for indications of safety, they wilfully lay themselves open to this deadly delusion. What a number there are who know, or might know, that they are on the road to hell; that they cannot miss; and yet they go on! And then how many people there are who rake cinders; that is, when thoughts of death, or judgment, or hell, obtrude themselves, how readily they cover them over with hopes of escape, or some good intentions to be better, before it is too late! How often parents do the same for their children, for they cannot bear to think of their being lost for ever; so they hope that somehow they will be changed before they die! How often preachers rake cinders also, by addressing their hearers as if they were all safe, and only wanted a little teaching now and then; and it may be a little warning occasionally! They cannot bear to tell them plainly that they are *lost now*, and may be lost for ever, if they do not repent and believe the Gospel; they would rather "be persuaded better things of them, and things which accompany salvation," though they know for certain that there are many unsaved ones in their congregation. They entertain them with good hearty services and pleasing sermons, and then let them go on their way to the solemn end, perfectly unconscious of any danger.

The Lord Jesus had no such false charity as this. He has told us plainly that we are all perishing creatures, and that there is no hope for any one of us while we are still on the broad road to ruin and in an unchanged state; that we must be born again or we cannot see the kingdom of God; that we must believe on the Lord Jesus Christ, who died in our stead on the cross, or perish for ever. Preachers therefore ought to be more faithful, because life is so uncertain, and the warnings of God so sure.

Well did John dream that they did not look like human beings, who were raking cinders to keep the fire out of sight.

After some days I got light on the subject of this awful dream, and hastened to tell John that I had found the way out of that fearful place for him. He would not hear me for some time; but I told him, that the prodigal son said, "I will arise and go to my Father, and say unto Him, I have sinned." "You see, John," I continued, "he came back the way he went, and he found pardon; that is the way for you."

I then knelt down and prayed, and he knelt with me at his table. There he remained for four hours, without speaking a word, until I was thoroughly exhausted and obliged to go. No sooner had I gone, than John's heart failed him, and he burst out crying aloud, and said to his wife, "Oh, Mary, what shall I do? what shall I do?"

"Take the book and read," she said, pushing the Bible along the table to him. It was open at the fifteenth chapter of St. Luke, where he read the words aloud, "I will arise and go to my Father, and will say unto him, Father, I have sinned." The spell was broken and the string of his tongue loosed, so that he cried aloud for mercy.

This was no unusual thing in one house or another; but in this particular dwelling it was wonderful. His next-door neighbour, who had often heard the sound of cursing and swearing there, but never the voice of prayer, was so astonished, that he rose and came to the door to assure himself of the astonishing fact. It was quite true; surely it was John's own voice praying. So, lifting the latch, he went in and shouted, "Glory to God!" The louder William shouted, the louder John cried for mercy. When listening to his friend, who pointed him to "the Lamb of God, who taketh away the sin of the world," he found that

"There is life for a look at the Crucified One;"

and then they shouted and praised God together.

It was a joyful meeting when I saw him again, and thanked God with him for the marvellous change which had been wrought in his soul. His very face was altered; and instead of the restless and defiant glare there used to be in his countenance, there was rest and cheerfulness.

I pointed out to him, from that same portion of the Word of God which had been blessed to his soul, that there was something more to be had than the pardon that he had already received; that there was also the best robe, the ring, the shoes, and the feast of rejoicing. The Father's arms round the neck of the prodigal son is a token of forgiveness—the robe, of righteousness divine which is imputed to us; the ring, of our union with Christ; the shoes, of strength, even grace, with which we walk; and the feast of rejoicing, the believer's privilege of joy and thanksgiving.

John's conversion was a remarkable event, and caused a great sensation; crowds of his fellow-workmen used to stand round him while he told his wonderful story. "Oh," he said, "I used to say there was no hell, when all the time

I had it burning in my heart; but, glory be to God, I am saved from hell to heaven!"

He seldom prayed in public after this, without begging the Lord to loose the string of the tongue; for, as he said (speaking from experience), "so many are held captive by that dumb devil." He became a true missionary for souls, and was very zealous in his testimony, especially amongst his old companions, who worked in the same factory: he had the joy of seeing many of them brought to the Lord.

John seemed to realize unseen things in an unusually striking way. He was a man who in his sleep had vivid dreams, and who in his waking hours pondered much upon eternal realities, so that he spoke as one who lived in sight of another world.

CHAPTER XXXV.

The Dismissal.

1860—61.

F this work at Hayle was not "a success," in every sense of the word, I do not yet know what success in parochial ministry is. If large congregations may be counted; many communicants taken into reckoning; with frequent services, and schools full of children—we certainly had these. But above all, we had a continual ingathering of souls, who will testify throughout eternity of the blessedness and reality of the work of God during the time I was there.

It so happened that as we approached the term of three years, of which I had been premonished when I first came, that my dear friend, Mr. Aitken, came to pay us a visit. He preached with more amazing power than ever. His appeals were altogether overwhelming, and I do not wonder that the people fell on their knees, as they did then and there, and cried aloud for mercy.

A newspaper reporter who came to hear this "great man" preach, was at first observed to be writing very diligently; then he paused, and his hand fell; then his pencil and book went from his grasp; presently he himself fell on his knees, and began to cry for mercy. We were curious afterwards to read his report.

In it the grateful man acknowledged his indebtedness, and the blessing he had received. As to the sermon, he likened it to one of the storms of the great Atlantic. He said, "At such a time it is interesting to stand on the shore and watch the sea, and to note the power of wind and waves while the storm is raging. Even then it is sometimes terrific enough; but how much more so when the wind veers and the mighty waves come rolling in one after another, and breaking with tremendous force upon the rocks on which we stand! So it was with this preacher. All eyes were fixed on him when he gave out his text, and proceeded with his usual introduction. Now and then he alarmed and roused us with the power of his oratory; but when he turned to apply his subject to the consciences of the people, he became irresistible. Immediately, there was heard on all sides a cry for mercy. The stentorian voice of the preacher was audible above all others as he went on to apply the Word with unrelenting force, till very few hearts, however hard, remained unbroken."

This was a memorable day with us. Twice was the church filled and emptied; and again a third time, in the evening the people crowded in and filled the place. Far into the night we wrought amongst the anxious and broken-hearted, bidding them to look at the Crucified One and live.

Mr. Aitken was not a man who raked cinders over the fire, but rather raked them off, and that in true kindness and love; but with terrible and awful plainness he showed the danger of trifling with the Gospel, and presuming upon God's love and forbearance.

On Monday evening we invited the people to assemble in the large schoolroom, which was filled to excess. Here I thought that the schoolmaster's desk would have been demolished under the tremendous energy and force, both mental and physical, of this preacher. At the first sign of a breakdown among the people, the great, tall man, in his long coat or cassock, came majestically striding out from behind the desk. That was enough. A hard rough-looking sailor, who was sitting by, with his eyes fixed on Mr. Aitken for a long time, fell on his knees and began to roar aloud for mercy, and very many others followed his example.

I asked this man afterwards what it was that had had such an effect upon him? "Oh," he replied, drawing his breath, as if he had scarcely yet recovered from the shock, "that big man was bad enough the other side of the desk, but when he came forth to the front, I didn't know what would happen to me. I was obliged to cry out for mercy; I couldn't help it."

The "big man," like the "Stormy Petrel," was just in his element in such a scene. In the gladness and joy of his heart he rejoiced and shouted, "Glory—glory be to God!" in a way which no one else could imitate or follow.

In the midst of this scene of confusion (as it must have appeared to an outside observer, if such an one was there), sat a woman, looking on at the people praying and praising God, when all at once Mr. Aitken turned suddenly upon her and said, "And you, my sister!" Immediately she gave a scream, and was down on her knees in a moment, crying for mercy as loud as the loudest.

If Cornish people like a noise, they certainly had it that evening to their hearts' content. As I have said before, when there is a real power of the Spirit present, the outpouring of the heart with noisy demonstration is joyous to those who go with the stream, and are in sympathy with it; but if those present stop to doubt the propriety of such an outcry, and begin to rebuke those who make it, then I think the answer that the Lord gave the Pharisees would still be applicable: "I tell you that, if these should hold their peace, the stones would immediately cry out" (Luke xix. 40).

It was a great triumph, and the rams'·horns did more execution in these two days than the silver trumpets had done in as many years.

The next day, as soon as Mr. Aitken had gone, the rector came to see me. He appeared to be somewhat embarrassed at first, but after a little time said (looking on the ground), "You know I am no revivalist. I do not like all this uproar. I cannot have it." He then went on to say that he wished me to leave, for though he had given a guarantee that if I succeeded, he would build me a church and endow it, he could not do anything of the kind now, for he did not consider my work any success whatever—quite the contrary. "These converted people (as you call them) are no churchmen!"

I replied, that I had taken his voice as from God in inviting me, and I supposed that I must take the same for my dismissal, if he really intended it; but I urged upon him to consider the matter well before he broke up the work which was going on there, for whatever he thought about it it was undoubtedly a work of God, though one certainly not very common in churches

Without saying another word he took up his hat and went away. His departure was so abrupt that I could not believe he intended me to receive this as six months' notice. Consequently, I went on with my work as usual, finding plenty to do, more especially after Mr. Aitken's energetic visit. There were many new converts to add to our classes; anxious ones to be guided and led to Christ; and broken-hearted and despairing ones to be comforted and built up. The work under such a preacher is by no means finished with his visit, however long or short it may be; but, on the contrary, it may rather be said to begin there.

After some months, the rector came again to remind me that he had given me notice more than five months before, and that he wished me to leave at the beginning of the year, as he had secured the services of a clergyman whose views were in accordance with his own. I was much grieved at this, and could only lay it before the Lord, and beg of Him to order all according to His will.

The following morning, without any seeking on my part, I received an invitation from Bath, asking me to come and take charge of the district of St. Paul's, in the parish of Holy Trinity. Thus was the door shut behind me, and another opened in front. This was so unmistakable, that I could not but be satisfied, and acquiesce in the manifest will of God; though, naturally, I felt great sorrow at having to leave the people and the work I loved so well. I said nothing about my dismissal, but went on with my various engagements as usual, though I had only a little more than three weeks left me.

By some means it appeared in the newspapers, that I was appointed to a district in Bath, and another clergyman was named as my successor at St. John's, Hayle. This fell as a great blow upon my people, who were both grieved and angry; but I could not comfort them, any more than I could help myself.

The last Christmas-day came and went, a sad and sorrowful day it was; then the last day of the year, and the last night. We held our watch-night service as usual, thanking God for the mercies of the past, and entered upon the new year with thanksgiving and prayer.

Thus ended my work, and eventful sojourn at Hayle, a little more than three years after it began. A very sorrowful trial it was, and one of bitter disappointment; but the Lord's leading was clear, and I have since proved that it was all

THE QUAINT OLD PICTURE. 315

right, though at the time it was most mysterious and very dark.

A few weeks before leaving Hayle, as I was sitting by the fire one wet afternoon, my eyes fell on a little coloured picture on the mantel-piece, which had been the companion

of my journeys for all the twenty years of which I have been writing. It was a quaint mediæval illustration of Moses lifting up the serpent in the wilderness, copied from a valuable manuscript (Book of Prayers) in the Bodleian Library at Oxford.

As I looked at the engraving before me, I began to suspect for the first time that there was a design in the arrangement of the figures, and that it was really intended to convey some particular teaching. I took it in my hand and studied it, when I observed that the cross or pole on which the serpent was elevated stood in the centre, dividing two sets of characters, and that there were serpents on one side, and none on the other.

Behind the figure of Moses, is a man standing with his arms crossed on his breast, looking at the brazen serpent. He has evidently obtained life and healing by a look. On the other side, I observed that there were four kinds of persons represented, who were not doing as this healed one did to obtain deliverance.

First, there is one who is kneeling in front of the cross, but he is looking towards Moses, and not at the serpent, and apparently confessing to him as if he were a priest.

Next behind him is one lying on his back, as if he was perfectly safe, though he is evidently in the midst of danger; for a serpent may be seen at his ear, possibly whispering "Peace, peace, when there is no peace."

Still further back from the cross there is a man with a sad face doing a work of mercy, binding up the wounds of a fellow-sufferer, and little suspecting that he himself is involved in the same danger.

Behind them all, on the background, is a valiant man who is doing battle with the serpents, which may be seen rising against him in unabating persistency.

I observed that none of these men were looking at the brazen serpent as they were commanded to do. I cannot describe how excited and interested I became; for I saw in this illustration a picture of my own life. Here was the way of salvation clearly set forth, and four ways which are not the way of salvation, all of which I had tried and found unavailing. This was the silent but speaking testimony of some unknown denizen of a cloister, who lived in the beginning of the fifteenth century, in the days of ignorance and superstition. But notwithstanding this darkness, he was brought out into the marvellous light of the Gospel, and has left this interesting record of his experience.

Like him, I also had fought with serpents, for I began in my own strength to combat with sin, and strove by my own resolutions to overcome. From this, I went on to do good works, and works of mercy, in the vain hope of thus obtaining the same for myself. Then, I relied in the Church for salvation, as God's appointed ark of safety; but not feeling secure, I took another step beyond, and sought forgiveness through the power of the priest. This I found was as ineffectual as all my previous efforts. At last, I was brought (by the Spirit of God) as a wounded and dying sinner, to look at the Crucified One. Then (as I have related), I found pardon and peace. Ever since it has been my joy and privilege (like Moses pointing to the serpent) to cry, "Behold the Lamb of God, which taketh away the sin of the world" (John i. 29). "I have determined to know nothing but *Jesus Christ* and Him crucified;" that is, to tell only of the person and office of Jesus Christ our Lord.

Nearly twenty years have elapsed since the period at which this book closes,* and, during all that time I have verified the truth and reality of the teaching and experience I have recorded in this volume. All these years, with their months, weeks, and days have passed by, and have found me continually rejoicing in the work of the Lord—often wearied in it, but never of it—often tempted to falter, but

---

* I may, perhaps, at some future time, give an account of these latter twenty years.

always enabled to persevere. I have seen many rise and start well, who have collapsed or retired; many who have blazed like a meteor for a short time, and then disappeared from the scene.

May I here, in a few parting words to the reader, tell how it is that I have been kept. I believe it is—First, Because I have never failed to insist upon the absolute necessity of conversion, saying in the words of the Master, "Marvel not, Ye must be born again" (John iii. 7). Secondly, Because I have preached nothing but what is taken from the Word, and required nothing to be believed for Salvation and Edification, but what can be proved thereby. Thirdly, Because I have exhorted living souls with purpose of heart to cleave unto the Lord; firmly believing that He who died to save, rose again from the dead, and lives to keep His people.

When we are saved, we are debtors to God, to devote ourselves to His service, and for His glory: besides this, we are debtors to men, to make known to them the grace which we have received; and we, as faithful stewards of God, should be ever ready (and not ashamed) to preach the Gospel, for, "It is the power of God unto salvation to every one that believeth" (Rom. i. 16).

www.ingramcontent.com/pod-product-compliance
Lightning Source LLC
Chambersburg PA
CBHW021155230426
43667CB00006B/411